Family Hospice Care
Pre-planning and Care Guide

Harry van Bommel

Resources Supporting Family and Community Legacies Inc.
Scarborough, Ontario, 1999

Cover Illustration by Diane Huson.
Author's cover photograph by Doug Walford.

Canadian Cataloguing in Publication Data

van Bommel, Harry
    Family hospice care

Previous eds. published under title: Choices.
Includes bibliographical references and index.
ISBN 1-55307-002-X

    I. Terminal care. 2. Terminally ill–Home Care. 3. Home nursing. I. Resources Supporting Family and Community Legacies Inc. II. Title. III. Title: Choices.

R726.8.V32 1999   362.1'75   C99-901508-7

I wish to thank Barry Ashpole, editor of The Pain Management Newsletter published by Knoll Pharma Inc. for permission to reprint revised versions of 'success stories' in Chapters 4 and 8 that first appeared in the newsletter in 1997 and 1998.

Resources Supporting Family and Community Legacies Inc.
11 Miniot Circle
Scarborough, ON
M1K 2K1
Canada
(416) 264-4665
harryvb@inforamp.net
www.inforamp.net/~harryvb
Printed and bound in Canada by Webcom Limited.

In memory of my parents and grandfather who taught me so much about the hospice philosophy of care:

Jacoba Christina Henrica Maria van Bommel-van Enckevort (1926-1980)
Johannes Fernandus Gerardus van Bommel (1925-1984)
Franciscus Hubertus van Enckevort (1889-1981)

In thanks to Rieky Haas, Philomena van Enckevort, the van Ryswyk family, the van Soest family, and other family members, friends and neighbors who have allowed me to share in their experiences and learn from their wisdom.

Dedicated to Janet, Bram and Joanna who teach me every day about physical, emotional and spiritual love and caring.

What You Must Know

Remember to talk to a professional health care provider (e.g., nurse, doctor, pharmacist or physiotherapist) or legal and financial professional (e.g., lawyer, accountant, tax expert) **before trying any** of the tips and techniques in this book to make sure you are doing them correctly. This book is not intended to replace professional help or advice but to supplement it and initiate further, informed communications. Any use of the information is at the reader's discretion. The author and publisher specifically disclaim any and all liability arising directly or indirectly from the use or application of any information contained in this book. Health care providers and/or legal and financial professionals should be consulted about your specific situation.

Table of Contents

Foreword

On behalf of the Saint Elizabeth Health Care Foundation, I am pleased to offer *Family Hospice Care* to Canadian families free of charge. This is the second charitable publication we have sponsored - the first, *Caring for Loved Ones at Home* received such positive accolades from the community, the Foundation decided to fund another.

Established in 1997, the Saint Elizabeth Health Care Foundation raises charitable funding to enhance and expand the health care services offered in the home and community.

Recognizing there is a need to provide information to people who are caring for loved ones at home with terminal or life-threatening illnesses, the Foundation embraced this very important initiative. *Family Hospice Care* is a practical and informative resource that is intended to help family members and friends meet the physical, spiritual, emotional and informational needs of their terminally-ill loved ones.

This copy of *Family Hospice Care* was made available to you as a result of charitable support. If you would like to help us make this book available, free of charge, to more Canadian families, please make a charitable donation to the Saint Elizabeth Health Care Foundation using the donation form included at the back of this book. Also, we would very much like to hear from you - let us know if this book met your needs or if you have suggestions for improvements. We have included a brief evaluation following the donation form - your comments will help keep this book up-to-date!

In closing, I would like to thank Harry van Bommel for presenting the Saint Elizabeth Health Care Foundation with the opportunity to partner in this invaluable project and for his time, research and expertise in the development of this book.

November, 1999

Sister Roberta Freeman, C.S.J.
Board Member
Saint Elizabeth Health Care Foundation

Saint Elizabeth
H E A L T H   C A R E

Acknowledging the Sponsors

We would like to thank the following individuals and sponsors for making this book available to you, free of charge:

Saint Elizabeth Health Care Foundation undertook the sponsorship of printing and distribution of 75,000 copies. Their sponsorship is a testament to their ongoing commitment to helping family, friends and neighbors provide basic, practical and comforting hospice care for loved ones at home.

The Military & Hospitaller Order of Saint Lazarus of Jerusalem, which is celebrating its 900th anniversary in 1998-1999, has been involved in providing and supporting hospice programs throughout the world since its beginning in the Crusades. The Order funded the initial pilot project for this book and for *Caring for Loved Ones at Home*. Through that sponsorship we were able to determine how many free books were needed for home and hospice care programs to offer to their patients and families.

DISCLAIMER: The views expressed in this book are those of the author and not necessarily those of any of the sponsors.

Acknowledgements

This book is a major revision of my *Choices for People Who Have a Terminal Illness, Their Families and Their Caregivers*, published and revised in 1986, 1987 and 1993. The people I acknowledged in that book deserve on-going credit for their invaluable contributions.

Although numerous people are mentioned in this section, each individual's contribution was very important.

I thank all the people at NC Press for their efforts: **Caroline Walker, Janet Walker, Ruth Chernia, Lisa Dimson, Rani Gill, Elina Guttenberg, Ron Lovering, Lynn McClory,** and **Elizabeth Whitehead.**

My heartfelt thanks to the people who shared their personal stories with me: **Carol Brock, M.D.; Frances Elliot, R.N.; The Reverend Keith Nevel** and **Hans Peters.**

The following people and organizations provided information and assistance for which I am grateful: **American Civil Liberties Union; Anglican Book Center; The Connecticut Hospice Inc.; Malin Kurz, Joe Gilhooly** and **Edward W. Keyserlingk,** Law Reform Commission of Canada; **The Medical Post; New York Task Force on Life and the Law; Dr. Cecily Saunders** of St. Christopher's Hospice; **John Toye;** and **Carol Williams** plus many of the organizations listed in the book.

I want to thank the people I interviewed throughout the research for this book, with special thanks to the following: **Nell Bushby** of the Bessie Dane Foundation (hospice program on Salt Spring Island, BC); **Marcia Darling,** Manager of Marketing Services for the Toronto Trust Cemeteries; **Mary Devassy, M.D.,** a family practitioner; **Jo Dixon, Llona O'Gorman** and **Marie Teitge** of Hospice Victoria; **Stephen Fleming, Ph.D.,** a psychologist and professor at York University in Toronto; **Peter Hanson, M.D.,** author; **Bob Hatfield, M.D.,** and **Diane Yackel** of Hospice Calgary; **Paul Henteleff, M.D.,** Director of Palliative Care Unit, St. Boniface Hospital, Winnipeg, Manitoba; **Dorothy C.H. Ley, M.D.,** Executive Director of the Palliative Care Foundation of Canada; and **Ken Walker, M.D.,** author.

Several people read most or all of the manuscript and provided useful suggestions for improvements: **Estelle Altman, Leslie Balmer, Carol Brock, Colleen Burns, Janet Klees** and **Bill Weiss, M.D.** Any content errors that remain are mine.

Special thanks to the following people for their help with the second and third revised editions of *Choices:* **Balfour Mount, M.D.**, Director of Palliative Care Service at Royal Victoria Hospital in Montreal; **Dame Cicely Saunders, DBE**, founder of St. Christopher's Hospice in London, England; **Warner Montgomery, Ph.D.**, and **Rieky Haas**.

In this major new edition -- *Family Hospice Care* -- I want to thank **Deb Thivierge** and the **Huson** family who gave up their homes for several weekends so that I could work uninterrupted. Also the **Augustinians at Marylake Monastery**, who welcomed me and provided me with a quiet, spiritual environment over half-a-dozen weekends to work on this book. I am grateful to you all.

Beverley Powell-Vinden did the final edit and typesetting of this book. Her efforts make this book more concise, easier to read and her nursing background adds to its final usefulness.

To the reviewers of this particular edition (1999), I am grateful to:

Bonnie L. Barry, is an oncology social worker and bereavement counselor at Mount Sinai Hospital in Toronto. Her suggestions on how to rewrite *Choices* were incorporated into the first draft of this book.

Carol A. Brock, M.D. reviewed her story from the first edition of *Choices* and updated the information.

Burnaby Palliative Care Program team members: **Leanne Baird**, Hospice Program Manager; **Kathy Bodell**, Clinical Process Leader; **Kate Doyle**, Social Worker; **Theresa Guscott**, Palliative Care Unit Patient Care Manager; **Judy Hedberg**, Home Care Liaison Nurse; and **Eve S. Sample**, Clinical Pharmacist; who each took portions of the manuscript for review and who all submitted valuable recommendations.

Michèle Chaban, M.S.W., Ph.D. is a masters trained social worker and a doctor of philosophy. She works at Mount Sinai Hospital in Toronto in Oncology and Palliative Medicine. As a thanatologist, Michèle teaches at the Faculty of Social Work and the Faculty of Medicine's Continuing Education program at the University of Toronto. Her extensive suggestions and revisions added depth and detail to all the aspects of hospice care.

Maureen Cooling, R.N., E.T. is an Enterostomal Therapist with a community nursing agency who was most helpful in explaining various symptom management techniques. I am indebted to her for sharing her expertise.

Carla Crowther, B.Sc., R.N. is a case manager for the Grey-Bruce Community Care Access Center in Owen Sound, Ontario. Her thoroughness is very much appreciated.

Susan Delmar is a young mother and widow whose perspectives added specific tips and suggestions that will help patients, spouses and young children going through the experience of a spouse and parent dying.

Shari Douglas, R.N. is the palliative care coordinator at the Grey-Bruce Community Care Access Center and is President of Shari Douglas and Associates. Her professional experiences in her local community and her active participation in provincial and national health care and palliative care organizations provides us with unequaled insights and suggestions.

Anne Gardner, CLJ and **Peter Gardner, KCLJ,** are from the British Columbia Commandery of The Military and Hospitaller Order of Saint Lazarus of Jerusalem, and provided very specific and practical recommendations to make the book more useful for patients and families.

Dr. Gillian Gilchrist, MB., ChB., retired as the Medical Director of the Palliative Care Service at Oshawa General Hospital (Ontario). Her professional expertise is outstanding in this field and her comments brought both reinforcement for what was written as well as specific suggestions on how to enhance the material.

Douglas Graydon, is the Pastoral Counselor at Casey House Hospice in Toronto, and added thoughtful revisions to the chapters on spirituality and legal documents and decision making and I am most grateful.

Peter Hargreaves, M.D. is Medical Director at The Lions Hospice in Kent, England. He reviewed the material from the perspective of caregivers in a free-standing and community hospice.

Robert E. Hatfield, M.D. (interviewed for the first edition of *Choices*) is a palliative care physician in Calgary with extensive experience. His comments added specific information that will be invaluable to patients and their families.

Blair Henry is Client Services Coordinator at Trinity Home Hospice. He updated some of the information in Chapter 19 on creating your own support circle/team to assist all of us who work in formal or informal circles.

Anne Isenberg is a graduate of the Seneca College Palliative Care Certificate Program and is an active volunteer with Bereaved Families of Ontario. Anne's personal experiences with grief, her research and work in this field, her experience as a writer and editor, and her friendship have enriched the content of this book for which I am grateful.

Larry Librach, M.D., CCFP, FCFP is the Director, The Temmy Latner Center for Palliative Care, Mount Sinai Hospital, Toronto. His thorough review and recommended changes to the final draft of the chapters on pain and symptom control and what to expect at the end of life have made these chapters truly useful and accurate. I am grateful for his thoughtful approach to providing easy-to-read medical information.

Marilyn Lundy, R.N., PHN, the Coordinator of Palliative Care for Saint Elizabeth Health Care provided updated information to the draft manuscript with my appreciation.

Eileen McArthur has been a volunteer in a hospital palliative care unit and a trainer of palliative care volunteers. Her review of the material from her personal and volunteer perspectives was invaluable.

Eleanor G. Pask is the Executive Director of The Childhood Cancer Foundation -- Candlelighters Canada. Her thorough and thoughtful review has provided excellent improvements throughout the entire book.

Mary Lois Rennie, is a hospice practitioner, volunteer and educator. Her hospice and personal expertise plus her meticulous editing of this book have added immeasurable practical information for patients, families and care providers.

Anna Towers, M.D. of the Palliative Care Program at McGill University in Montreal and a physician at the Royal Victoria Hospital reviewed the manuscript and provided excellent recommendations to improve the chapter on pain and symptom control. Her expertise is most welcome.

Sue Watts, R.N. is the Day Care Manager for the Lions Hospice in Kent, England. She reviewed the manuscript from both the perspective of caregivers in a free-standing and community hospice.

I am also thankful to the following for reading the manuscript and for providing general comments and recommendations that have enhanced the book: **Margaret Clarke**, Executive Director, Hospice and Palliative Care Manitoba; **Frederic S. Martin**; **James McGregor, M.D.**, former Assistant Professor in the Departments of Family Medicine and Oncology at Queen's University in Kingston, Ontario; the Head of Palliative Care Services at Hotel Dieu Hospital and Palliative Care Consultant to the Kingston Regional Palliative Care Center and Kingston General Hospital; now in practice in California; **Peter J. Mortimer-Rae, KLJ, OMLJ**, Commander of the Calgary Commandery of The Military & Hospitaller Order of Saint Lazarus of Jerusalem; **Sid R. Wallace**; and **Rob Wedel, M.D.**, Medical Director, Palliative Care Program, Lethbridge, Alberta. My thanks go to **Robert Clarke** of The Military and Hospitaller Order of Saint Lazarus of Jerusalem for securing the helpful editorial comments of some of the people listed above.

Personal thanks and gratitude for their support to **Paul Clark**, an active volunteer at all levels of palliative care in Canada for over 20 years and to **David Irwin**, a palliative care supporter and enthusiast, and Chair of the

Palliative Care Commission at The Military & Hospitaller Order of Saint Lazarus of Jerusalem.

Over many years, I have spoken to thousands of people across Canada in workshops; college and university courses; at professional and volunteer inservices, and at provincial, national and international conferences on issues of dying, death and bereavement. To those who took the time to talk or write to me with their experiences, stories and practical advice, I thank you.

To the members of the palliative care associations to which I belong, I am grateful for their information, advice and stories. These groups include the **Canadian Palliative Care Association**, the **Hospice Association of Ontario**, the **Toronto Palliative Care Council**, **The National Hospice Organization (U.S.)**, **The Ontario Palliative Care Association**, and the former **Palliative Care Work Group of Toronto**.

I am also grateful to many hospice groups across Canada whose self-published manuals and brochures for their volunteers, patients and families are full of helpful information and tips, consistent with the material in this book.

To those who speak and write about palliative care, I am grateful for their re-affirming that much of the information in this book is not unique but shared by most of us. In particular, I would like to thank **Dr. Cicely Saunders** and **Dr. Thérèse Vanier** (retired) of St. Christopher's Hospice in England for their insights and expertise as founding members of the hospice movement internationally during interviews given in the summer of 1996.

I am grateful to **Rubin Cohen** and **Dr. Hung Der** for their personal and genuine encouragement of this work.

My loving thanks and gratitude to my best friend and wife, **Janet Klees**, for always encouraging my work and for challenging me to do my best. Her first editing of the manuscript made it more concise, readable, useful and relevant to families caring for a loved one. To our children, **Joanna** and **Bram** for reminding me that the hospice philosophy of care is quite natural to a child. I am grateful to my family for constantly reminding me what is possible when you balance love, gratitude and service.

Part 1: First Things First

Introduction: How to Use This Book

I assume that many people will read only some of the chapters in this book, depending on needs and available time. For those of you with limited time I assumed that you want quick and practical information, so I have kept most of the chapters crisp and to the point. I have repeated some of information in more than one chapter. Although this might prove tiresome to those of you who read the entire book, I believe it is important to keep each chapter as a separate and complete unit for easy reference.

This book is for family members and friends of someone who has a terminal or life-threatening illness. Its purpose is simply to provide information on how you might meet some of the physical, emotional, spiritual and information needs of your loved one who is ill and the rest of your family and friends involved in the care. The book is also designed to encourage open, honest and regular communication and cooperation between patients, families, and health care professionals and volunteer caregivers.

Occasionally I have written something directly to the person who is ill. The rest of the time, the information is directed at family members and friends. Patients are encouraged to read as much, or as little, of the book as they wish. As a family member or friend, you might read through the material and highlight those parts that you think your loved one might benefit from the most.

The book is not designed to make anyone a nurse or palliative care specialist. I hope that the book gives you enough information on how to get the help you need from experts in the field. They are your main source of information. This book is intended to supplement their help.

The book is designed to look at practical concerns like: effective pain and symptom control; living and dying at home, in a hospice or in a hospital; patient, family, and caregiver rights and responsibilities; ways to encourage open communication; legal and financial planning; ways to improve overall cooperation including finding and using personal and community resources.

I am not a medical expert, so I have relied on the knowledge and advice of people who are experts in their respective fields. The information in this book comes from personal experiences, interviews, workshops and conferences, written materials from numerous organizations, and in sources listed in the book.

From my own personal experiences I believe that people need **clear, brief and practical** information. The majority of those actively involved with people who have a terminal or life-threatening illness do not have the time to read long, detailed or theoretical books. They want something that can help today. This book, then, includes many **lists, forms and numbered ideas** to make it easier to find and use what you need. For those who want more detail, or want to study clinical studies or academic presentations, I have included a comprehensive list of recommended readings.

My parents and grandfather all died within a five–year period. They were not afraid of death as much as they were afraid of how they would die. In all three instances I was fortunate enough to be one of the people helping them to live at home until they died. Had we known more about proper pain control techniques, hospice and home care alternatives, patient and family rights, financial planning, etc., we could have provided even better care. We wanted to do so much more for the people we loved but we didn't know how. We didn't know where to get the information about how to provide better care.

Terminal illness does not mean a failure to cure. It does not mean that the disease has to rob us of our ability and need to love and to care. Terminal simply means "last" and in that sense of the word, a terminal illness is simply our last illness.

Personal control is all too often lost when a diagnosis of a terminal or life-threatening illness is made. People who have been in charge of their careers, their homes and especially their own minds, find themselves powerless to direct their lives. A sense of control comes from understanding what the options are and making decisions based upon reliable information. Knowledge decreases fear while increasing personal control.

Physicians, nurses and other caregivers are not strangers to the frustrations of terminal or life-threatening illnesses. Until recently, their education contained little information about end-of-life care and ways to help their dying patients. These dedicated people were taught how to cure people, so to admit there is no cure goes against all of their professional training. They also feel a loss of control.

All of us have different experiences, religious and moral beliefs and ways of making decisions. Patients and families may decide to leave most of the decisions in the hands of their medical caregivers or they may choose to actively make their own decisions based on counsel from caregivers, other family members, and spiritual leaders. My goal is to ensure that people know they have options and that they can exercise control over their medical treatment.

Although the focus of this book is primarily on patients and families understanding their options, I have a great deal of empathy for the role of the professional and volunteer caregivers. Often, final decisions about a person's life and death are left to these people. Their role is crucial and our understanding of how it affects us is very important to total patient care.

I have tried to write in a style that reflects the importance of both women and men in the caregiving professions. It is hard to find the exact words to describe the different roles people have. I have used **patient** rather than consumer or client because most of us who have been patients understand the word means 'someone who receives treatment'. (We also know too well that patience is a major requirement for anyone who receives treatment.)

I have used **family** to include both people who are part of one's immediate family and those we define as members of our family through friendship and love. Family can also include people whose relationship to the patient is emotionally significant but uncertain, conflicted or even hostile. Such people care for the patient but do so unwillingly or reluctantly. **Caregivers** include professionals and volunteers who help care for our loved ones.

A **primary caregiver** usually is a family member or close friend who provides most of the physical care for a person at home (e.g., wife, husband, lover, best friend).

The words **palliative** and **hospice** mean exactly the same thing. I will use both terms. The hospice philosophy of care is about trying to meet the physical, emotional, spiritual and information needs of people with a terminal illness or life-threatening illness and their families.

Many of you reading this book are presently involved in a personal and/or professional way with someone who has a terminal or life-threatening illness. I encourage you to adapt the book to your personal or professional needs. I have designed this book to meet the concerns and interests of as many different people as possible. For professionals in the field, I believe this book is very useful to your patients as a basic understanding of what their choices are while encouraging them to work with you for the best care possible.

I strongly believe that improving communication and cooperation between caregivers and between programs and services will lead to greater comfort and peace for a person who is dying, and personal satisfaction for those who are helping people to live as fully as possible until they die. This goal is reached every day in Canada when people have proper pain and symptom control, and receive emotional, spiritual and informational support and loving care.

Note: This is a relatively short book given all the topics it hopes to cover. Therefore, we cannot cover every kind of situation you, or a loved one, may experience. *Adapt the information in this book to meet your needs.* Some people who use this book will need it for only a short time. Others may need it for several months or longer. *If you cannot find what you need in this book, ask your Home Care Case Manager, family doctor, or visiting home nurse for more specific information.* There is a lot of information out there and these people can help you get it quickly. Also look in the reference and organizations' lists at the back of this book for more information.

My sincere best wishes,

Harry van Bommel

Chapter 1   What To Do In An Emergency

Do not call 911 if someone has died a natural, expected death at home. Instead, call the most responsible physician (e.g., your family doctor, doctor on call, palliative care physician) who can tell you what you should do. When a death is expected to happen at home, talk to your doctor about what you should do before, during and after the death.

Call 911 or your local hospital, fire department or ambulance service in almost all other emergency situations where you cannot deal with whatever is happening.

You can call 911 in Quebec if a person has died a natural death at home. Legal arrangements have been made with response teams not to resuscitate a person who has died a natural death at home. Talk to your family doctor about your specific circumstances before calling 911.

Talk to your physician and health care team about **who should be called** in what type of emergency. Keep a list of their names and telephone numbers by the telephone and in your pocket. What may originally feel like an emergency may only need some telephone help from your doctor, nurse, home care case manager, social worker or hospice staff or volunteer.

If you are expecting to care for someone at home, and have enough time to prepare, take an emergency first aid course or upgrading program or a home care course for family members. There are also family health care programs offered through local organizations including St. John Ambulance, The Red Cross, community colleges, YMCAs, and others. The more you know what to do in an emergency situation, the more comfortable you will feel. Focus on probable or possible emergency situations based on the individual medical circumstances involved.

As with all good planning, you should think about what you will do in different situations **before** they happen. Just as we should plan our escape route from our home if there is a fire, we should also know what to do when we are caring for a loved at home who has a terminal or life-threatening illness. The more we ask others about what we might expect to happen, the more we can prepare to deal with anything that comes along. Every person's situation is unique so you need to adapt the general information to your specific circumstances.

Chapter 2 Getting Organized:
'To Do' Checklists For Families

Concerns When Someone is at Home
Who Can Help You
Other People Who Can Help and Whose Telephone Numbers You Should Have
Handy
Checklist After Death
After the Funeral/Memorial Service

One of the causes of feeling overwhelmed when caring for someone is trying to keep track of the information you need or already have. The following checklists can be used whether the person you are caring for is at home, in the hospital or other facility. The lists can help you near the beginning of caring for someone and/or near to the end of their lives. **Adapt the lists to suit your own needs and ignore the rest.**

Also check the medical, personal information, legal, funeral and financial forms in Chapters 13, 15, 16, and 17. These forms are meant to hold the information you need to complete some of the task in the checklists below. **Remember** you do not have to know and do everything at once. Use the checklists to pace yourself. Most of the tasks do not need to be done right now.

Concerns When Someone is at Home

❒ Do you know enough about pain and symptom control to help the person who is home? If not, how can you get the information you need quickly from the physician, home care nurse, pharmacist? (Also check Chapter 8 on pain and symptom control.)

❒ Do you know what to do in a medical emergency at home? Who do you call? When? For what type of emergencies?

❒ Will the physicians make house calls?

❒ How can you reach the physician day or night?

❒ Has the person who is ill decided if they want to be resuscitated if they stop breathing? Have they put it in writing? Where is it? If they want to be resuscitated, learn CPR.

☐ Has the person written out a Power of Attorney for Personal Care and Property decisions saying who will make medical and financial decisions on their behalf if they cannot speak for themselves? Where is it kept? Who is the person? Does the family know who this person is and will they work with, or against, this person? If the person has not made someone their substitute decision maker, either get them to sign the form if they can or have the immediate family agree to have one spokesperson for the person. It is not legal but it helps you to make decisions at home and with physicians. These forms are available at provincial government health or justice ministries, some bookstores, doctors' offices, or your own lawyer.

☐ Are you using all of the relevant and available home care resources such as visiting home nurses, social workers, homemakers, occupational and physical therapists, dieticians, massage therapists, chiropractors, speech therapists, palliative care volunteer programs? Are you using other resources in the community including spiritual supports, professional and community volunteers as you need them? (Check the chapters in Parts 3 and 7 on hospice care and community resources.)

☐ Does the person's life insurance policies pay for extra home care support? Do the policies allow the person to take some of the money out before their death to pay for extra costs? (For example, some policies that normally pay out $100,000 to a beneficiary, now allow the person's whose life is insured to take out some of that, say $25,000, to pay for extra home care costs.) Check with the insurance agent or the insurance company to see if the person qualifies.

☐ Has the person written out a legal will to prevent legal difficulties about their estate after their death? Where is it kept? Who is the executor (person in charge after death)?

☐ Where is the information kept on bank accounts, investments, life insurance, safety deposit boxes, credit/charge cards, and vehicle ownership and insurance? When possible, you might want to change bank accounts into joint accounts so that only one person has to sign to deposit or withdraw money. This is also true for safety deposit boxes. In this way, accounts and boxes are not frozen until after the estate has been probated or settled.

☐ Has the person signed an organ donation form? Where is it kept? What restrictions exist around organ donation because of the person's disease or if the person dies at home? (Age, disease or location of death are some of the criteria used to determine if organs are acceptable for donation. Find out in advance so that the family is not left feeling rejected if organ donation is not accepted.)

☐ Has the person made any pre-funeral arrangements? Where is the information?

☐ Some companies give partial refunds (called 'compassionate travel policies') if you need to travel for the death of an immediate family member. An immediate family member is usually a: spouse, child, brother or sister, grandparent, grandchild, in-law or legal guardian. A proof of death certificate is required. The application form is available from the companies offering this refund and is usually completed within 90 days after the death.

☐ Do you have a plan to get some support and relief for yourself? Who can you turn to in your neighborhood for immediate help? Who might help you by staying with your loved one for a few hours while you take a break? Who can stay for longer periods of time (e.g., a weekend) so that you can visit friends or family elsewhere or go to a hotel for a weekend of spoiling yourself? Are there respite services available that can care for your loved one while you take a few days off? (Check Chapters 18 and 19 on community supports and support circles for some ideas.)

☐ Do you feel comfortable talking with professionals, volunteers, neighbors and family members helping you and your loved one? (Check the chapters in Parts 3 and 5 on hospice care and emotional and spiritual care for some tips).

When looking at funeral costs it is helpful to check out:

• If the person is a honorably discharged Canadian veteran with insufficient funds for a proper funeral, The Last Post Fund (800-563-2508) will help. Also call War Veterans Allowance: 1-800-387-0919.

• Veterans Affairs Canada may also have funds available for funeral costs. Contact your local branch office.

• If the person dies from a work-related illness or accident, the Workplace Safety Insurance Board (formerly the Worker's Compensation Board) may cover some of the funeral costs.

Who Can Help You

Family Doctor or Most Responsible Physician

❏ Will he or she make house calls?

❏ How can you reach them night and day with questions, or in an emergency?

❏ Will they sign the death certificate and/or come to the home to legally declare the person has died? This means the person does not have to go to the hospital to be declared dead there. (Note: the laws requiring a physician to declare a person has died at home vary from province to province. Check with your family physician.)

Home Care Case Manager

This person co-ordinates the nurses, homemakers, suppliers, equipment providers and other agencies.

❏ Do you know how to reach them day and night with questions, or in an emergency?

Pharmacist

This person often knows the most about your medications, how they interact with each other, side effects, etc.

❏ Do you know how to reach them day or night with questions, or in an emergency?

Palliative Care Program/Service

This may be a program in your hospital or in your community that helps to meet your loved one's physical, emotional, spiritual and information needs. For example, some communities have pain and symptom control coordinators. Your local home care program can tell you what is available.

❐ Is there a palliative care program/service in your community?

❐ Do you know how to reach them day or night with questions, or in an emergency?

Other People Who Can Help and Whose Telephone Numbers You Should Have Handy

❐ Your priest, minister, rabbi or spiritual leader.

❐ Private nursing and home care companies to supplement your care.

❐ Red Cross which provides some services, equipment, volunteers and financial aid.

❐ Disease specific group (e.g., Cancer Society, AIDS Committee).

Checklist After Death

Sometimes it is helpful to have a checklist of things that need to be done after the death of a loved one at home. (If the death is at a hospital, free-standing hospice or other health care facility, you are helped to do whatever is necessary.) Some of the tasks may already be done. This list gives you direction at a time when decisions are expected from you. Sit down with your family and divide the various tasks so that no one has too much to do. If the executor of the estate is someone other than a family member, then you may leave many of the legal, financial, tax and other requirements for him or her to complete.

The forms included in this book provide you with much of the information that is required by a funeral home, executor, lawyer, family physician, etc. If there was no time to fill in these forms, some of the following suggestions will help ensure that most things are covered.

❏ Call the family physician and ask for further directions if you have not pre-planned for this situation together.

❏ If you are alone at the time of death call someone right away to give you emotional support and to help arrange the next few days' activities. You may be exhausted and need help right away.

❏ Call your funeral home to arrange for the transportation of the body to the funeral home. Make an appointment to finalize the arrangements. If your loved one left specific instructions, then arrange to follow them as completely as possible. If there were no instructions, decide on the type of funeral and whether the body will be buried or cremated.

❏ Collect the various information forms included in this book so that you do not have to remember all the information.

❏ Arrange for family members and friends to take turns answering the door and phone.

❏ You may need some immediate grief or bereavement support for family members either through a formal counselor or your spiritual leader and friends. Ask for the comforting support you need right now.

❏ If you are not the executor then notify him right away and ask for his help.

❏ Decide whether you wish flowers and/or donations to a charity (assuming you have no instructions from your loved one).

❏ Make a list of the immediate family, friends and colleagues from work you want to notify by phone or telegram.

❏ Decide if you wish specific people to act as pallbearers and put a check mark beside their name on the list in Chapter 17.

❏ Make a separate list for people who live far away and whom you wish notified by letter and/or printed notice.

❏ Prepare a copy of a printed notice if you wish to use one.

❏ You or someone else should call or telegram the people on the list to notify them of the death.

❐ Different religions require different arrangements. For example, Roman Catholics usually use Prayer Cards at the funeral service. If you are Roman Catholic, your church or funeral home can suggest a printer who will do these quickly. Other religions require other specific things to be done, so check with your cleric or funeral director for help.

❐ If small children belonging to the deceased or to a survivor are not attending the funeral, arrange for help until after the services are over.

❐ Coordinate the supply of food for the next few days.

❐ Arrange for help with daily household chores.

❐ If people are coming from out-of-town, arrange a place for them to stay and eat.

❐ Arrange for the care of any family pets.

❐ Take precautions during the funeral services to protect the home against burglaries. Have someone housesit.

❐ Write an obituary. Funeral directors can offer suggestions but some or all of the following can be included: name, age, place of birth, cause and place of death, occupation, educational background, military service, memberships held, volunteer work, and list of the immediate family. Give the date, time and place of services. If the funeral director does not provide this service you can deliver or call in the obituary to the newspaper yourself. Most newspapers charge for this notice.

❐ Decide what to do with the flowers after the funeral.

❐ Arrange to have someone pay the clerics, organist, and others who need payment the day of the funeral.

After the Funeral/Memorial Service

The paper work and bureaucracy of dying, the insurance policies, the probating of the will, etc., can be very frustrating. Some of the following steps need to be done right away and others can wait. Pick and choose where, when and how to use your energy. Whether you are the executrix of the will or helping someone who is, it is important to expect delay, frustration and illogical procedures. Except for the last step of sending thank-you cards, the executrix of the will usually carries out all of the following steps. If this person is not a member of the family, she needs information and help from the next-of-kin during some of the steps. (Check Chapter 17 on preparing funeral arrangements for more information.)

❏ When you get information from any officials, **take note of their name, the date you spoke with them and what they said.** This is especially true with large bureaucracies where each person may give you different information.

❏ If the deceased lived alone, notify the utilities and post office. Have mail forwarded to your address or the executor's address.

❏ If the deceased rented his home, notify the landlord and arrange a time when you can move all the belongings.

❏ Get several copies of the death certificate. You need these for insurance, banking and other legal matters. The funeral director usually arranges to get these for you or you can get them yourself from your provincial ministry responsible for births, deaths and marriages.

❏ Fill out the person's financial status form as at the time of death.

❏ Notify insurance company(ies) about all appropriate policies.

❏ Check with your local Health and Welfare Canada office about any death benefits, and spouse/family benefits. Check with your funeral director, home care case manager, your lawyer and accountant, palliative care service to find out if new programs exist that might be helpful. Some programs are not widely known so not everyone on this list may have the same information. Ask them what specific documents you need to get these benefits.

❏ Also check with the Canadian Ministry of Veterans affairs for any military benefits.

❏ If the person received any government checks, those departments have to be notified of their death (e.g., Old Age Pension, Canada Pension Plan (CPP), Employment Insurance, Family Benefits).

❏ Check with credit unions, trade unions, fraternities, the Royal Canadian Legion, credit card companies, auto clubs, special associations or organizations that the deceased was a member of, for similar pensions and other benefits.

❏ Collect all outstanding bills and pay them. In cases of large bills, mortgage payments, business debts etc., you should get the advice of a lawyer and/or accountant.

❏ Cancel all credit cards right away.

❏ Notify the following organizations of the person's death: driver's license bureau, charitable organizations the person contributed to, post office, pension/government health insurance and other government agencies (e.g., to cancel Social Insurance Number), and organizations or associations that the person was a member of.

❏ In the case of car insurance and registration, the insurance must be changed to the name of the new owner before car registration can be changed.

❏ Notify the land titles office in your province if the person owned property.

❏ Different jurisdictions have different regulations about how to probate a will (if it is necessary at all). Check with your local government to see what the regulations are. For simple estates, it is often possible to settle the will out of court without the help of a lawyer, however, family reform laws are more common and lead to more restrictions to estate settlement. When in doubt, speak with a lawyer. You may also ask your insurance agent, funeral home director or other professionals who deal daily with these questions. They may advise you or refer you to an estate lawyer.

❏ Complete the person's income tax form at the end of the year. If the estate is large or complicated, get the advice of an accountant or tax lawyer.

❏ Distribute the assets according to the person's will and auction off or dispose of the other assets as required. Large estates do require certain laws to be followed and again you should get legal advice on the proper procedures.

❐ Make a list of people you wish to send thank you notes to such as those who attended the funeral; family members and friends who sent condolences and/or charitable donations; and physicians and other caregivers who gave the deceased and family good care.

Note: I began by saying that this process can be very frustrating and emotionally draining. It is important to recognize that the grieving process continues and that these steps are often an important part of that grieving. Cleaning out closets, selling furniture, closing bank accounts are all emotionally traumatic and take their toll on you but they also help you to release some of the your emotional pain. With painful memories, take the time to remember more than the pain. Remember the person, the pleasures you shared together as well as the pain. Recognize your personal needs and take time to pamper yourself. You deserve it.

Take the time you need, **ask** for the specific help you deserve from other family members and friends (they may not know how to offer help) and use this opportunity to acknowledge your real loss.

Chapter 3   A Summary Of Some Of The Basics

Some people will not have time to read each chapter of this book thoroughly. The following general points are a good preview and review. More detail is given in specific chapters. Use the Table of Contents and Index to find the answers to your specific concerns.

This book is based on the assumption that we can choose how we cope with terminal or life-threatening illness. This book suggests ways to provide medical and family supports to a person who is dying but the book is not meant to imply that this period of living until death is simple or without physical and emotional hardships.

Hospice or Palliative Care

The words palliative and hospice mean exactly the same thing. I use both terms. The hospice philosophy of care is about trying to meet the physical, emotional (including social), spiritual and information needs of people with a terminal or life-threatening illness and their families.

Pain and Symptom Control

Most people can be relatively pain free, comfortable and alert until they die. The days of people shouting out to die because the pain hurts so bad should be over.

If a patient is suffering severe pain, get the doctor in charge to check with a palliative care specialist who can suggest methods to reduce the pain now. We have all the knowledge and skills, right now, to manage overwhelming pain. All of the pain may not go away. Most of us suffer from some physical pain from aging, arthritis, back problems, etc. However, unbearable pain is not necessary.

The secret to effective pain control (relief) is giving the **right drug(s)**, in the **right amount**, in the **right way** and at the **right time**. This balance requires physicians and other hospice team members to do proper, ongoing assessments of a person's pain and to consult with others who may have information that is helpful. Proper pain medication usually prevents overwhelming pain from returning while keeping the patient alert. If pain does suddenly increase (called "breakthrough pain") extra medication must be immediately available to relieve it. In those rare cases when pain cannot be relieved enough, a person can be placed in a drug-induced coma for a period of time to alleviate the pain. No ones needs to suffer the type of unmanaged pain that we may have witnessed our parents and grandparents suffer.

Once pain is managed, other symptoms like vomiting, bed sores, and dry mouths are more easily controlled.

Personality

People's basic personalities do not change when they find out they have a terminal or life-threatening illness or if they are grieving. How they dealt with stressful or traumatic situations in the past is likely how they cope now.

Your Role

Caring for others in such a personal and intimate way as hospice care is one of the most fulfilling and life-defining opportunities in our lives. When you care for someone else you know in your heart, mind and soul that you are making a real difference in that person's life. Caregiving gives us that unique opportunity to remember what is truly valuable in our lives and within our families and community. Caring is not always easy. It can be physically exhausting, mentally taxing and emotionally draining. It can also be exhilarating, rejuvenating, peaceful, joyful and awe inspiring.

Choose a role that is comfortable and supportive to the person who is dying and to those who are grieving. You should also get the support from family and friends you need to help you. Hospice care is about mutually caring for each other during this time.

Part 2: Hospice Stories

Chapter 4   Personal Stories of What is Possible

The following stories highlight some of the main points in this book. We often learn best through the stories of actual people. I have summarized their thoughts, with their permission, as if they were speaking directly to you. Some of these stories appeared in my first book *Choices*. Their advice and insights are timeless so I have reproduced them here. Others were first published in *The Pain Management Newsletter* published by Knoll Pharma Inc. in 1997 and 1998. The story by Dr. Cicely Saunders is based on an interview in the summer of 1996.

Dr. Cicely Saunders

Dr. Saunders is the modern founder of hospice care. Her previous careers as a nurse and social worker opened her eyes to the needs of people with a terminal or life-threatening illness. After completing her medical studies and working with terminally patients, she decided that a free-standing hospice providing excellent physical, emotional, spiritual and information supports was needed. She founded St. Christopher's Hospice in London, England in 1967. She is now retired from medical practice but still works regularly at St. Christopher's Hospice.

The last person that I cared for was my husband, Marian, because I am not in clinical work now. He used to sit back and say 'I'm completely happy. I have done what I had to do in my life and now I am ready to die.' I don't think you can do better than that. He died in 1995. He was nearly 94. He is the artist that did all the pictures around St. Christopher's Hospice.

He had about 4 life-threatening illnesses during his last 10 years and he was in and out of here but he was basically at home for those 10 years. He came in here for the last six weeks.

We have been looking at what spirituality really is in this day and age when so few people talk in religious language. I think it is the essentialness of what it is to be human in your own culture and relationships. Therefore, what we owe people is respect and attentive listening which enables them to realize that they are valued as themselves. I think that is the essence of what we are looking at in spiritual care. They may have a feeling for the beyond and I think we should be very ready to see what can still give them delight. And also what are their important symbols. All of that may be a key into how they see the beyond. So far as my husband was concerned he was not awfully traditional but he was Polish Catholic and completely sure of where he was going and that it was all right.

The medical director here looked after Marian absolutely beautifully and the knowledge of how to do that was being given by him. My own knowledge of my own journey through bereavement and so on before was a help. The most important thing, I suppose in a way, was our love for one another. We had very good memories. The thing that helped me most afterwards was that at the back of my little diary I had written the things he had said to me over the course of about four years. After he died I wrote them all out and as an artist, he was saying to me "You are my complementary color". Also, "We have found ourselves. I am safe. I am happy" and things like that. They were very constructive and helpful.

"Ann"

Dr. Jim McGregor was an Assistant Professor in the Departments of Family Medicine and Oncology at Queen's University in Kingston, Ontario; the Head of Palliative Care Services at Hotel Dieu Hospital and Palliative Care Consultant to the Kingston Regional Palliative Care Center and Kingston General Hospital. He has since moved to the United States. Once of his patients was "Ann." This is his description of how his team helped care for Ann's pain and symptoms.

Ann is a 47-year old woman with metastatic cancer of the lung. In mid-November, 1996 on a Friday, she arrives at the hospital with abdominal pain and nausea. Her greatest concern, however, is not just with her physical pain and uncomfortable symptoms. She is supposed to get married the following day and wants to know if someone can help her enough so that she can make the service. I see Ann on the Friday afternoon.

Ann cannot get from her bed to the bathroom without vomiting. Her nausea may be caused by the simple act of moving around. She feels full and bloated on small amounts of food and liquid. To try and ease her pain and symptoms, we prescribed a different nausea medication and put Ann on continuous subcutaneous medications using a portable pain pump that she can wear under her clothes and with which she can walk about.

Ann's nausea and pain were well controlled within hours. She remained on the pain pump and attended her wedding the next afternoon and evening, to her own amazement and that of her family. She returned to hospital that Saturday evening after the reception. She was tired from both the excitement of the day and her condition. By Monday she was able to begin taking some of her medication by mouth. On Tuesday the pump was removed and Ann was released from hospital on Wednesday to begin her married life with her new husband.

"Mr. G."

Andrew Féron, M.S.W., C.S.W. is the social worker on the Palliative Care Unit at Parkwood Hospital in London, Ontario. He was part of the team caring for Mr. G. Mrs. G. talked about her husband's suicidal wishes and she asked "how could we allow her husband to go on living when 'No decent human being would allow an animal to suffer like this without putting it out of its misery'".

Mr. G was a 70-year old man with recurrent carcinoma of the nasal cavity. His pain and symptoms were well managed. He was dearly loved and cared for by his family at home until Mr. G's cancer ate away his mouth and nose, leaving a gaping tumor from his eyes to his chin that became infected with maggots. Mrs. G. could no longer cope with his illness and he was brought to our unit. He wanted help to die.

Mr. G's physical symptoms were well managed but his emotional suffering and that of his family's were unmanageable. Our team struggled with how we could 'be present' during Mr. G's last days. At times it was even difficult to relate to Mr. G. as a person because, without a face, he lost his identity. To be so ill and helpless that death offers the only release is a fate so awful to think about that it becomes understandable why some people want to discuss euthanasia or assisted suicide in their own particular case. Although I am opposed to euthanasia and assisted suicide, this case tested my beliefs.

No one on the team could imagine Mr. G's suffering but all could sympathize with his request to die. I admitted to Mrs. G. my humanity and the fact that I also struggled with feelings of frustration at not being able to do anything directly to ease Mr. G's emotional suffering or improve his quality of life. I talked about the pain I saw in his eyes as he witnessed peoples' reactions to his appearance. I acknowledged the wonderful care that Mrs. G. had provided and assured her of the value of her continued involvement. I allowed her to vent her anger, frustration, exhaustion and grief. Verbal communication with Mr. G. was almost impossible and he did not have the strength to engage in another relationship with a well-meaning professional. By supporting the family, I empowered them to support Mr. G. in his suffering.

The answer of how best 'to be present' with Mr. G., without helping him to die, came from Mr. G's six-year-old granddaughter. The team had recommended that she not come to visit her grandfather as his condition was deteriorating quickly in these, his last days.

Little six-year-olds can be quite persuasive and she insisted on seeing her grandfather. She was told in advance what he would look like and what the room he was in looked like so that she would not be frightened or surprised by what she saw. When she got to the room, she rushed in, ran to her grandfather, gave him a big hug and said, "I love you Grandpa". She saw the man she loved inside the sick body. She touched his heart and showed the rest of his family and the palliative care team the answer of how 'to be present'. It is easier said than done, of course. It takes unconditional, child-like love.

"Hans Peters"

Like many veterans I am not afraid of death; I am afraid of how I will die.

Hans Peters was a farm manager in his mid 50's. He was widowed a few years before his own death. This is his story compiled from several interviews. He had a lot he wanted to say to people. He wanted to help others understand what dying means so that people could benefit from his experiences.

I am dying but I am not afraid of death. I stopped being afraid of death that May morning in 1940 when I looked up from milking our family cow to see a Nazi soldier pointing a rifle at me. I fought later in another war and saw death all around me. Through my experiences I became more afraid of how I would die rather than death itself.

I won't live much longer now. My doctors tell me I have emphysema. It feels like a tight chain around my chest. You breathe and breathe and don't seem to get any air into your lungs. For the last few weeks I've been breathing oxygen from a tank. It makes my mouth dry and I can get "high" if I breathe too much of it. I've been smoking steady for 45 years now and this is the result, but what the hell -- when I was a kid on the farm my father gave all his sons a pouch of tobacco on the day we graduated from elementary school. My wife kept telling me to stop smoking but it was too hard for me to do and I enjoyed it so much. When my wife died I smoked even more and cared about it less.

With emphysema you can live for many years, so they say. But I have a brain tumor too, which my physicians can't operate on so I will die pretty soon. One of the many doctors who looked after me was surprised that I didn't worry too much about death. She was a young neurologist and really upset by the news she had to give me about my illness, especially that I only have a few months to live. She hadn't experienced death as often as I had and was afraid of how I would react to her news.

After the initial shock wore off I took stock of my life and with few exceptions was quite pleased. I had married the girl of my dreams and our kids have grown to be good, hardworking and loving people.

You know I was a farmer. When the doctor found out I was a farmer, she told my kids that farmers understand death much better than other people. Farmers understand how seasons affect the life-cycle: in spring, life begins; in summer, life grows and becomes productive; while in the fall, life's work is harvested. Of course the winter season is that short period when life ends, only to begin again very soon in a new form. No big deal.

I believe in God and in an afterlife. When my wife was in a coma she saw heaven and said it was more beautiful, glorious and exciting than even our love for each other or the birth of our kids. She described her vision as her standing on one side of a flowing yet shallow river. She told me: "I had to make a choice of whether to cross the river or return to my family. It was the hardest choice I've ever made for heaven was so beautiful. I chose to come back here because I knew I couldn't leave you yet." She told me of the most peaceful world she had ever seen. I believed her then and I am comforted by the memory of her words now.

Death isn't scary for me anymore. How I die is what keeps bugging me.

Now that I know I am dying I have a few suggestions for my friends. It is very important to me that they accept the fact that I am dying. It doesn't help me to hear them say that I am looking better or that I will be up and about soon. I won't. When some of my friends do not accept that I am dying it makes it difficult for me to talk about what I feel and what my hopes are for them. By what they say (or don't say) and what they do, they are telling me they don't want to face the fact that I am dying; nor I guess their own death one day.

When some people are unable to talk openly, it also makes it difficult for my kids because they have fewer people to lean on. Fortunately, I have family and friends who do accept the natural process of my dying. It is their gift to my kids and me that can never be repaid.

What would I suggest to employers who have someone with a terminal illness working for them? Terminal illness does not mean that a person is useless. It means so much for people to feel useful and needed. Do not let them go "for their own good." As long as they can work, with some help from others at the job, please let them work. Some people can even do some of their work at home. Let them. Employers and employees need to realize that working together during this difficult time can help them both.

What about my medical treatment? Doctors and other medical staff often mean well but they sometimes forget they are dealing with people. When things first began happening to me it was all too fast for me to think clearly. My kids were very worried and, therefore, they took over asking the questions that needed to be asked e.g., What is happening? How soon can he come home? Is there anything we can do? What are his chances of recovery? What things do you think we need to know to help us to help him? Often these questions were dodged because there were no clear answers. There were educated guesses, however, and I think we deserved to know what they were.

I was brought into emergency five times before coming home to die and in three of those times I was given too much oxygen which made me "drunk" for days. I don't remember my son's birthday because I was "out of it" for three days. The frustrating thing for my family was that the first two times it happened, no one believed my kids when they told doctors that I wasn't acting as I normally would. They said my kids were exaggerating about what they saw and were being too protective of me.

When my kids finally got the doctor to explain why I had appeared intoxicated or senile for a few days at a time they were able to protect me from it recurring the next time I was rushed to the hospital. In other words, when they knew the facts, or educated guesses, of what was happening to me they could work together with the medical staff to give me the best care I could get.

So often in the hospital I heard other patients complain that people weren't listening to them. It seems to me life would be easier if everyone worked together, for it would spread the knowledge around to the people who know the patient best and who can assist him the best. Nurses often complained of the same thing. They admitted the doctors were extremely busy and, therefore, only had five-to-ten minutes to spend with each patient. What infuriated them was that they were the professional staff who saw the patients the most yet their opinion was often not even consulted, never mind listened to.

People make life so complicated when really it is quite simple. Imagine all the lawsuits that would never be laid against doctors, nurses, and hospitals if the patients and their families were involved from the beginning. A simple consent form isn't enough. Knowledge gives me self-confidence and some form of control which after nearly 60 years of living I have gotten used to having.

Perhaps one day, writers and the rest of the world will talk more with people who are dying. Better yet, let's get the children and the politicians to talk to us. They could learn a lot about living from people who are dying.

There are three things that keep coming back to me these days and maybe you can use them for your book. It will be the last time I guess that anything I say will mean something to more than just my kids and friends.

Faith in God makes accepting death easier. Faith in people will give people, like me, a more dignified death in the future than is possible today.

Employers need to understand that one day they will die as well and, therefore, they should benefit from the presence of someone who may be dying but hasn't given up on life or given up on being productive.

Friends need to understand as well that dying people still have the normal needs that we all have. I still think of having a good time, playing cards, reading the newspaper, getting into a good political argument. I enjoy laughing even though at times I need to cry. If my wife were alive, I would still enjoy sex and the comfort of a kiss and a hug. I also need to talk about my death which is not meant to be morbid or to remind you that you are going to die one day too. Dying is not scary all the time but sometimes I feel I have to handle it all by myself because people don't understand what it's like.

My kids have been super for they hug me and let me hug back. They talk about how they feel and about how I feel. They help me make plans and try to insure that I get the best treatment available. Sometimes they love me too much and that makes me sad because I know I must leave them. That is the hardest of all.

I hope that my life has meant something to my family and friends and also to people who have met me briefly: during the war, with my community work or just because I happened to smile at a stranger one day not knowing that he, too, may have lost a dear friend recently.

I also hope that when it is time for me to go I can say goodbye with some dignity to help my kids to build their strengths and their love. How I leave them will be in their memories for the rest of their lives and I hope I can make it loving and special, for they deserve at least that much.

Hans died with his children beside him at home. His children grew stronger and their love for each other and their parents did increase. They are very proud of their parents, just as their father and mother were proud of them. They hope to write a family history one day, so that their children can learn from the grandparents they will never know.

Dr. Carol Brock

Dr. Carol Brock is a family physician who has taught family practice to physicians at a community hospital. I met Dr. Brock in the mid-1980s at her home where our short interview turned into a two and one-half hour discussion of the physician-patient relationship.

It was clear from the beginning that Dr. Brock had sensitivity to the needs of her patients. Her choice of family practice was based more on her personal philosophy of what a family physician should be than what she had been taught about medicine during her professional training. The following is a summary of what Dr. Brock felt then, and now, about what were the most important things to pass along to other family physicians, their patients and patients' families.

The most important role of family physicians, when one of their patients is dying, is to pay attention -- not just to their words, for words often say what patients think they should say, but also to their body language. Looking into their eyes can help physicians understand their patients' fears and needs. Each situation is unique. For example, a patient or family member may come asking for your medical advice, when what she really needs is to have her hand held and told that her fears are natural and surmountable.

People will come to you at different times during the period when they or a loved one is dying. They come very soon after learning about their terminal illness from a specialist. They come during the living process leading to death and their family members will come to you after the person has died. What they need most often is someone who knows them well, listens unconditionally and explains in clear language the medical process of the illness and what they can expect to happen.

Although the listening and counseling is crucial to patient care, there are also the practical components to medical care that the family practitioner can help with. In effect, the family practitioner should be the patient's advocate with all the other members of the medical world: the hospital, specialists, social workers, home care personnel and even the clergy when that is appropriate.

Assuming there are family members and/or friends available to help the patient, you can talk to them in a family conference and help them make group decisions. A family conference permits people to volunteer how they can help the patient best: housekeeping, driving to and from the hospital or appointments, or acting as the single family spokesperson with the medical specialists. During a family conference each family member can also talk about what they find difficult to do: bathing the patient, talking about death and dying, or answering phone calls from other family and friends who want to know about the patient's condition.

In effect, the family physician is helping the family to stop for a few moments during a very traumatic time, review the various options available to them, and consider what decisions must be made. This is naturally an ongoing process but once the family begins to work together (if this is possible), then the physician's time commitment does not have to be as great. As a family practitioner you can also suggest that your patients turn to the people closest to them for emotional, spiritual and physical support. It may appear obvious that people do this on their own, but so often people find it difficult to decide honestly what they really need in the way of support. People do not want to be a burden to someone else.

As a family practitioner, you can suggest that your patients relax in a comfortable chair, in a quiet place and think about what they really need in a physical, emotional and spiritual way. You can repeat often to your patients that once they have decided what they need, they must force themselves to ask for help. When people lived in smaller communities it wasn't as necessary to ask for help because people naturally helped each other. In today's urban world, we feel uncertain and are afraid to ask for help and our family and friends often feel they would be interfering if they offered their help.

If a patient asks for help, but the person they ask cannot cope with the terminal illness, the patient should ask someone else. If the first few people asked cannot give the patient the supports she needs, she, with the help of a family member or friend, should persist and ask someone else. I realize this is easier said than done but patients need support and family practitioners can help them get it.

Physicians or friends who say "There's nothing left to do." are doing a great disservice to the person. You have to help him find hope, and a way to cope, when all appears hopeless. There is always something you can do even if a cure is no longer one of the options. People can live a full life until their death, if they are given physical and emotional support.

People who are dying can put their financial and legal matters in order to save their survivors a great deal of frustration. They can also spend valuable time with their families and friends talking about future hopes and reminiscing about happy times in the past.

Families and friends can provide physical and emotional support by supplying prepared foods or baby-sitting. Being there yourself and being yourself are the most important things you can do. Words are often not as important as listening, holding a hand, sharing a tear and saying "I love you." A simple open-ended question like "How are you really feeling?" will permit the person who is dying or grieving to say as much or as little as she wishes.

One of the hardest things family and friends are asked to do is to listen repeatedly to someone who is grieving. It may appear that the person is living in the past, yet it is a common response to grief and sorrow and repetition makes the past and the death real and the healing effective.

Patients afraid of dying may ask their physicians very difficult questions, such as, "What are God's reasons for dying now? What are the physician's own beliefs about euthanasia? What will happen to their families? Will they die in pain and will they die alone?" Most often people want an honest answer from their physician, not a church sermon remembered from the physician's childhood days. If you, as a physician, believe in an after-life, speak honestly about your belief. If you disagree with euthanasia in all cases, explain why. With the families, the physician can discuss how survivors of other patients dealt with the death of a loved one. Fears about pain are real and modern pain and symptom control techniques can take that pain away while keeping a person mentally alert. If you are unable to explain or prescribe adequate pain control, refer the patient to a physician who specializes in this field.

Patients are often afraid of dying alone but they may not talk about this fear. People, generally, do not want to be a burden to others. Reassure patients that you or a colleague are available to help at any time (patients don't usually abuse this offer) and discuss with the family ways to ensure that the person is never alone during the final period before death.

As a family practitioner I often see situations where there is little, unified family support. Part of the family wants one thing for the patient and another part wants something totally different. These are difficult situations at best and again the physician's primary concern is the patient's needs and desires. If it is possible, get the patient to designate a spokesperson for himself and encourage the family to concentrate on the patient's wishes rather than their own. If the situation is more difficult, try and bring other people into the picture who might help, such as a cleric, a social worker, or a support group like the Cancer Society, a Bereaved Parents group, etc.

Choices made by a patient, family and physician about treatment and medications are not always the right ones. It takes time and coordinated effort to find the right combination of medication and treatment for each patient's individual needs. If everyone works together as a team then the right choices are found more quickly. As a family physician, I believe everyone does his or her best at this time and if you come to the death of a loved one feeling you've done what you could and that I, as your family physician, have helped, then the death is an easier thing to accept for all concerned.

When I taught family practice to general practitioners a decade ago, I noticed, at first, an unconscious narrowness of mind when dealing with patient's emotional needs. This is not a condemnation but rather an observation. Many physicians are chosen by medical schools for their academic excellence rather than their interpersonal communication skills and aptitude for working with people.

Physicians are receiving more training in listening and communication skills today. Being human, they vary in their interest and evolving ability to attend to patients' emotional needs. The pre-requisite is having, and consciously taking, the time to be with the patient, wherever the patient is at. There is a learning curve to getting more comfortable with the wide variety of patients let alone with their dying and death. Good physician-patient communication and connecting at the human-to-human level leads to more dignified living until death for both patients and their physicians.

A personal note. I have changed my own personal ways of dealing with death and dying. I have learned many valuable lessons of living from my patients who were dying. I have also gone through soul searching to examine how my role as physician must sometimes change from that of curing patients to helping patients work with the choices available to them here and now. Personal friends, patients and reading books in various fields, including life-after-death issues, have helped me to understand even more clearly that there is still loving, giving and productivity when patients live until their death.

Rev. Keith Nevel

I met The Reverend Keith Nevel over lunch at "the-best-kept-secret-in-town" restaurant in the mid 1980s. This beautiful restaurant with its towering ceiling, quiet and aristocratic atmosphere was the backdrop for our discussion on the role of the clergy in working with people who have a terminal illness and their families.

The Reverend Nevel was the Anglican Chaplain at a palliative care unit. He was also the Consultant on Aging for his Diocese. He died several years ago. He was a person with great humor and insight which put me (and I assume his patients and their families) immediately at ease. When I asked Mr. Nevel the important features of chaplaincy he was very clear. "Be yourself above other things. If chaplains are uncomfortable with any aspect of aging or dying they cannot be very helpful to the people they visit."

The best a chaplain can do is to bring out the patient's own wealth of spiritual resources if the patient wants that to happen. Difficult situations, such as the death of someone you care for, challenges some people while making others feel vulnerable and alone. When they ask for our support we must provide it in an unconditional way.

Chaplains should be neutral religious figures except to members of their own particular church. Sometimes patients do not want to see me or any of the other chaplains and that is fair game. Humor allows me to ask them openly if they would like to speak with me; it also allows them to say yes or no, without feeling that I am putting them on the spot.

People all hope for a peaceful and pain-free death. I have found that the degree of peacefulness is often a measure of coming to terms with your own spiritual beliefs. I say this not in terms of church attendance but rather in how people use and understand their own spiritual resources. In my experience, I have found that people who have used religion for social reasons during their lifetime will benefit little from their faith at the time they are dying. This situation is reversible with enough time but requires people to seriously examine their relationship with God in the past and how they can strengthen their spirituality in the present.

Being an active member of a church does not protect us from difficult times, but rather, how we use the spirituality of our faith. People who have worked out their spirituality, whether in church, or not, can use their spiritual resources at time of great need. They may want to build upon their spiritual resources with a spiritual leader, like a chaplain, or they may do it by themselves or with others. Their attitude can often be expressed in the sentence: "Some people believe in the existence of God; others believe God."

People with no religion are often open to talking about spirituality because they haven't used the church as a social vehicle in the past. They are open to discussion and will debate their ideas and feelings and try to resolve any inconsistencies they may feel. One needn't accept a church's particular teachings to believe in God; what is important is whatever God may mean to that person.

One of the concerns of palliative care is the family. There is, however, a middle-class assumption that the family is always there to help patients with their death. Families often have major differences that are not immediately resolved when patients finds out they are dying. In fact, the family can often inhibit how we help patients. Our first priority is the individual patient but the family also requires our support and understanding.

We must remember that people often die the way they live. If they faced life's rewards and challenges with humor, insight, and concern for others, they will probably die in the same way. If they have been unsatisfied with their life; if they have major difficulties with their family, they will probably die in the same way. People do not dramatically change because they know they are dying. If anything, their dominant characteristics become even more evident.

The chaplain's role is to offer to help both the patient and the family resolve differences, individually and together. Sometimes someone else may be more effective in helping the patient and family such as a favorite nurse, a psychologist or a family friend. The principle here is to be flexible and meet the individual needs of the patient and family. I'll give you some examples from my own experience to make my points clear.

One of the major fears of people who are dying is that they are alone and forgotten. I visited one woman and before I could say hello she looked at my clerical collar and said: "Thank God I haven't been forgotten. Someone still cares." At times, my clerical wardrobe gives comfort to people who feel alone and my greatest joy is sharing time with them and listening to their hopes and fears without placing any judgments on them.

I mentioned how important humor can be. One man that I visited spoke about his religious experiences, good and bad. We talked about our faith, our view of an afterlife and his hopes for his family. He had not attended an Anglican service for quite some time but wanted to have communion before he died. I suggested that perhaps his family should share in this sacrament and he asked them to come the next day.

The man's wife had given him *The Joy of Stress* by Dr. Peter Hanson for Christmas and we were discussing the book when the family arrived. They were skeptical of my motives. They worried about an anticipated lecture on church attendance. To break the ice I mentioned Dr. Hanson's book and the man's wife asked me if I had read it. "I have, but I liked *The Joy of Sex* better." The family didn't know how to react until I began to laugh loudly and joyfully. The 19-year-old son joined in the laughter and we were able to talk openly and comfortably for the next half-hour. The communion was a joy to share with them. Like all church rituals, the communion service brings people together and makes a particular celebration real and concrete. It can be comforting and hopeful. It becomes a fond memory for the family after the person's death.

I receive a great deal more from the people I visit than they receive from me. During my own difficult times I look back on the lessons they have taught me. One deeply religious woman once told me about how her view of dying had changed over time. For months she had said that she was ready to die. After some introspection she discovered that what she had really meant was that she was ready for God to take her only on her terms. She would die when she was ready to go, and not a minute sooner. Her view changed. She became ready to go when God was ready to take her. Her change in perception was very comforting to her, for a heavy decision had been lifted from her shoulders. She died a most peaceful death.

I cannot speak too highly of the palliative care philosophy. The idea of spending more time listening unconditionally to patients is wonderful. Ideally, every member of the team works toward adapting the circumstances to the individual's needs.

One Roman Catholic woman had lived with a man outside of marriage for many years. She believed her actions to be "sinful" and could not speak to the Catholic Chaplain or other members of the palliative care team about her guilt. When the team found out about her situation they began to ask casual questions that permitted her to talk if she wanted to. A simple question about her frequent male visitor like: "How is he doing today?" permitted this woman to bring up a painful subject without fear of judgment or a lengthy lecture.

I have talked about how families can sometimes compound problems rather than help resolve them. I once spent many weeks talking with the young mother of an eight-year-old girl. The mother was dying of cancer and felt she had a major spiritual problem. After some discussions we found that her real problem was her father, who used her faith against her. He told her that if she was really faithful she would not have cancer. He used Biblical quotes to show her that she was unworthy when I was trying to help her see her own spiritual strength.

The history of this family included child abuse and the power of the father over this young mother was so negative that my efforts did not give her the great sense of peace and comfort she deserved. Fortunately, however, she was able to plan ahead for her daughter's future by arranging a guardian for her. This gave her some peace of mind. The situation was frustrating for all members of the palliative care team because we could not overcome the power the woman's father had over her mind.

Fear of the afterlife is another area that makes some people's deaths difficult. People who believe they have committed major sins may wish to confess them to a cleric in hopes of getting to heaven. What has surprised me most is that many of these confessions deal with decisions or mistakes someone has made decades ago. The fear of death reminds them more of their errors than of their successes.

One woman, about 55 years old, confessed to hating her stepfather. Her guilt made her fear death and what her life-after-death would be like. After we talked for a while, I found that her stepfather had abused her as a child and that her mother, knowing of the situation, had done nothing to protect her. She professed great love for her mother but after more chats she admitted her real hidden anger and hate. This type of confession and the talks we had afterward helped her see her life and feelings more honestly and she was better able to deal with her own death.

I have a few thoughts for people interested in chaplaincy work with people who have a terminal illness. The most important skill is to be yourself. Remember that the people you are dealing with are the same adults they were before they found out they were dying. Treat them with the respect they deserve, not paternalistically.

Perhaps a criticism of palliative care teams is permitted. In my own experience I have found that patients who are strong, independent and know what they want are treated differently from patients who are more ill and therefore more dependent. Staff of palliative care units give a great deal of themselves because of the nature of their work. They want to give everyone the gift of a peaceful and dignified death. When their efforts are turned down by someone more strong willed, the staff may begin to pay less attention to them than to patients who are more dependent and eager for staff's company. This is quite natural but a tendency that must be observed and addressed so that if patients change their mind about how much care they want, the option for more care is always there.

My last suggestion to caregivers, especially chaplains, is not to take yourself too seriously. Sometimes there is not enough humor in our work for we are dealing with dying people. People in the last stages of life have much to offer us. If humor can help us to put our lives and our circumstances into a larger perspective, even in the midst of the radical changes in our lives, then I am all for it. I think we can help families look back on this period in their lives with a touch of humor added to the memories of love, talking, sharing, anger, fear, frustration and every other emotion that is such a part of living.

Part 3: Hospice Philosophy of Care

Chapter 5 Hospice Care: The Dignified Way to Live Before You Die

Definition of Palliative/Hospice Care

The words 'palliative' and 'hospice' mean exactly the same thing. I use them both.

The hospice philosophy of care is about trying to meet the physical, emotional, spiritual and information needs of people with a terminal or life-threatening illness and their families. Hospice care is as much a philosophy of providing care as it is a specific program or an institution.

The hospice philosophy of care assumes that everyone -- patients, family members and friends, and professional and volunteer caregivers -- all have knowledge and skills to give each other and all need to receive support as well. Although the emphasis is on meeting the patient's and family's needs, there is an assumption that doctors, nurses, social workers, chaplains, and all other professional and volunteer caregivers also need support. This philosophy of mutual support is one of the distinguishing features of hospice care as apart from acute care.

In today's technological society palliative/hospice care is actually a return to a more humane, patient-oriented philosophy and system of care that encourages people with a terminal or life-threatening illness, their families and caregivers to work together and, where possible, permits a person to die at home.

When someone hears a physician say: "There is nothing more we can do," it is frightening. In fact, much can still be done to make someone's life rich and fulfilling, pain free and productive. When curing is no longer possible, caring is. About 400 B.C., Plato wrote that the mind and the body are one and should not be treated separately. In modern hospice care, the primary goal is to work with a patient and family in the three areas of physical, emotional and spiritual care.

Dr. Paul Henteleff, past medical director of the St. Boniface Palliative Care Unit in Winnipeg, Manitoba, and the first president of The Canada Palliative Care Association believes that dying decently is what we should be aiming at. People should feel wanted. People should not be misled by false hope. People should have the pain and symptom control they need. People should not be diverted from making the best possible use of their life -- whatever that means to them.

Dr. Dorothy C. H. Ley, was a pioneer in the Canadian hospice movement. She agreed that hospice care is a philosophy rather than a program or service. The hospice care philosophy has been used in small and large communities alike. In fact, hospice care often develops naturally in communities where citizens have long worked together with local medical professionals, family, neighbors and fellow church members to provide total care for people who have a terminal or life-threatening illness. Urban centers are beginning to establish hospice programs drawing on community resources and interest to benefit patients and their families.

The hospice movement has expanded rapidly in Canada since the mid 1970s. Originally it was mostly for cancer patients. Hospice is slowly beginning to help people with other terminal or life-threatening illnesses. More services are needed, however, as many Canadians do not have access to the hospice philosophy of care.

History of Hospice Care

The roots of hospice care go back to five ancient traditions of people caring for each other. These traditions date back thousands of years. At the most primitive level, people removed vermin from each other's hair and bodies and helped each other with grooming, scratching, and other basic hygiene.

They would teach each other knowledge and skills, especially their young ones. They tried to heal or tend to the sick, injured and wounded even though few of them got old. Over time, and at a deeper level of caring, they shared each other's possessions especially with the poor within their group. They would also show hospitality to strangers, travelers, wanderers and pilgrims as long as these people were no threat to them. Ancient trading routes developed along these lines.

Formal hospices were places of shelter provided by religious orders to pilgrims on their way to the Holy Land during the Middle Ages in Europe. Travelers found food, refuge and spiritual encouragement to prepare them for their continuing journey. These hospices were modeled on various Greek and Roman institutions.

In the 19th century, Mary Aikenhead opened the first modern hospice in Dublin. She founded an order of nuns called the Irish Sisters of Charity. These sisters provided various medical and spiritual services including care for people who were dying. She began her order in her own home and coined the name, hospice. She saw death as the beginning of a journey, so her hospice was a place of refuge, just as in the Middle Ages, but for a different kind of journey.

At the turn of the century, the Sisters of Charity opened St. Joseph's Hospice in London. The spread of the modern hospice movement did not begin until Dame Cicely Saunders opened her St. Christopher's Hospice, in 1967, also in London. Dame Saunders worked in England as a nurse, then as a social worker. She met David Tasma, a patient who had a terminal illness, in a London teaching hospital. He was a Polish refugee from Warsaw. They discussed his needs for improved pain control and their ideas for a special kind of physical, emotional and spiritual care. He left her five hundred pounds to help establish such a center after his death.

Dame Saunders left social work to study medicine and trained at St. Joseph's as its first full-time medical officer. After her training she worked with the community to establish St. Christopher's Hospice. It is the oldest established terminal-care facility to combine teaching and research with patient care. It's early concentration on excellent medical management of pain and symptoms distinguished it from other hospices.

In the United States, millionaire Nathaniel Hawthorne's daughter, Rose, watched her friend, Emma Lazarus, die of cancer. (Emma Lazarus' poem is inscribed on the Statue of Liberty.) Rose Hawthorne founded the order of Dominican nuns, Servants of Relief, and opened a hospice-like home in 1899 in New York City. It wasn't until 1971, that Dr. Sylvia Lack established a modern hospice program in New Haven Connecticut. Dr. Lack studied with Dame Saunders before coming to the United States. She began with a home care program and opened a hospice center in 1978 with the support of the National Cancer Institute.

In Canada, palliative care began in the mid 1970s with units at The Royal Victoria Hospital in Montreal and at St. Boniface in Winnipeg. From the experiences at the Royal Victoria Hospital, Dr. Balfour Mount and his team prepared an extensive hospice care manual for professionals.

At about the same time, community-based hospice programs evolved across Canada. These grass root, non-profit organizations were started by concerned community members who wanted their loved ones to live at home until their deaths rather than die in hospitals. Many started with only volunteer help. Some now have paid staff, especially palliative care nurses, to help assess and meet the needs of people living at home with a terminal or life-threatening illness.

There are many ways to provide hospice care but the most important features are the same no matter where the service is provided.

Features of Hospice Care

By definition, hospice care is anti-dogmatic, and constantly strives to adapt to the individual needs of the patients, their families, and of a particular community. The modern philosophy, however, is rooted in Christian, white, middle and upper class society beliefs. To become universal, hospice care will need to become even less dogmatic through multicultural and multi-faith approaches to care.

The four areas of concern in hospice care are the physical, emotional, spiritual and information needs of the patient and, where applicable, those of the family. Hospice care can be provided in someone's home or in institutional settings. What hospice programs offer to patients and their families is very dependent on where the care is given. Some aspects of care, however, are the same no matter where the person lives.

By emotional care, I include having the patient and family involved in decision making, in listening to their feelings and needs and showing them respect and compassion. Emotional care includes providing opportunities for patients to express themselves in valued, creative ways. They may do that through art, music, crafts, or games they enjoy playing. These opportunities are therapeutic without, necessarily, involving 'therapy'. Emotional care also looks at how people of different ages within a family deal with dying and death. Grandparents have different experiences with dying and death than their children and grandchildren. Ideally, this mix of experiences can help family members cope better with their emotional ups and downs. When this is not so, outside help may be needed. Emotional care in hospice also looks at the needs of professional and volunteer caregivers.

The spiritual roots of hospice come from the concept of 'the hidden Christ'. In medieval times, poor travelers were treated lavishly by hospice members because there was the underlying assumption that any visitor could be the second coming of Christ. Therefore, all visitors were treated royally and without cost. Modern spiritual care refers more to the patient and family's personal experiences of suffering and death as well as their concerns regarding life-after-death, their belief or disbelief in God, and encouraging the inner spiritual strength most people have regardless of any religious affiliation. Spiritual care is available through a chaplain or spiritual leader as well as through the general contact between patients, families and their caregivers. It is up to the patient and family if they wish formal religious guidance and assistance.

The emotional and spiritual care offered to a patient is especially important when the patient has no family or friends nearby. The hospice caregivers are able to offer the support, understanding and compassion to patients at home or in an institution that patients have not traditionally received in our modern medical systems. The added comradeship possible, for example, within a hospital palliative care program with other patients, and the opportunity to share thoughts and feelings with them, makes hospice care a vital service to these patients. Another example are people with AIDS who have, until recently, not received the unconditional support and compassion of the community. AIDS hospice and home care programs have been developed in various North American cities to meet the needs of people with AIDS, while also educating the public about the illness and the goals of hospice care, in general.

The goal of hospice care is not to cure a terminal or life-threatening illness but to provide comfort. Hospice care is not about prolonging life heroically when someone is near death. Surgical procedures are recommended only if they can help a patient's physical comfort. Few tests are carried out unless they, too, can help improve comfort. The primary concern is the comfort and caring support of patients and their family. **Patients early on in their active treatment can also benefit from hospice's excellent pain and symptom control regardless of the person's disease or prognosis. Waiting until pain becomes unbearable or until a person is labeled a 'palliative care patient' makes pain control more difficult.**

The most common concern of patients with a terminal or life-threatening illness is their fear of pain and uncomfortable symptoms. The first priority of hospice care, therefore, is pain and symptom control. When pain is controlled, the patient's dignity is easier to maintain, the person can think more clearly and concentrate on their emotional, spiritual and information needs. Painkillers (analgesics) should be given routinely and in sufficient quantities. At the same time, medication is given to offset some of the side effects of painkillers while giving the patient maximum mental alertness. Patients often have a noticeable period of relief after their pain is managed. The patient and family may assume that the person is actually getting healthier or is cured. This is not true. Effective pain and symptom control help people feel better but do not cure a disease.

Once pain and other symptoms of an illness are under control the patient and family have time to consider their own emotional and spiritual needs. A major concern of patients and families at this point is how a patient dies. According to Dr. Cicely Saunders, proper pain and symptom control in cancer patients may help patients to be alert and communicative until a short time before death. They often slip into unconsciousness and die in the way most of us would like, in their sleep.

When we talk about emotional and spiritual care it is not an idealistic vision of a perfect world. There are very specific ways to help patients and families emotionally and spiritually. Emotional needs of people dying, their family and caregivers are described more fully in the chapter on emotional needs. Generally speaking, emotional support includes listening unconditionally to peoples' needs. This listening can be done by all the caregivers and includes having the patient and family actively involved in making decisions.

Often when patients are prevented from making decisions, no matter how large or small, they become very anxious, irritable, angry or unsure of themselves. They stop trusting what people close to them say. Their increased negative emotions add to their physical discomfort. Their physical discomfort adds to increased negative emotions and the vicious circle may never end. Hospice care is a way to change this circle into a positive cycle of total physical, emotional and spiritual care. Earlier access to hospice care may help reduce some of this anxiety, harm and trauma and provide information to help patients make further treatment decisions.

In institutional settings, rules are kept to a minimum. Families are encouraged to bring special meals to the person dying and eat together as a family. Cultural customs are important and respected. Family contact is crucial, so the family is encouraged to participate actively in their loved one's care.

When the patient's condition permits, frequent back rubs, walks, recreational activities, relaxation exercises, music, art and visits by friends are all encouraged. There are no specific visiting hours. Pets are sometimes allowed to visit. People are encouraged to bring their own photos, plants and other things to make them feel more at home. Patients have choices in their meals including home cooked food. They are allowed to smoke or have an alcoholic drink and are encouraged to do things they would normally enjoy doing.

Questions are answered honestly and the caregivers are respectful of a person's privacy and decisions. What we might call small things are encouraged. For example, caregivers refer to their patients as Mr. or Mrs. Smith rather than "dear," or "honey," unless the patient enjoys such terms of endearment. Respect and personal care is very important.

When someone dies, hospice care for the family does not end. Many hospice programs have a bereavement component that encourages continued communication with the family during their time of grief.

The caregivers' role in bereavement may begin with a letter or card signed by all the staff and/or volunteers and sent to the family about three weeks after someone's death. There may be a follow-up call to see if the family wants to come in and visit or to have a hospice person visit them at home. The family may choose to join a support group with other grieving families in order to share their feelings, anger and hopes. Respect for the family wishes is very important so the caregivers always leave a door open, day or night, for someone to call in and chat for a bit.

To find out about hospice programs in your community you can check with your doctor, the hospital social work department, hospital discharge planner, or one of the national associations for hospices listed in this book. Be sure to check about costs, if any, and whether your insurance company covers some or all of the costs, and if there are competing services, to ensure that you are choosing the correct one.

Types of Hospice Care

The following is a list of various types of hospice care. Different communities choose different models. A program may incorporate smaller existing programs, co-ordinate services between various agencies, or the community may choose a specific model better suited to its needs and financial capabilities.

Informal Hospice Care

Coordinated by a person's family and physician who want to care for the patient without formal help from agencies or institutions. They may use a support circle of friends and volunteers to meet the needs of the person who is dying.

Home Care

Goes by various names including 'hospice care without walls' or in Ontario, Community Care Access Centers. Home care is a program through which professional case managers co-ordinate someone's medical care at home. The managers can bring in whatever professionals, services and equipment that are possible within their service.

Home care is often the key component of any hospice care program. These programs may be affiliated with a specific hospital, hospice unit or coordinated through public health agencies. Sometimes home care is strictly a community response to a need and is coordinated through a volunteer organization. In some communities the home care program is the only hospice care component available. With home care, the patient remains at home until death, rather than in a hospital or nursing home, and is treated by visiting nurses, doctors, therapists, clerics and other caregivers. Principles of pain and symptom control, emotional and spiritual care are followed.

In almost all hospice programs, home care is considered the most important component because people who are dying are usually more comfortable in their own environment. Only in situations when the family and caregivers cannot provide quality care do patients go to the hospital, a hospice care facility or a long-term care facility.

Community Hospices

Organizations, primarily run by volunteers, to meet the needs of people with a terminal or life-threatening illness with no charge for services. The hospice organization may have some paid staff, especially nurses to help volunteers assess the needs of their clients. Community hospices work closely with a patient's family physician, other health care providers, and local home care programs.

Free-Standing Hospice Facility

A facility separate from any other institution that provides only hospice care. Patients are often referred by a family physician or by a specialist seeing the patient in a hospital. Depending on the resources of the facility there may be space available in emergency situations. These facilities generally do not have operating rooms, specialized life-support systems or other features of an acute care general hospital. St. Christopher's Hospice in England is the first modern example of a free-standing hospice. There are few free-standing hospices in Canada.

Free-Standing Hospital-Affiliated Hospice

A separate building housing a hospice center but affiliated to a specific hospital (often a teaching hospital) such as Casey House in Toronto.

Hospital-Based Palliative Care Unit

A separate hospice unit within a hospital which provides all the services of a freestanding facility except that patients are within easy access of hospital personnel and facilities. Because pre-existing facilities can be restructured, such units are less expensive to begin than a freestanding facility.

Hospital-Based Hospice Team

Rather than a separate unit within the hospital, a hospice team goes to the patients in the various wards within the hospital. The team educates the regular caregivers in pain and symptom control and encourages the emotional and spiritual care of specific patients. Hospitals with limited resources or those wishing to test the hospice program, may have only a single person (often a nurse) introducing the program to patients and staff.

Extended Care Services

Hospice programs may also be found in institutions such as nursing homes, long-term care facilities, military hospitals and prisons.

The Hospice Care Team

When people are dying of a terminal or life-threatening illness it is practically impossible for them to do it alone (even if they want to). Hospice care is a philosophy. As such it permits professionals and volunteers to work together to help someone who is ill. Even in communities where there is no official hospice care, neighbors, family physicians, clerics and friends can work together as a team to help someone in need.

I will speak briefly about each potential member of this team. The nature of hospice care means constant improvements and changes so that the hospice care team in your community may include any or all of the following specialties: physicians, nurses, pharmacists, clerics, therapists, dieticians, psychiatrists or psychologists, social workers, homemakers, other home care providers and volunteers. Often members of the hospice team, such as a psychologist or chaplain, are not full-time. I have listed the most common members of a team first.

Patients, family members, friends and close neighbors are members of the team because they are most intimately involved in the care of the person who is dying on a day-to-day basis. They are probably untrained in what to do and will make honest mistakes in an effort to be most helpful. They require and deserve the knowledge and support of the trained professionals to help make their support all the more practical and meaningful.

Home Care Case Manager assesses a patient's home-care needs and co-ordinates the services including visiting home nurses, homemakers, therapists and needed supplies. Home care case managers work for local home care organizations.

Physicians act as medical coordinators of the team. The special nature of hospice care has led to some physicians specializing in this field with emphasis on pain and symptom control and the physical comfort of their patients.

Nurses play a key role in coordinating, teaching and providing hospice care. They help provide the excellent pain and symptom management patients need along with some of the emotional, spiritual, grief and bereavement care for both patients and their families. They may spend the most time answering questions and listening to comments the patient and family have. They are often in the best position to advocate for the highest quality of care possible for the patient and family.

Social Workers are involved in various aspects of hospice care: client advocacy; long-term individual, family and group counseling; crisis intervention; short-term casework; financial planning; pre-admission assessment to help all caregivers look at the whole person; and discharge planning to help people know what community resources are available to them and how to access them. They may also be involved in helping family members deal with age differences, educational and cultural differences, and conflicts.

Client advocacy (representing the patient to other caregivers) is a key role because social workers are able to help people understand and use community resources, find sources of financial aid, and coordinate home care services. As a patient advocate, they can also help resolve differences with other caregivers over the patient's treatment.

Long-term therapy can include discussion with the patient and family to help them with any emotional or communication difficulties they may have. The social worker may also coordinate or participate in bereavement programs for the family after a person has died.

Crisis intervention by a social worker may include helping to resolve problems that are compounded by a person's illness. An example might be helping a patient in a hospice settle a dispute with a landlord over back rent. A social worker may often offer help in cases where the patient has no family nearby or in cases where the family is unaware of ways to resolve various problems.

Short-term counseling may be one-to-five interviews with the patient and/or family talking about their questions and concerns that have not been discussed with other members of the hospice care team. The social worker can help assess any problems and help people plan and evaluate any follow-up help.

Pharmacists play an important role in recommending medications and educating physicians, nurses, other caregivers, patients and families about the appropriate use of medications. Pharmacists can explain: a) possible side effects of each medication, b) effects of mixing various medications together, and c) the effects of food, liquids and complementary therapies on specific medications.

Homemakers may come from either a commercial or government agency. Homemakers can provide day-to-day services such as preparing meals, cleaning your home, doing grocery shopping and running errands. They may be in your home more than any other caregiver so it is important that the patient and family enjoy that person's company. However, it is important to remember that homemakers are not nurses and cannot be expected to provide medical care.

Volunteers are very important to an effective hospice care program. Their expertise and available time mean a great deal to the patients and family. Volunteers may have experienced the loss of a loved one or may be interested in helping people through a very special time of life.

Volunteers make such care possible, especially in smaller communities, by reducing the cost of providing hospice care. The use of volunteers allows full-time caregivers to concentrate on their specific areas of expertise.

Volunteers generally receive specialized training so that they become expert at listening to people and offering help that the patient and family need and ask for. Volunteers do a lot of home care visits to make sure that the proper services are available and provided. They also act as a patient advocate so that the patient and family never feel alone. Volunteers may come to the family through a hospice program or through the creation of a support circle of family, friends, neighbors, and colleagues.

Chaplain/Clergy Mother Teresa of Calcutta once said of her ministry that it was her role to take one person at a time and love that person for that time. In this way, acts of love and compassion can help a Hindu be a better Hindu, a Christian a better Christian, a Jew a better Jew, a Moslem a better Moslem, a Buddhist a better Buddhist.

Upon request, the hospice chaplain or clergy can help patients, their family and perhaps some of the caregivers. Each patient's preference for spiritual counseling is followed. Patients may ask to speak with their own clerics, to the hospice chaplain or they may choose not to speak to anyone about their spirituality.

The chaplain or clergy often act as an interfaith spiritual leader, spending time listening impartially to the needs and ideas of patients and their families. They also participate in preparation and performing of funeral services if the family wishes. After a patient's death, they may also continue to support the family during their time of grief.

Chaplains and clergy also guide other caregivers in answering spiritual questions. Someone may hesitate to ask a chaplain or clergy about the meaning of life but they might ask a nurse or homemaker.

Dietitians do a great deal to help provide meals that reduce constipation and other side effects of medication and treatment. Dietitians also encourage patients and families to suggest or supply their own favorite meals such a mom's home-cooked chicken or dad's special cake. People will generally eat more if they can eat the food they are used to.

Dietitians also understand that patients with certain illnesses prefer different types of food or need the food prepared in a different way. They might also make suggestions on how to 'present' the food so that it looks more pleasing especially when the patient doesn't feel like eating.

Occupational Therapists try to strike a balance between home management, self-care and leisure activities by increasing the patient's knowledge and skill to live within a life-threatening situation.

Home management includes homemaking, childcare and parenting. Self-care includes personal hygiene, grooming, feeding, dressing, mobility, and adapting one's disabilities to their present needs. Leisure activities include the patient's personal interests and hobbies for self-expression and amusement.

Physiotherapists For every patient, the primary goal of any therapy is to keep them as independent as possible in their particular circumstances. A physiotherapist is concerned with providing physical and breathing exercises to help a patient remain independent. Exercises include limb movements, improved breathing techniques to minimize the effects of physical exertion, and recreational games. Breathing exercises can prevent pneumonia while muscle exercises prevent muscles from wasting away.

Physiotherapists try to avoid telling patients they cannot do something but rather let the patients decide what they can and cannot do. They can also educate families and nurses in proper physical care. They use simple techniques rather than cumbersome exercise machines.

Art Therapists Art therapy allows people who enjoy art to participate actively in self-expression. Many artistic forms are possible and this recreational exercise is not meant to "keep people busy and out of the way" but, rather as an enjoyable and expressive activity. Art is a way to communicate for people who have trouble talking about their needs.

Music Therapists Music therapy can be as simple as providing patients with their favorite music to listen to. Music soothes and comforts people and can raise someone's pain threshold. Music therapy may also include active participation in playing or writing music and songs, listening to music with people who share your taste or listening to a live performance. Music therapists have an understanding of the physiological and psychological effects of music on people.

Art and music have always been therapeutic for people. One does not need a therapist to enjoy the benefits of any of the creative arts. The therapists, however, can help to enhance a patient's own appreciation of the arts and meet some of their physical, emotional and spiritual needs.

Psychiatrists and/or Psychologists help patients, family and other caregivers cope with different situations and help them accept what is going on. They usually let the patient take the lead, much as the clerics do. If the patient, family or other caregivers do not wish to see the psychiatrist or psychologist then their wishes are respected. Both of these professionals can help identify mental conditions that might benefit from extra help including clinical depression, traumatic events from a patient's past that they want to deal with or specific counseling for anxiety about death and dying.

The philosophy of hospice care encourages a relaxation of limits around a particular caregiver specialty. It is not uncommon to see an occupational therapist listening to patients discuss the pain they used to have, a physician fluffing pillows, a patient comparing her religious beliefs with that of a nurse, or the chaplain helping a patient with his meal.

There are regular meetings of the hospice care team to coordinate the over-all activities of the team, during which, each team member presents a specific patient's needs or concerns. This open communication ideally keeps everyone on the team informed about each patient and family. Coordinating care may be more difficult when many different agencies are involved. More effort is being made across Canada to coordinate care more fully and easily between hospice care providers at different agencies and institutions.

Of course, a patient's chart is also used to write in specific information about the patient's physical, emotional, spiritual and information needs. These charts are used by the different team members on different shifts to keep up-to-date on what the patient and family may need. These charts may also provide information on the patient's thoughts and feelings about her care, fears and hopes. Patients often have access to these charts and are encouraged to write in them to share their own ideas and feelings directly with the caregivers. Sometimes, a separate communication book is left by the bedside for anyone to write in to improve communication between the various caregivers and the patient.

Another important team member has sometimes been called the patient advocate. This advocate can be any family member or friend who is with the patient. A more specific advocate role may be played by a specific family member or friend who acts as spokesperson for the patient who may be unable or unwilling to communicate with the caregivers.

The advocate, working with the caregivers, makes sure that:

- the patient is fed the prescribed food when they are best able to eat it,

- the patient's medication and treatment is accurate and given at the proper times,

- any tests or examinations have been approved,

- the physician and other caregivers communicate with her about all matters relating to the patient,

- the patient is given a sense of control and respect.

The modern hospice movement is still relatively young and, therefore, constantly changing. From the patient/family point of view, it is important that you find out what services are available, what they cost, if anything, and whether or not they meet your needs.

You now have an understanding of the philosophy of hospice care and can use that knowledge to help hospice care in your community. When people work together, the end result is an overall improvement of services for patients and families and increased professional satisfaction for the caregivers.

Chapter 6   Patient and Family Relationships With Professional and Volunteer Caregivers

Understanding the Physician
Understanding Patients and Their Families
What Physicians Can Learn from Their Patients
Some Do's and Don'ts of Improved Communication
Resolving Communication Problems

This book concentrates on how people can work together for the improved total care of someone who has a terminal or life-threatening illness. A key relationship during this period is the one between the patient-family and their various physicians. While this chapter concentrates on this relationship, many of the points are also valid for relationships with other caregivers. Mutual respect and open communication are just as important with nurses, clerics, therapists, and other caregivers as with a physician.

The medical world is going through a rapid and tremendous change. There are increased pressures on caregivers including the added responsibilities to other medical personnel, intervention by governments and insurance bodies, limitations on payment for consultations, telephone advice and sometimes the type of service caregivers are allowed to give. The increased demands by patients, families and consumer organizations compared to the relatively slow response of the health care system causes even more tension.

The changes in the health care system requires everyone to recognize the financial and resource limitations at this time. Limited hospice programs, medical services, long waiting periods, and caregiver time all affect the kind of care a patient can expect. Understanding these limitations will help people to have realistic expectations of the type of care available to them while also encouraging them to find ways to adapt to the specific limitations of their case.

There may a natural apprehension by the patient and family toward physicians, especially doctors they do not have a comfortable long-term relationship with. Most of them are afraid of their illness but are forced by circumstances to rely on the expertise and advice of people they may not know. Added to this anxiety is the reality that medicine has not cured the patient of a terminal or life-threatening illness. They may have lost trust in the 'system'.

In the past few years, there has been more awareness that when the patient and family work together with their physicians, everyone benefits. Open and honest communication relieves the patient and families' anxiety, while the physicians feel more job satisfaction and less personal stress. When such communication does not happen, it is up to the physician and family to provide the energy, patience and wisdom to improve the situation. Patients may be too mentally and physically drained to give extra effort to improve communication.

Understanding the Physician

Caregivers endure stresses that everyone can help diminish by working together. The professional stresses of a physician include:

- Heavy workload (it isn't enough to be a physician these days; you must also be a business person, a politician, and a bureaucrat);

- Deciding how much patients should know about their serious illness if the patient does not ask for more details themselves. Although most patients prefer to know the truth about their illness, there are patients who do not want the physician to tell them the full truth. This could be for cultural or personal reasons. They may prefer that the physician speak with a spouse, parent or adult child instead of to them.

- The increasing paperwork requirements of governments and insurance companies;

- Little time to learn new treatments and methods;

- Little time to deal with personal stress;

- Increasing numbers of lawsuits; and

- A decreased public respect for the medical profession in general.

A common complaint against physicians is that they are uncommunicative. Dr. Peter Hanson, the author of *The Joy of Stress*, explains why some physicians may appear uncommunicative. Physicians, especially specialists, have often gone directly from high school, to university, then to medical school, and finally specialty training. They have limited experience or training in communication skills with people outside the medical community, especially people from different cultural and economic backgrounds.

Many graduates from medical schools have either a domineering, paternalistic personality or an analytic, detail-oriented personality. These personality types can make communication difficult. Some of these physicians are basically quite shy and do not realize that they are being uncommunicative. With diplomacy and persistence patients and families can help physicians become more communicative in today's chaotic, rapidly changing health care system. However, during a time of terminal or life-threatening illness, the patients and families probably do not have the skills, energy or patience to "draw out" the physician. It is up to physicians and all health-care providers to acquire the necessary communication skills needed to help patients and families through such fearful and uncertain times.

Many physicians are uncomfortable with patients who are dying. After all, medical training is designed to cure patients. Medical training has indirectly seen death as a failure of modern medicine. Dealing with the emotional stresses of patients dying is not part of most medical training. Medical ethics about life and death decisions are only now offered in some medical schools. If physicians are uncomfortable talking about death and dying they should tell their patients. Patients may be able to help their physicians understand what it is like to be dying. At the same time, patients can feel useful by helping their doctors. If physicians remain uncomfortable, they must refer their patients to someone who can meet some of their emotional and spiritual needs. Of course, patients or their families may also look for a different physician who can meet their specific needs.

Some eminent physicians have written about physician-patient relationships. Sir William Osler was a 19th-century Canadian physician and scholar. He began the Internal Medicine department at Johns Hopkins Hospital, helped begin the Rockefeller Foundation and taught students like the Mayo brothers (of Mayo Clinic fame). Sir William believed that it is more important to know what type of patient has a disease rather than what type of disease a patient has. He gave his patients both medication and lots of optimism. That optimism is just as important to someone who is dying. It takes the form of encouraging a full life until one dies and helping teach grieving families learn from the lessons of their recent loss.

Norman Cousins in his book *The Anatomy of an Illness* describes a visit he had with Dr. Albert Schweitzer in Africa. Schweitzer explained his philosophy of medical practice. He believed that each person carries his own doctor inside of him. He goes to a physician because he does not recognize his own strength. A physician's greatest asset is his ability to bring out the doctor within his patients. By helping patients gain a sense of personal control over their lives, physicians are also achieving a professional satisfaction that they are making a positive difference in the lives of their patients.

Understanding Patients and Their Families

Total care looks at a patient's physical, emotional, spiritual and information needs. Studies show that people who have a terminal or life-threatening illness want many of the same things including:

- To be relatively pain free;

- To be alert and aware of what is happening to them;

- To have the companionship of their family and friends;

- To be accepted as the person they have always been;

- To maintain their individuality and inherent dignity;

- Not to die alone (this is especially true in cases where people, most often women, have already lost their spouse);

- Not to be a burden to their family and caregivers;

- To have familiar things around them: photos, plants, music, flowers, favorite food, pets;

- To be cared for and remembered with love and respect; and

- To have their family continue living and loving after their death.

Patients and families suffer most when communication with their physician is poor and the relationship is uncooperative. Patients need a spokesperson, advocate if you like, who has the energy, commitment and time to encourage, even demand, improved communication with the physician. It may not be easy to find such an advocate because of many people's fear of anything medical.

Trouble with effective communication can happen if the patient 'doesn't want to bother the doctor' with information, symptoms, pain or concerns. This deference to physicians was taught to older people and many of them find it hard to be assertive and expect an open and honest communication with their doctor. Other communication problems may happen if there are family problems (e.g., children arguing over what is best for 'mom' or 'dad'). If the patient has no one nearby for support, medical appointments and conversations become even more physically and mentally exhausting. These difficulties can be partially overcome if everyone understands that the difficulties must be discussed and resolved in order to develop open communication and real cooperation. The people with the most energy and experience must make sure that difficulties are overcome for the sake of the patient and family.

There are, quite naturally, patients who have a difficult time adjusting to a terminal or life-threatening illness. They may fight their illness or completely submit to it. They may communicate very little with their families or not cooperate with their caregivers. These are difficult times for everyone involved and require a continued effort by the family and caregivers to meet the individual needs of the patient. People need a sense of control that comes only from making decisions, even if they are considered wrong. While you cannot force patients to agree to all the changes going on in their lives you cannot stand by as if the consequences of their decisions do not affect you personally. Patients need to be told what the consequences of their actions are and how they affect the family and other caregivers. Sometimes the situation will improve for everyone concerned but, realistically, some people can never communicate or cooperate enough so they can live fully until their deaths. It is immensely frustrating to watch someone make decisions that you strongly believe diminishes the fullness of their remaining life. They likely have frustrated you in similar ways over many years. We wish it could be different but there is often not enough time to resolve all the problems someone has.

Language barriers prevent health care providers from completely understanding their patients and the families. Some programs have translators and others use the ATT telephone company's instant translation telephone service. Whenever one uses a translator, however, you must recognize that the person may not be providing literal translations and may try to summarize what you have said. There will be errors. For matters of critical importance, it is necessary to repeat the conversation using different words to ensure that the message is clear and accurate. Make sure that using an inappropriate translator does not upset cultural norms. For example, a young male translator for an elderly female with gynecological problems may be very uncomfortable or ineffective.

When a family member translates, it is important to accurately translate rather than choose what to translate.

What Physicians Can Learn from Their Patients

There are many things physicians can learn from their patients, especially those who are dying, and from their families. Professional development programs also help physicians become more comfortable with their patients' deaths as well as their own deaths. Physicians can learn from their patients:

• Facts about their condition. This seems obvious but some symptoms are not adequately addressed by the physician because the patient does not talk about new symptoms, there are time constraints or the physician or patient do not know enough about proper pain and symptom control. Physicians must ask enough questions to get at the answers and must ask the right kind of questions. Taking case histories is one of a physician's greatest skills and we can expect them to do it well.

• New treatments that patients have read about in a popular magazine or seen on a television program that the physician has not investigated. Admittedly, some of these treatments are not proven but discussing them with patients help to get them more actively involved in their treatment. That sense of control improves a patient's self-image and decreases their anxiety.

- Patients are the only people involved in every medical appointment, test and treatment. They were there for every pain, symptom, test and operation. They can, and should be asked, to offer vital feedback on their present treatments, feelings and fears.

- Patients, with the physician's encouragement, can express their needs and, therefore, help the physician in determining further treatment.

- Patients remind physicians of what it means to be human. Many of our wisest physicians have learned their wisdom at the bedside of their dying patients.

Some Do's and Don'ts of Improved Communication

From the physician and other caregivers' points of view there are proven techniques that patients and families can use to improve their relationship.

Some Patient and Family Do's

- Know your caregivers' names and help them to remember yours.

- Communicate with them about your physical and emotional needs and feelings. Speak openly about your concerns and fears and ask your physician if she can recommend someone else who can give practical information to you about what is happening, e.g., pharmacists, social workers, nurses, and health information organizations. Some books, videos or Internet sites might also help you.

- Cooperate fully once a decision on treatment is mutually decided. If you have ongoing concerns, speak to other members of the hospice team.

- Write down the important questions to ask (usually in groups of three) and have a family member or friend with you to record the answers.

- Respect the caregiver's time while expecting the same in return.

- Ask concise questions that can be answered in a few minutes. Questions like "Why did this happen to me?" require more time and thought. Ask for extra time with a hospice team member to look at such important questions of life's meaning, self-worth, and spirituality.

- Offer a time limit for discussion (e.g., 11-12 minutes) and stick to it. In this way you build up a trusting relationship with the caregivers and they know you respect their time.

- If you have a large family, choose a family representative and let the hospice team know who is picked and how to get hold of them. Ask the family representative to be with the patient when the doctor, nurse or social worker provide information or ask for decisions.

- Encourage family meetings with the doctor, primary nurse or social worker to understand what is happening now and what might happen in the future.

- Ask the hospital or hospice to bring in the discharge planner (person who helps you get community services once you leave the hospital) early in the discussion rather than at the last minute. Discharge from a facility into your home should go as smoothly as possible to reduce anxiety and encourage a clean transfer over to community resources. Patients have little control over how they leave a facility and what services are waiting for them. A call to the local home care program by the patient's family or advocate might help the transition by making sure that all the necessary services are in place when the person gets home.

Some Don'ts

- Do not ignore medical instructions after a mutual medical decision has been made. If you ignore treatment decisions, you must let your physician know.

- Do not ask too many questions, over and over again, (it is better to record the physician's answers).

- Do not bring up questions about minor ailments of other family members and friends in hope of free medical advice. If your family and friends have significant difficulty dealing with your illness, then it is good to ask your physician or other hospice care team members for help.

- Do not keep telephoning with questions that are better answered by other experts like a nurse, pharmacist or therapist.

- Do not wait to communicate new pains or negative symptoms until they have become serious problems.

- Do not forget to communicate emotional needs.

- Do not get a second medical opinion without telling the principal physician unless your principal physician is uncooperative. Also consider the extra emotional and financial burdens involved in getting a second opinion to make sure it is worth the cost to you.

- Do not follow other medical or complementary therapies without consulting the principal physician because the different therapies may conflict. Although one's cultural or personal beliefs may discourage such open discussion of alternatives, it is important that you do nothing that makes the patient more ill.

- Do not forget to treat the caregivers with respect or concern.

Some patients choose not to follow the above suggestions and, in effect, choose not to communicate and cooperate. Whether we agree with their decisions or not, it is their decision and they must be respected (unless they injure someone else).

Resolving Communication Problems

When open communication does not seem possible, there are other options available. When the problem has become serious, bring in the hospital, hospice or community social worker to see if improvements can be made. Other caregivers such as a cleric, nurse, facility's patient advocate representative, or psychologist may also be helpful.

Where the communication cannot be improved, the patient or family can do one or both of the following (although I recognize that during such an emotional time these suggestions are not easy to follow) especially in rural areas where choices may be limited:

- Change specialists on the advice of your family physician or another caregiver.

- Change hospitals or the service you are using.

If it is the patient or family that is uncooperative, the physician might recommend a different physician or hospital. She must legally continue care until the patient has found a new physician.

Many communication problems are not usually one person's fault. People have different personalities and for whatever reason, some people do not communicate well with each other. If both people recognize the problem and accept the situation, the caregiver can help find someone to replace him.

In hospice care, both the patient and the family receive support. A physician may find it easier to speak to a single member of the family rather than the whole family. Recognizing that the patient's comfort is the physician's first concern, the family can arrange to choose a member to act as spokesperson and minimize the time a physician needs to spend with the whole family. Other members of the hospice care team can provide specific supports to the family.

Communication is talking in a common language about common goals. Expect excellent communication from the people you talk to. Make your own best effort to communicate well with them or have someone speak on your behalf. Good communication can make the difference between dying well and dying horribly. It also makes the difference in how grieving family members remember the last days of their loved one and the support they received before, during and after the person's illness.

Chapter 7   Care for the Caregivers

Immediate Needs
Long-Term Needs
Practical Supports
Professional and Volunteer Caregivers

Caring for others in such a personal and intimate way as palliative care is one of the most fulfilling and life-defining opportunities in our lives. When you care for someone else you know in your heart, mind and soul that you are making a real difference in that person's life. Caregiving gives us that unique opportunity to remember what is truly valuable in our lives and within our families and community. Caring is not always easy. It can be physically exhausting, mentally taxing and emotionally draining. It can also be exhilarating, rejuvenating, peaceful, joyful and awe inspiring.

Immediate Needs

When I began caring for my parents and my grandfather, I was concerned about their physical needs first and then their emotional and spiritual needs. I was not interested in people's advice that I needed to take better care of myself, get more help at home, or even that I should get back to work. I may not have been prepared for the demands of taking care of loved ones at home but I had a life-time of preparation in a loving family to want to be with my parents and grandfather in their last months.

What other people did not understand was that I had a whole life ahead of me. Later on I could eat well, sleep longer, work and enjoy myself. Right then, I only had a few months to be with my mother, my father and my grandfather. I was not trying to be a martyr. I was not ignoring my own emotional and spiritual needs. I was fulfilling them as best I could. Taking care of my loved ones was demanding, fulfilling and terribly important to me. I did it for me as much as I did it for them. They needed me. I needed them.

Yes, I hurt myself physically by ignoring my diet, exercise and time to be alone. After my father's death I could barely move my neck for months.

However, I was fulfilling one of my greatest needs to be with my parents and grandfather, revel in our love and our family history. No family is perfect. No family has perfect relationships within it. However, I would never have any of the regrets that begin with sentences like: "If only I had...." What a legacy that time together is for me. I am a better husband, father, friend and neighbor because of those intense times.

Would I do it differently today? Yes. I know more now. I can take better care of myself so that my loved ones are not as worried about me. People who are dying still worry a great deal about the people who are caring for them. By taking care of ourselves, we can minimize some of that worry.

I hope some of what I present is helpful. Do what you need to do to make this time as fulfilling and meaningful as possible. You will not have this particular opportunity again.

Long-term Needs

Although we might hurt ourselves in short-term caregiving situations, we must be wiser when we care for someone for a long time. It might be all right to use caregiving as an excuse not to eat and drink well, exercise or sleep well. However, when you do this for any length of time you will hurt yourself dramatically **and** you will hurt the person you are caring for.

Just as patients need support to meet their physical, emotional, spiritual, and information needs, so do family members and professional and volunteer caregivers.

Knowledge and experience can deepen our reservoir of hope and courage. Eileen McArthur explains: "As a volunteer in palliative care and later as a trainer of palliative care volunteers, I gained an understanding and a good deal of insight which served me well when I was faced with the impending deaths of my mother and my brother. My hospital experience provided me with the knowledge and experience that helped and supported both my family and me when we became the caregivers for our loved ones. The stories in Chapter 4 of this book are very similar to many of my personal and hospital experiences of the human drama and emotions observed. I saw courage, great courage, in patients and their families and I also witnessed great sadness, disappointment and guilt. I consider it a privilege to have been involved with a palliative care unit in a hospital and I know that this interest in helping to provide a 'good death' for the terminally ill will never wane."

Practical Supports

- We hear only about 20% of what someone says and forget about 80% of that within one day. That leaves us remembering only about 4% of our conversation. During times of great stress, we probably forget even more. As we look at ways to improve how we care for ourselves and for others, we must always remember this simple fact. Most problems and conflicts between people stem from this simple fact. You 'know' I said one thing and I 'know' I said something else. If we fight over who is right, we will never improve our communication and improve our relationship. If you have a conflict, assume there was a communication problem and start over. That might help fix most situations.

- Active listening is a skill that involves listening to what a person says while also questioning what they might not be saying, and why. Active listening also involves looking at the person's body language to see if what they are saying is consistent with how they look. Never assume you can 'read' someone's body language. Use the person's body language as clues to use in questions. For example, if someone is saying they are very happy to see you but they are wincing at the same time, find out if they are in pain or discomfort or if they are thinking about something else while talking with you.

  You can always tell when people are **not** practicing active listening. If there is no silence in a conversation then people are thinking up their own replies to someone's comments while the other person is still talking. This is not active listening. A good listener uses the silence after someone finishes talking to think about what was said and, perhaps, rehearse what they want to reply.

- Take care of yourself physically, emotionally and spiritually. That means that you need to eat some healthy food (get neighbors and friends to do some cooking for you and you can freeze it until you are ready) and healthy drinks. Pray or meditate to feel the comfort that this gives you. Take some time for a quick walk around the block or some other light exercise. Sleep as much of a normal sleep as you can. Get others to give you extra time for 'cat naps'.

- Remember that caregiving is mutual. The person you are caring for must be allowed to give some care to you in return, if they can. Too often we do not want to 'bother' the person with our concerns, worries or needs. They need to be wanted as much as you do so let the caregiving be mutual. As their illness progresses, they will not be able to do as much of that. However, there is a special gift that even people in comas offer us: they give us quiet time to think about what is important in our lives and what we may want to do with the rest of our lives that makes sense to us. Use the time well because it truly is a wonderful gift.

- You need to get as much information as you want to understand what you can do, how you can do it well and where you can turn to for help. Practical advice is available in books like *Caring for Loved Ones at Home*.

- The more connected you are to your family, friends, neighbors, colleagues from work, your community and your cultural and spiritual community, the better you are able to deal with the ups and downs of caring for your loved one who is dying.

- In periods of overwhelming stress, you might find it helpful to concentrate on a quote or prayer. At one point in caring for my mother, I did not think I could go on. She was throwing up and all I could do was hold the vomit tray and help as best I could. I thought I was going to be physically ill myself or faint. I remembered a paraphrased version of a verse from the Bible and I kept repeating it over and over again to focus me on helping her rather than becoming sick myself. The verse helped me concentrate on something other than my fear. The verse as I remembered it from John 14:27 was, "Peace I give you, my peace I give unto you: not as the world giveth, give I unto you. Let not your heart be weary, neither let it be afraid." Your own religious or poetic background may help you find a similar quote or prayer.

- There are some mistaken ideas about the kind of person you need to be to care for someone at home:

You need unlimited energy. What, in fact, you really need is enough support from others so you can all pool your energy together to help the person who is ill.

You have to accept all the responsibilities on your own shoulders. No one's shoulders are that big, so share the responsibilities so you have more time to enjoy each other's company.

If you look after yourself, you are selfish. How little we must think of the person who is ill to think that they do not care about our well being. If you do not take care of yourself you will probably make the person who is ill feel worse about their situation. This is a mutual experience and everyone must help each other and themselves stay as healthy and comfortable as possible.

If you are exhausted, you must really care about the person who is ill. Plan to take some time off (often called respite care). It may mean taking a few days off from caregiving. It may mean the person you are caring for goes to a hospice or respite program for a few days to get their pain and symptoms under better control while you rest at home. When my grandfather was ill, I took a few days to travel to my niece's baptism. It wasn't easy leaving him (for either of us) but we knew it was necessary and my niece and I now have a lifelong memory to share of that important event.

People should know what we need and offer it to us. It just isn't going to happen that way for most people. People need specific requests to know how they can help you. You have to ask -- even your own family -- so that their help can be specific, useful and timely. Most people do not know how to offer help but are most willing to help if asked.

You might ask for help with practical chores around the house. You might ask someone to pray with you in quiet. You might ask someone to go for a walk for an hour to enjoy the fresh air and company. You might ask someone you know who works in health care to answer some questions about your loved one's care. You might ask someone to watch some television with you or go to a movie together. You might ask someone to stay with your loved one while you go out for an ice cream.

The more you ask different people to help in different ways, the more support you will get. If you do not ask, and people do not know how to offer, you will be alone.

God will take care of you. God will help you spiritually and emotionally. At the same time you need to help yourself. Get support from family, friends, special groups, telephone calls with loved ones far away, moderate exercise, massage, books, good nutrition (and some special treats that may not be on the nutritionists' top ten list!), some time away for a night or two rest (called respite care), some fun everyday, writing a journal or diary, sleeping a little more, a walk in nature, reading a good book, some calming music, silence and a talk with a favorite pet. Most of these things do not have to take a lot of time but all of them will help give you an extra bit of energy. This is not selfish; it really is about meeting the loving needs of the person you are caring for and some of your own needs as well.

Don't spend a lot of time thinking about your feelings. When we think about how we are feeling and when we take the time to express our feelings through talking, crying, walking or praying, we can move beyond our own feelings and be more supportive of others. When we block off our own feelings, we are more likely to block out other people's feelings too. Denying our feelings may provide us with temporary relief from dealing with them, and this denial can be very necessary when faced with overwhelming responsibilities and feelings. Long-term denial, however, may lead to, or worsen, physical or mental illnesses that could be prevented or minimized. Eventually, you will deal with your feelings. Our bodies and mind forces us to deal with them, whether we want to or not. If you deal with your emotions every day, it minimizes the chance of being overwhelmed by denied emotions later on.

- Sometimes when we try to care for someone else we lose sight of what is helpful and who else may need us. A mother caring for a dying child is torn between being with that child as much as possible while also wanting to be with her husband and other children. This most troubling dilemma must be faced squarely with the help of one's family and friends. We cannot be all things to all people but we cannot completely isolate ourselves from others who need us even as we care for someone we truly love.

- Sometimes it is necessary to say no. No, you cannot do everything for everyone. No, you cannot stop working. No, you need to see your children. No, you need some time for yourself. Saying no can be very difficult for those who see their role as caregiving. In North American society, we still assume that caregiving is mostly for women. This puts a completely unfair responsibility on women, especially those who are caring for several people at the same time and prevents men from reaping the benefits of caring for others. Caregiving can be exhausting if left to a few. It is in sharing the care, women and men together, that minimizes the health risks of caring while fulfilling some of our most fundamental cravings for feeling needed and feeling part of a family and community.

We are under the illusion that it 'is better to give than to receive'. This illusion supports our intuitive feeling that "I'd rather be helping someone who is dying, than being the dying person myself." This sets up an unequal relationship. At some point, you will be the one receiving someone's care and if they treat you unequally you will resent it too. Saying no is one way to show respect and caring. Just as children who are grieving need boundaries and rules, so do adults. Show that you understand that you need care as well by saying no to others that may be demanding too much care from you.

When you recognize the equality of caregiving and receiving care, you enter in the realm of true love and compassion. You will be a real person again rather than a caregiver or server. You can find that well of true love that you have shared before the person's illness. You can become husband and wife, brother and sister, parent and child again and revel in those wonderful relationships. You can find that balance between love, gratitude and service that is so fulfilling.

- It can be very helpful to have a private space where you can go to hide, sleep, re-energize, pray and think. Even if it is just down the hallway, it is a place to recover your energy and perspective.

- Sometimes when I get overwhelmed by what I expect of myself and what others might expect from me I take a deep breath, close my eyes and ask myself four questions:

What is it that I can do to help my loved one?

What is it that I cannot do to help my loved one no matter how much I wish I could? (e.g., I cannot cure them. I cannot make them work out problems with other family members. I cannot make them take their medication if they do not want to.).

What is it that my loved one can do to help me?

What is it that my loved one cannot do to help me no matter how much they wish they could? (e.g., They may not have the skills to communicate all their feelings to me. They may be incapable of knowing how much you love them.)

This exercise helps me focus on the possible rather than become overwhelmed by the impossible.

- There is now a wealth of books, videos, and audiotapes with the stories of people in similar circumstances to you. Borrow them from the library. Ask for copies from friends who ask what they can do to help. People have found ways to make caregiving both more enjoyable and less demanding. Learn from them and teach others.

- Consider having a support circle, like the one described later in this book, to help you and the person who is ill. Such a circle can minimize some of the chores or tasks you do not enjoy as much yourself, so that you can concentrate on those things that have the most meaning for you.

Professional and Volunteer Caregivers

Much of what is in this book about helping the patient and family members during a person's illness, and the grieving afterward, holds true for professional and volunteer caregivers as well. You are human beings first and some people will affect you more visibly than others. When my mother died, our family physician, the visiting nurse and the homemaker sat together and cried. They did not pretend to be strong or professional distant. They did not worry about embarrassment and most importantly, they did not go away. They stayed and expressed their feelings honestly. It was their greatest gift to the rest of my family for it showed us their concern without words and how my mother had touched their lives.

Hospice care bereavement programs follow many of these suggestions by allowing people to express their feelings, keep in contact with some of the caregivers, and use the sense of touch to express concern.

When we look at caregiver stress, I will separate caregivers that work in palliative/hospice care from acute care doctors, nurses, therapists, clerics, psychologists and the others.

Acute Care Caregivers

People who work in hospitals and medical centers are used to treating patients who are there for active, cure-oriented treatment. Generally, health care systems do not provide them the time, training or staffing to provide excellent hospice care. Most give the best clinical care possible in very difficult circumstances. Some may have some of the following stresses:

- Difficulty in accepting that a patient's physical and psychosocial problems cannot always be cured or controlled.

- Difficulty in knowing when to get palliative care for their patients. In some areas, there may be little or no palliative care services available that can add to the stress.

- Difficulty in deciding how much to tell a patient about her condition.

- Difficulty in coping with the severe constraints of time and low staffing ratios involved in patient care and administrative responsibilities.

- Frustration at being involved with a patient's family whose emotional resources have already been drained by the patient's illness.

- Disappointment at being unable to fulfil the patient or family's expectation of dying a good death.

- Depressed because they have no time to deal with their own grief when a patient is dying or has died.

- Anger at being critically reviewed by the public.

- Difficulty in deciding how involved to get with the patient and the family especially outside of normal working hours.

- Frustration in their inability to give the kind of care they want to give.

- Difficulty with their inability to be a good communicator.

Palliative/Hospice Caregivers

The stresses of palliative/hospice caregivers differ from those of acute care staff. Although they often have more time to help patients and families, their professional position has been given less credibility because they are dealing with people who are dying. There are no miracle cures and there is an erroneous assumption that their work is, therefore, less rewarding or valuable.

With added time to spend with patients and families there are added concerns and problems to deal with. The philosophy of physical, emotional and spiritual support is not always easy to fulfil. Some patients have not accepted that they are dying. Some patients and families have major unresolved problems that frustrate the caregivers' hope for a peaceful and comforting death for a patient.

The relative newness of palliative/hospice care means that the systems have not been perfected, and may never be perfected, to everyone's satisfaction. In designing the program, frictions between well-meaning caregivers occur because each has certain beliefs about what they think is the palliative care program.

Caregivers grieve someone's death in their own individual way. In cases where they have come to know patients and their families closely, the grieving is more acute. There are few people outside of hospice care who can understand the mixture of personal satisfaction and professional stresses that these caregivers have. One of the advantages of working in hospice care is that professional stresses are more clearly identified and addressed. The following list describes some of the differences between acute care and hospice care personnel:

- There may be less conflict regarding a patient's death because hospice care is concerned with comfort rather than prolonging life.

- There may a lower patient/caregiver ratio in hospice care so that time and administrative stresses are reduced. This ratio depends on the particular hospice care model in place. Freestanding hospices and hospital units have lower staff ratios, for example but consultation teams in hospitals may not.

- There is a team spirit in hospice care and an acceptance of the hospice care philosophy that includes more formal and informal supports for the professionals and volunteers involved. Although team spirit exists in acute care as well, there is often little time during work to provide each other support to enhance that spirit. Financial cutbacks threaten to reduce the amount of time that hospice care teams can provide mutual support as well.

- There is more open and honest communication between caregivers and the patient and family which decreases the likelihood that different caregivers will not share some of the information they have.

- There is great patient/family satisfaction and approval of hospice care teams that reflects well on the caregivers. In the home, hospice care teams have been invited in to help which adds a special dimension of intimacy and satisfaction.

- There is often specialized training for hospice caregivers which prepares them for their work. Part of this training is recognizing the cultural and religious diversity of people in North America. We cannot expect a first generation Chinese person to have the same general attitudes toward dying, death and bereavement as a fourth-generation Canadian with Italian and Scottish roots.

- There are fewer unpredictable situations as many terminal illnesses have a relatively well understand process toward a natural death. Symptoms may still change quickly, however, hospice care teams can help prepare patients and families for what is likely to happen in the months ahead.

Hospice care offers people an opportunity, every day, to make a dramatic and measurable difference in someone's life. What an opportunity to fulfil one of our greatest needs -- to feel needed and to know that our life has meaning.

Part 4: Physical Needs

Chapter 8 Pain and Symptom Control

Defining Pain
Describing Pain and Symptoms
Pain Control Medications
Myths about Pain Control Medication
Other Pain Control Techniques
What Prevents Adequate Pain Control?
General Symptom Control Techniques
Complementary Therapies
Specific Symptoms

Most people can be relatively pain free and alert until they die. The days of people shouting out to die because the pain hurts so bad should be over. No one needs to suffer overwhelming pain anymore. Even in the rare situation of extreme or complex pain, patients can be given short-term relief through drug-induced sleep. Some people still suffer unbearable pain: (a) because they and/or their medical team believe it is typical to suffer a painful death, (b) because the dying patient is being over-treated for their illness but under-treated for their pain, (c) because the patient is not receiving good hospice care including effective pain and symptom control, or (d) because patients or their families are fearful of taking pain medication.

If your loved one is suffering severe pain, get the doctor in charge to check with a palliative care specialist who can suggest ways to stop or greatly reduce the pain now and in the future as the condition changes. We have all the knowledge and skills, right now, to manage most pain. All of the pain may not go away. Most of us suffer from some physical pain from aging, arthritis, back problems, etc. However, unbearable pain is not necessary.

Generally:

- Only about 40% of people with cancer have pain during most of their illness. Most cancers do not cause pain.

- Most people with advanced cancer have some pain. Much of this pain has been poorly controlled.

- According to physicians involved in hospice care, where there is pain, it is controllable in over 95% of the cases.

The secret to effective pain control (relief) is giving the **right drug(s)**, in the **right amount**, in the **right way** and at the **right time**. This balance requires physicians and other hospice team members to do proper, ongoing assessments of a person's pain and to consult with others who may have information that is helpful. Proper pain medication usually prevents overwhelming pain from returning while keeping the patient alert. If pain does suddenly increase (called "breakthrough pain") extra breakthrough or rescue medication must be available right away to relieve it. In those rare cases when pain resists all treatment, a person can be helped through a drug-induced coma for a period of time to alleviate the pain. No one needs to suffer unmanaged, severe pain that we may have witnessed our parents and grandparents suffer.

Once pain is managed, other symptoms like vomiting, bed sores, and dry mouths may be more easily controlled.

Did you know that one of the most common causes of vomiting for patients with widespread cancer is constipation? Or that vomiting is not the rule for patients with advanced stomach or bowel cancer?

Don't be surprised if you didn't know these facts and don't be surprised if some of your physicians don't know them either. Pain and symptom control is a relatively new field requiring some specialized training. A family physician, or a specialist in cancer or heart diseases, while knowledgeable, may not know the latest techniques of pain and symptom control. As a patient or family member/advocate, you need to ask if the physicians are up-to-date on pain and symptom control techniques or ask them to refer you to a pain management specialist when the need arises. If a patient is in severe pain, and the medication and help they are receiving is not working quickly, they need the help of a pain specialist right away. Ongoing, unrelieved pain is not necessary. A person has a right to good pain control.

Defining Pain

Pain is always subjective because it is what the patient says it is and not what others think it might be or should be based on their experience.

Pain is different than suffering and caregivers must distinguish between the two in order to provide total care to a patient. **Pain control** deals specifically with keeping a patient relatively pain-free and alert physically. **Symptom control** deals with other physical-comfort needs of patients with symptoms like nausea, vomiting and bed sores. **Suffering** includes a person's physical pain and symptoms **and** the emotional, mental and spiritual pain that are part of a terminal illness, e.g., fear, anxiety, loss of faith, grief or guilt.

I use the term 'relatively pain free' in describing physical pain because patients generally have more than one pain at a time. They may have several pains associated with an illness like cancer, but they may also have arthritis, back pain, various physical disabilities and other pain. Most of us are never pain free especially as we get older. Proper pain control means that we can easily tolerate whatever pains we may have.

Pain can be broken down into three categories:

- Acute pain: toothache, appendicitis, broken leg, after-surgery pain, pinched nerve and pain from various types of tests or treatments. These pains end in a relatively short time.

- Chronic pain: arthritis and other similar disorders which last for more than six months but are not life threatening.

- Terminal-illness pain: pain from an illness in its last stages (remember many illnesses have no pain associated with them). When pain exists, it is likely to increase over time but patients **should not feel pain** before their next medication is given. If the person continues to feel pain, the physician should increase the dose regularly, even daily, or change to a stronger medication.

Pain is a physical sensation that is modified in the mind by a patient's emotional or spiritual experiences. An example might help explain this best. Madame E. was 57 years old and in extreme pain from colon cancer. Madame E. was being treated on a palliative ward at Hôpital Sainte-Croix in Drummondville, Québec. She was given different types of pain control (including a pain pump, morphine, and other medications) but none managed her pain satisfactorily. The palliative care team was at a loss of what to do as they had had very good pain control of similar cases.

Her husband was physically present with Madame E. but not seen as very emotionally supportive to her and they shared little eye contact. Their only known daughter (30 years old) was shy except around her anxiety about Madame E.'s pain. Both husband and daughter were constantly requesting more help for Madame E.'s pain but short of inducing sleep (which the family did not want), there was nothing left to do.

The answer of how best to help Madame E. came during a very sad television telecast of the funeral of the 14 women murdered at the Ecole Polytechnique at the University of Montreal on December 6, 1989. Anne Plante, Head Nurse of the Medical and Palliative Care Floor takes up the story. "All the rooms on our floor are single rooms except the room where Madame E. was staying. The patient in the bed next to her had the funeral on the television as did all the other patients on the floor. There was complete quiet on the floor. No one was calling nurses for help. There were no tears or talking, just silence from the patients as the funeral was shown. Madame E. was the exception. She was sobbing.

"I went to Madame E. to ask her what was the worst part of living for her right now. This question usually helps us understand some of the emotional and spiritual as well as physical needs of a patient. It brings us to the central needs in someone's life right now."

"It's Suzanne," answered Madame. E. Through further discussion, Anne Plante was able to find out that Suzanne was Madame E's eldest daughter who died 10 years ago at the age of 21. She was about the same age as the women whose funeral she had been watching. No one in the family had mentioned Suzanne until then.

Suzanne had leukemia and had agreed to an experimental treatment which involved a lot of pain. Her mother felt she had unduly influenced Suzanne into taking the treatment and still felt guilt for the pain Suzanne had suffered.

Madame E. talked about her daughter and her own guilt. Her husband and other daughter were also able to begin to talk about Suzanne. The husband felt useless as he watched first his daughter and then his wife suffer painfully. The other daughter was terribly worried that she would be the next female family member to get sick, suffer terrible pain and die. The family had a cousin and sister-in-law who had suffered pain before their deaths.

They assumed that pain was a natural consequence of dying. At the time of Suzanne's illness, none of them had received any support to communicate openly with Suzanne. They never got to say a proper goodbye or to ask Suzanne if she had any regrets about trying the experimental treatments. There were a lot of unresolved feelings about Suzanne's own courageous decision to try the treatment because no one had talked to Suzanne at the time. The family was reliving, with Madame E., the same closed communication they had had before. They were not talking to each other about their fears, hopes, regrets or their love for each other.

With the help of the nursing team, the family was able to talk about their past grief and losses and to talk about their present fears. This open communication about Madame E's emotional needs caused her to feel less pain. The way the pain was managed did not change but the patient's emotional responses changed, which eased her pain.

The nursing team also helped prepare a 'goodbye ritual' for Suzanne that the family participated in with their family priest. Through prayers and some personal goodbyes they were able to let go of some of their past grief to concentrate on their present emotional needs.

Madame E. came to understand that Suzanne was a mature young woman who decided to take the treatment in hopes of a cure. She was courageous in her choice just as Madame E. had been courageous to offer her support during the ordeal.

Madame E. lived another three weeks with her pain well controlled; she was able to talk with her family until just before her death. The family felt through this experience that open communication drew them closer together to support each other. After Madame E's death, her husband and daughter continued that open communication and grew closer together.

The palliative care team also learned the importance of going beyond the physical needs of a patient to find out what emotional and spiritual needs may need attention as well. They do this now whenever they first meet the patient and family.

Describing Pain and Symptoms

Pain is a very subjective and individual sensation. One person's headache may force him to bed while another person's headache may allow her to continue to work. Culturally, people have different beliefs about how much pain one should tolerate before getting help. All of these factors contribute to how we feel pain and how we describe it.

The following checklist allows you to describe your pain and other symptoms as clearly as possible. If you have more than one pain, make that clear to the physician as well. If you or a family member/friend can, write down the answers to these questions for your doctor. **Your physician's assessment of your pain is the key to effective pain management.** Give them the information they need to be most helpful.

- Where in the body did the pain or symptom begin?

- When did it start (date and time)?

- On a scale of 1-10, with 10 the worst pain you have ever had (e.g., broken arm, back pain, severe toothache), how would you measure your pain most of the time? After you take painkillers? Before your next dose?

- Describe any other symptoms you have had.

- What were you doing at the time of the pain or symptom?

- To what degree does your pain or symptom limit your normal activities (e.g. breathing, going to the bathroom, eating, moving, sexuality, sleeping or socializing)?

- How long does the pain or symptom last? (an hour, all day?)

- Is the pain or symptom constant or does it change?

- Does the pain or symptom stay in one place or spread out to other parts of your body?

- What makes the pain or symptom worse?

- What makes the pain or symptom better?

- What medications have you already tried for the pain and how well did they work?

- Other information?

Words to describe pain can be difficult. You might try one or more of the following:

aching - like the overall discomfort you sometimes feel when you wake up in the morning and your body is sore from sleeping in a wrong position

burning - like the pain from putting your hand on the stove

cramp - like a leg cramp from too much swimming

drilling - like a pain you might have if an electric drill was used on your body

hammering/ pounding - like a hammer or drum stick hitting you

knotting - like a bad stomach ache

pinching - like getting pinched by a friend in the play ground when you were a child

shooting - like an electric shock

stabbing - like a mild pin prick to your finger or a more severe knife wound.

Pain Control Medications

Pain has different degrees of intensity. Pain control experts and the World Health Organization (1996) recommend the following 3-step medication ladder to control pain:

Step One	for mild pain	non-opioid [+ added drug(s), if necessary]
Step Two	mild to moderate pain	opioid [+ non-opioid and added drug(s) if necessary]
Step Three	moderate to strong	strong opioid [+ non-opioid and added drug(s) if necessary]

Special Notes

- The steps go from weakest (Aspirin) to strongest medications (opioids like morphine) only when the pain persists or increases without relief.

- For breakthrough or intermittent pain, physicians may prescribe 50-100% of a regular 4-hour dose to take as needed.

- For pain due to nerve damage, physicians may prescribe a tricyclic antidepressant or an anticonvulsant. Opioids are not successful with this type of pain.

- Added drugs (called adjuvant) are those used to (1) deal with adverse effects of other drugs (e.g., constipation, nausea); (2) enhance the pain relief effects of other drugs; and (3) treat psychological distress that aggravates physical pain (e.g., insomnia, anxiety, depression). Another example is the use of non-steroidal anti-inflammatory agents (NSAIDs) in managing bone pain.

- Medication should be given:

  - by mouth when possible

  - by the clock at fixed times before the last dose wears off (This is why nurses sometimes wake patients up to give them pain medication.)

- by the ladder above

- for the individual (for example, the range of oral morphine for an individual can be from 5 mg to 1,000 mg every 4 hours)

- with special attention to detail.

As the World Health Organization concludes: "The correct dose is the dose that works." (p. 22)

It takes time and experimentation to arrive at the exact combination of medications that will keep a patient pain-free and alert. Patients and families can shorten this process by recording and communicating with the physician and nurses any positive or negative results of new medications. Patients may take several different types of medications to control their specific type(s) of pain. Sometimes, when a dosage is increased or someone changes one medication for another, there is a period where the person may have some nausea and sleepiness. The sleepiness could also come from a lack a sleep before the change in medication and the person is just catching up. If symptoms last more than a few days, the physician must be told.

When discussing pain medication with the physician, it is helpful to have all the pill bottles with you that you are using now. This will improve communication and help the physician answer your questions.

Breakthrough pain happens even when someone has good pain control. This pain suddenly 'breaks through' whatever pain control medication you may have. It requires immediate attention to bring it under control. Many physicians prescribe an extra medication for patients to give themselves if they experience breakthrough pain. The patients report any breakthrough pain to their physician to see if any changes in overall pain control is needed.

Each few years, newer medications including longer acting ones come on the market, for example, patches with slow-release medications that enter the body from the patch through the skin. Some people also benefit from portable pain pumps that provide continuous medication, round the clock, without having to wake up to take it. The pumps have helped people remain relatively active both at home and outdoors. "Ann's story" in Chapter 4 is an example of this. It is important to know that fewer than 10% of patients require ongoing injections to manage their pain -- they can take the medication in pill form, as a suppository or as a skin patch.

Pain control through medication is a changing field with constant improvements. It is very important that doctors treating patients with a terminal or life-threatening illness check with a pain control expert for the most recent recommendations. Improved pain control means the patient can carry on daily activities for a longer time.

Myths About Pain Control Medication

Pain experts agree there are three myths about pain control that some physicians and the general public believe in; myths which limit the effective use of medication to control pain. There is a belief that medications given in higher-than-traditional dosages will cause:

- addiction to the drug,

- an increased tolerance to the drug which makes the drug ineffective,

- possible hallucinations from taking the drug.

Addiction Patients do not become addicted to opioid drugs when the medication is used for pain. When the medication is given on a regular basis to alleviate pain there are no "psychological highs" that is the basis of any addiction. Without such euphoria there can be no addiction.

Tolerance to a drug assumes that increasingly higher doses of the medication are needed to relieve pain to the point where the drug becomes ineffective. Studies by experts such as Dr. Robert Twycross of Sir Michael Sobell House in Oxford, have proven that patients can relieve pain by receiving morphine every four hours for over a year without having to increase the dosage. Other studies show that patients can have ever-increasing doses of oral medication to treat worsening pain with the medication still being very effective. Clearly, you don't start with large doses of medication. A physician needs to assess the proper dose and make adjustments as necessary. Expect this to take some time to get the dose right, however, do not tolerate unbearable pain -- ask for immediate relief.

As Dr. Anna Towers of Palliative Care McGill explains, in the vast majority of cases, if opioid doses need to be increased over time, it is because the patient's disease has progressed and they have more pain, not because they have built up a tolerance to the drug(s).

The key point again is that pain needs to be relieved.

The fear of increased tolerance or drug overdoses lead to a physician prescribing medication on a medical chart with the abbreviation "PRN" -- "when necessary." In other words, a patient must feel pain before he can ask the nurse for further medication, a situation that leads not only to unnecessary pain but also to increased anxiety and fear in a patient. The pain threshold is lowered requiring even a greater dose of medication the next time. The myth of tolerance came about because patients were made to suffer unnecessarily. According to the experts this practice of PRN must stop. Studies have shown that medication doses may have to increase over time, but at a slower rate of increase than many physicians expected.

Hallucinations do occur in about one percent of patients (this may improve with newer drugs and techniques). Some of the causes may be metabolic changes such as kidney or liver failure or a person may have brain tumors triggering them. Hospice care teams are well trained to help both the patients and their families deal with hallucinations.

The two major side effects of long-term opioids that are manageable are nausea and constipation. Severe nausea can be almost as uncomfortable as pain. Early attention to diet and medication can certainly help. Constipation causes more misery and health problems than almost any other side effect. It can lead to patients not eating, bowel obstructions, and confusion. It often leads to the emaciated look of cancer patients because they have not been eating. Again, early attention to diet, laxatives and exercise (if possible) will help.

Other Pain Control Techniques

There are other treatments for pain control such as:

- Radiotherapy: radiation is used to shrink tumors to reduce a patient's symptoms.

- Nerve blocks: for localized acute cancer pain, a local anaesthetic or nerve destroying injection is given to block nerves from sending pain messages to the brain. Results may be temporary or long-lasting.

- Hypnosis: a hypnotist can sometimes help manage pain.

- Neurosurgery: with the proper use of medication and other techniques, the need for neurosurgery should be uncommon. If other measures have failed, however, neurosurgery should not be delayed.

- Massage to soothe minor pains.

- Supportive devices like neck collars, slings to support limbs.

- Mentholated creams or ointments (like the ones used for sports injuries).

- Hot or cold treatments.

- TENS machines that provide mild electrical stimulus to diminish pain sensations.

- Complementary therapies or treatments such as acupuncture therapeutic touch, Rekai, meditation, prayer and imagery.

What Prevents Adequate Pain Control?

Patients and physicians ideally want to maximize control of pain and uncomfortable symptoms. Sometimes, however, their beliefs or seemingly small actions stand in the way of satisfactory control. A few examples:

Patients' Errors
- Believing the pain is not treatable.

- Not seeing a physician soon enough for help (do not wait for the pain to become unbearable before you get help).

- Telling the physician and family that the pain isn't strong. Being 'stoic' may be a way to hide their belief that greater pain means their disease is getting worse. They may also be afraid of the medication itself, or losing control, or 'having a needle'. Their beliefs may have existed for years and even passed down through the family. It will take time to deal with these beliefs.

- Failing to take medication. Some people choose not to relieve their pain for personal, religious or cultural reasons. Their decision should be respected and their families given extra support to watch their loved one suffer through the pain. The patient must not be coerced into taking medications but the option of changing their minds must be there for them.

- Taking the medication at the wrong times or inconsistently.

- Fearing addiction or drug tolerance even when these are not true.

- Believing painkillers are only for extreme pain or that opioid use will shorten their life.

- Stopping the medication because of side effects and not telling the physician.

Physicians/Nurses' Errors

- Ignoring a patient's description of pain.

- Not seeing through the patient's brave face.

- Prescribing pain killers that are too weak.

- Giving pain killers only when the patient says her pain has returned (effective pain control prevents the return of pain).

- Not giving enough information about the medication, its use and when it must be taken.

- Not knowing enough about different types of medication and how to move from one to another as pain increases.

- Not asking for a consultation with a pain specialist in difficult cases -- the earlier, the better.

To combat pain, we must recognize that pain is always real and unique for each person who has a terminal illness. Proper pain control requires the right drug(s) or treatment(s), in the right way, and at the right time. Proper pain control includes some experimentation to discover the right combination of medication and treatments. This requires the complete cooperation of the patient, the family and the caregivers. When the pain is under control, other symptoms can be addressed, so that the patient's suffering is reduced and he can remain alert and active for as long as possible.

General Symptom Control Techniques

Total pain is not merely the sensation of pain. Total pain is a combination of physical, emotional, and spiritual pain. The primary emotional component of total pain is fear. Fear can greatly aggravate a patient's physical pain, so fear, anxiety and other negative emotions must also be treated. Add to this list diarrhea, constipation, lack of hunger and energy, bed sores, lack of mobility and other symptoms and you will understand the need for thorough symptom control and relief.

Some of the symptom control and stress management techniques that hospice care or homecare providers use, other than medications, include:

Diet

Some foods cause constipation while others cause diarrhea. Knowing which foods cause what reaction can help caregivers to alleviate a specific symptom. Certain types of foods also provide better nutrition at a time when someone's appetite is less than normal.

Some food tips:

A broth before a meal helps to thin secretions in the mouth.

Thick soups and stews are a way to combine protein and vegetables with rice, barley or noodles.

Milk shakes with eggs, malt, cream, and high quality ice cream are good sources of calories and very tasty.

Soft and easy-to-swallow casseroles make good meals.

Omelets, soufflés, quiche and some pasta dishes are also good meals to prepare.

Follow the person's likes and recognize that these preferences for certain foods may change over time. Don't worry about cholesterol.

The eating environment is very important as eating is also a social event. People tend to eat more in the company of others, especially if the meal is not rushed. The setting can be quiet and relaxing or filled with the typical energy of previous family meals.

Some more tips:

Food that is nicely presented makes the whole meal more pleasant.

If the person is having difficulty eating with others, give them the privacy they need and another opportunity to share in a social, family time.

Use a hot plate to keep food warm during the meal.

Use special drinking cups to make it easier to drink and to prevent embarrassing spills.

Help the person wash up before meals.

Use a napkin or towel to protect the person's clothes during a meal.

Prepare food into small chunks if the person has trouble using a knife.Perhaps cut the food away from the table.

If you are helping the person to eat, offer a small amount on a spoon, wait until that bite is gone before offering more (do not rush the person), and do not wash solid food down with liquids.

Exercise

Extended bed rest can lead to bed sores, constipation, back aches, general immobility and loss of muscle strength because the muscles are not being used. Exercises, active or passive, can be done by the patient or with someone's help in bed or they can be done when the patient is out of bed. Walking, stretching and breathing exercises are excellent ways to exercise as long as safety concerns are addressed. People should use walking aids (e.g., cane, walker) if they feel weak to reduce falls. Ask the nurses or physiotherapists to provide some specific exercises. As someone gets nearer to death, of course, they do not need very much exercise.

Massage

Gets the blood circulating, invigorates the skin and can be very soothing and or exhilarating depending on the type of massage. Everyone enjoys a massage so it is not a surprise that they are excellent for the physical and emotional well being of a patient as well.

Prayer and Meditation

Done individually or together, prayer and meditation may have a powerful effect on one's ability to deal with total pain. Prayer may also bring a group of individuals together in a common spiritual approach to helping each other.

Occupational Therapy and Physiotherapy

Involves recreation, rehabilitation and physical activities based on a patient's physical capabilities. It encourages people to make decisions and participate in things that they have always enjoyed like a walk in the garden or a card game with friends.

Laughter

Increases production of endorphins (natural chemical painkillers in our bodies), reduces tension, distracts attention, changes expectations, and is an internal jog of organs for exercise. In another sense, laughter is contagious and lets people express their feelings in a less threatening way. It can change the mood of a place faster than any other emotion. Find a few good audio-tapes, CDs or videos of comedians like Bill Cosby and sit back and enjoy yourself while you reduce your pain or discomfort.

Relaxation Exercises

Deep breathing, visualization, hypnosis and meditation are all forms of relaxation exercises. They help to relax the body physically and mentally.

Listening

Perhaps no method of symptom control has a greater impact on a patient's fear, anxiety, loneliness and depression than someone who listens uncondi-tionally and answers questions in an honest way.

Heat and Cold Treatments

Applying heat or cold to various body parts can soothe and help to reduce pain.

Distraction

Helping someone to direct their attention away from their pain through music, television, family activities, reading, talking, playing cards, etc. can be very helpful for short periods of time.

The purpose of all of these techniques is to give patients a sense of control over their lives. Even if patients become bedridden, decisions have to be made about exercise, diet, etc. These decisions allow patients to make deci-sions about their care and give them a sense of control. Independence is very important to people and symptom control helps keep them independent for as long as possible.

Complementary Therapies

Complementary therapies are included in this chapter because I feel that family physicians must coordinate the overall medical treatment of their patients. Therefore, patients and their families should consult their physi-cians before trying any new therapies. If the patient wants to try a therapy, the physician may suggest resources and present both the pros and cons. In cases where the family physician does not believe in any form of complementary therapy, the patient or caregiver can research the therapy through their library, medical reports or organizations listed in this book. Regardless of the physician's opinion, it is important that patients inform their physicians about any therapies they are trying that may conflict with the medications or treatments the physician and patient have agreed to follow.

The increase in complementary health organizations and treatments force us to be more careful in choosing what is appropriate for us. Some family physicians may encourage their patients to try other treatments not offered by them as long as:

- The treatment is not harmful.

- Is not expensive (most fraudulent therapies are very expensive).

- The practitioners can prove their claims.

- The practitioners encourage continued communication with the family physician.

There are holistic physicians, nurses, therapists and others who have received traditional medical training. There are also those without a medical background who have taken certified training from a recognized training facility. There are other practitioners who cannot prove their abilities or their results.

The decision to try a complementary therapy is a personal one and should be made in consultation with your physician and other people you trust. Take precautions to ensure that you are dealing with committed and knowledgeable practitioners. I have included a list of organizations at the back of this book where you can call or write for more detailed information.

There are as many forms of complementary therapies as there are people willing to develop them. Some of these therapies result in physical and/or emotional improvements while others remain in the area of consumer fraud.

Holistic health is a system of care that emphasizes the whole person: physical, cultural, nutritional, environmental, emotional, spiritual and lifestyle. While it encompasses all safe methods of diagnosis and treatment including surgery and medications when appropriate, the difference between holistic care and traditional medical care is that patients take a more active role in their own care. Part of this holistic philosophy includes:

- Maintaining a positive attitude toward living to the fullest with hope, humor and inner calm;

- Reducing environmental and emotional stresses through relaxation exercises and recreational activities;

- Encouraging positive stresses through challenge, nature walks, sex, art and music appreciation;

- Eating nutritiously;

- Having caring relationships with others and providing support to others;

- Using prayer, meditation, visualization and imaging to optimize prevention and healing; and

- Seeking professional advice and counseling when needed.

I cannot go into detail here about all the complementary treatments available but I will list a few of the more commonly known ones. Many of these therapies are still not accepted by traditional medical people and remain controversial. I am not qualified to suggest that people try or avoid these therapies. There are many medical reports that support or oppose the use of these therapies. Some of these therapies are included in medical insurance benefits while others are not. Check your own policies. Consider the financial costs before deciding on any long-term complementary therapies.

The decision to try complementary therapies must remain with patients. Families and physicians can provide information both for and against a particular therapy but they must respect the patient's decisions unless such decisions will lead to harmful, expensive therapies. True holistic, complementary therapies are neither harmful nor very expensive. They can be powerful healing or comforting methods.

Acupuncture An ancient Chinese technique that can be used to neutralize pain messages going to the brain. Sterile needles are inserted through the skin in pre-determined points, often remote from the site of the actual disorder or pain.

Aromatherapy Using various aromas can trigger healing in the body. Just as the memory of a favorite person's perfume can trigger a comforting memory, other aromas can trigger physical and emotional responses. A trained individual can use the essential oils to help a person relax, relieve anxiety or insomnia, or to stimulate someone who feels sluggish or depressed. Patients and families can learn to use the smells to promote a sense of wellbeing at home.

Autosuggestion Also called autogenic training or self-hypnotism, autosuggestion uses meditative exercises and deep relaxation to help the body naturally balance itself when directed into a relaxed state. Proven useful in treating ulcers, constipation, blood pressure, migraines, asthma, diabetes, arthritis and pain, it is also becoming more popular as a stress management technique.

Biofeedback A self-directed relaxation technique to help regulate your own pulse rate, body temperature and muscle tension. It has, therefore, been effective for people with: high blood pressure, migraine headaches, muscle spasms, back and neck pain, and general tension. Like all relaxation techniques, biofeedback is useful in managing stress, fear or anxiety.

Chiropractic Care A philosophy, science and art to correct interference in the nervous system with the spinal column as the life-line of the system. Chiropractors manipulate the spine to return its vertebrae to a balanced state, thereby easing back and neck stress and pain. Practitioners also include preventive exercises and improved posture, nutrition and lifestyle programs to maintain a balanced system.

Herbal Therapy Based on Native American, Chinese and Eastern peoples' methods, herbalism has been used to supply vitamins and minerals the body needs without the danger of toxic side effects.

Homeopathy A treatment that gives people very small does of drugs or chemicals that in a healthy person would produce symptoms like those of the disease itself. The theory is that such treatment increases a person's own immune system responses to help cure or minimize the effects of a disease.

Music Therapy The use of music to evoke peacefulness, to release emotions or to bring back memories. The therapy can involve listening to or playing favorite music, singing songs or the writing of music or songs for therapeutic reasons.

Naturopathy Seeks to balance the relationship between the mind, body and spirit of the individual and his environment, in nature. Naturopathy attempts to improve the resistance within the body to the disease by nourishing it with natural foods and water in order to cleanse the body of its toxins. Emphasis is also placed on developing peace of mind through relaxation exercises, visualization and meditation.

Osteopathy A medical therapy that involves manipulation for correcting body ailments that may be caused by the pressure of displaced bones on nerves.

Therapeutic Touch A simple, ancient method of healing based on the principle of laying-on-of-hands using the energy in one person's hands to help balance the energy in someone else's body. The modern version, taught in some American universities to student nurses, relies on passing one's hands near the patient's body, rather than actually touching them.

Visual Arts Therapy Often called art therapy, this therapy uses visual arts like crafts, drawing, sculpting, jewelry design, photography, or video to help people express their thoughts and emotions in a visual way. One doesn't have to have previous artistic experience to enjoy the benefits of the creative arts.

Specific Symptoms

The following are some tips. Check with the visiting home nurse, home care case manager or family physician before following any of these tips to make sure they apply in your situation. The closer the person nears death, the less aggressive one can be about certain symptom control techniques. For example, someone in their last hours of life does not need to be moved every two hours to prevent bedsores or to have aggressive mouth care.

Note: Whatever the symptom, constant reassurance, talking gently with the person, appropriate touch and comfort go a long way to help with all of the following symptoms. It is your presence, your offer to help, your increasing knowledge and skills about what you are doing that provide the added comfort and safety that helps people through difficult moments. Your presence, as the person nears death, may also be comforting to you as you experience your own feelings and thoughts about what is happening.

Caring for Loved Ones at Home has illustrations and instructions for helping bedridden loved ones, lifting them, using bedpans, giving bed baths, etc.

Appetite Loss (anorexia)

Can occur very early on in an illness or as one nears the end of their life. As the body slows down, it needs less food and liquids. This natural loss of appetite does not mean the person is starving themselves or hurting their health. Offer the person small amounts of food on smaller luncheon-size plates and liquids in small glasses. Most will eat in the morning or early afternoon. They may have less energy to eat an evening meal. At some point the person may not want solid food at all and, again, this is natural as the body just doesn't need it any more. We have been taught that you must eat healthy foods to live well. It may be hard for us to stop offering food to our loved ones because it is yet another sign that they are nearing death. When should a person who has a terminal illness stop eating? Follow the person's hunger. If they are not hungry and their loss of appetite is because they are nearing their death, then continue to offer small glasses of water or juices every hour, or popsicles or ice chips. High calorie, high protein drinks may help the person to get enough calories. Intravenous feeding or liquids may be appropriate some times but usually do not lengthen someone's life or provide them comfort. It is important to take care of the person's dry mouth as they take in less food and liquids.

Drinking alcohol may not be wise depending on the medications the person is taking or their physical condition. However, an alcoholic drink before a meal may stimulate someone's appetite or may involve the person in a family tradition. Check with your physician about what is best.

Breathlessness (dyspnea)

A common and, perhaps, distressing symptom. Breathlessness **does not** lead to choking or suffocation. Simple breathing exercises, having the person sit or lay in a different position, and reassurance to reduce anxiety can help the person feel in control of their breathing again. Some medications may also help depending on the cause of the breathlessness. If their room is dry, use a humidifier. A room with a view outside can also help the person feel less claustrophobic and can reduce their breathlessness. Keep the room comfortably warm or cool. Oxygen treatment may help some people. An electric fan that sends fresh air across, but not into, the person's face may help relieve the sensation of breathlessness. Placing the person's bed or chair by an open door or window can also improve breathlessness. Calming music can relax and slow the breathing rate. Discuss this symptom with your physician.

Confusion/Dementia

Can be very upsetting to family members. The person they have known for years is acting strangely. Medication, environmental changes or physical changes can cause a person to be 'mixed-up' or not understand what is happening to them. Confusion may make them suspicious of everyone's behavior. The confusion may be temporary or may continue for the rest of the person's illness. This symptom requires immediate attention by the person's physician and nurses. Do not stop giving pain medication until the cause of the confusion is determined.

Some tips: if the person does not recognize you, identify yourself, tell the person where they are, what day it is, who might be visiting, plans for the day, etc. Use family photos and other personal items to help the person understand who they are and where they are.

Avoid arguments. Use simple questions to get a yes or no answer about specific things (e.g., Would you like your supper now?) Make sure the rooms are safe with furniture out of the way for easy movement, slippers and rugs that do not slip and proper lighting. Good lighting helps the person easily find things or move around safely.

Always remember that the person you have loved is still there. The hands that have comforted you are still there. The arms that have held you are still there. The person's personality may have temporarily or permanently changed, but not the person. Remember them. Remind yourself of them and then see the changes as the disease speaking through them. You will be a source of stability, love and compassion during a difficult time. When my mother went through days of severe confusion when she thought we were trying to kill her, it was immensely traumatic for all of us. She needed us during that time but it was difficult to watch her personality change so dramatically. When she recovered from her confusion (she had been awake and talking for over 48 hours) she had absolutely no memory of what she had experienced or said. She asked us who she had 'hurt' unintentionally so that she could apologize. The apologies were not necessary for us, but important to her. During the early stages of someone's confusion, family members may need more short breaks away from the person. These breaks give them some privacy to deal with the changes in their loved one's personality and allow them to openly express their feelings with a trusted person, away from their loved one.

Constipation

Often happens when we eat less, move less and if we are taking painkillers or other drugs. Untreated, constipation is a leading cause of vomiting, bowel blockage, and severe discomfort. Some tips: if the person can eat, a high-fibre diet and lots of fluids are helpful. Whole bran, stewed prunes, fruit and fruit juices, leafy vegetables and whole wheat bread and muffins are all helpful. Lots of liquids are important. A recipe of 1/2 cup applesauce,

1/2 cup of all bran, and 1/4 cup of prune juice helps improve bowel movements as well. Keep refrigerated. Medications may help and in extreme cases an enema may be needed to relieve discomfort. Constipation needs attention to reduce severe discomfort and to prevent sapping a person of their physical energy.

Depression

Can be mild or severe. People who are dying may have periods of sadness or what we call depression. This is quite different from a clinical depression that may, or may not, be linked to the person's illness or from untreated pain. Clinical depression can be treated and must be taken seriously. Depression may be incorrectly diagnosed as clinical (requiring medical treatment) if a patient is completely exhausted because of their illness, treatment or poorly managed pain. Milder depressions must also be taken very seriously and can often be helped by allowing a person some time to be alone with their thoughts and/or providing lots of opportunities for the person to talk about what specifically saddens them about dying. We all have different reasons for being 'depressed' as we come to terms with our lives and our deaths. Try not to superimpose your own reasons for being unhappy on the person but rather let them tell their story in their way over a number of times. Listening, without judgement and without a lot of 'free advice', can be very helpful. Maybe different people can be listeners too to provide the person with as much support as they need.

A simple, open-ended question like "What is it about dying that makes you unhappy right now?" may open the doors to a good discussion. When I asked my father this question, his immediate response was, "Well, if you were dying son, you'd be unhappy too." When I asked him what specifically made him unhappy, he took a few minutes to think of an answer and rehearse it in his mind. This was a long time for me to be quiet but crucial to encouraging him to choose his words carefully. His answer surprised me which was the beauty of asking a general question and letting him decide how much he wanted to tell me. He was most unhappy that he could not attend my wedding in seven months. Sharing his unhappiness allowed us to talk about our concerns, worries, fears and hopes for the future. He was able to participate more actively in our wedding plans than he had dared do before. Another useful question is "Are you afraid?"

Medication may be prescribed by a physician to help relieve depression but it is used in conjunction with the above.

Diarrhea

Is both uncomfortable and embarrassing. Many people define their personal 'dignity' with an ability to go the bathroom on their own. With diarrhea, especially if one is bedridden, this perceived loss of 'dignity' can be very difficult. There are medications that help with ongoing diarrhea. The rectal area needs extra attention to prevent soreness or rashes. A gentle washing after every bowel movement and using a barrier cream can help.

Few of us feel comfortable having someone help us with bedpans, bed baths and the like. It is important to treat a person with great respect, gentleness and understanding. Allow them to do as much as they can for themselves in private and only help where necessary. If you are very close to the person, remind them that they have done or would do the same for you. Using appropriate humor to 'lighten' the atmosphere can also be helpful. Use the opportunities provided by regular personal care to show your love and intimate respect for the person.

Assisting the nurses when they do the first bed baths at home is a good way to increase your own comfort and competence and may ease both you and your loved one into this new situation.

Use room spray to keep the living area smelling pleasant. Incontinent pads on the bed or adult diapers can provide some comfort. The skin needs extra attention if you use pads. Bowel incontinence may be caused when the bowel is blocked by constipation and should be treated immediately. Medication can be used to control diarrhea.

Hallucinations

Rarely occur as a side effect of medication. They may happen if the person becomes dehydrated, has recently changed medications, or experiences other physical or chemical changes. Encourage the person to relax and stay with them. Their hallucination may be something they are 'seeing' or 'hearing'. It may be comforting (e.g., seeing a dead relative in the room smiling at them) or frightening. Do not leave them alone during a hallucination. Hallucinations must be reported to the physician so the cause can be dealt with. Certainly any distress can be relieved with medication. Family distress at seeing a loved one hallucinate requires someone to ask professionals or volunteers to provide extra support to help you understand what is going on, why and what can be done or not done. The person may not remember hallucinating. Family and other caregivers need to be sensitive to the person's questions about what happened.

Hiccups

Hiccups that last for a long time can be very exhausting and distressing. Breathing exercises, carbonated drinks and some medications will help. Do not let hiccups continue for long before getting some professional advice from a nurse or physician.

Incontinence

Incontinence of the bladder (when urine leaks out) is just as traumatic for people as uncontrolled diarrhea. When we lose control of our bladders or when we have to wear adult diapers for the first time, it can be hard to get used to the idea. Our sense of personal dignity is so tied to bowel and bladder control that most of us need time to adjust to the idea that we have lost that ability.

That said, many people wear adult diapers and continue to lead full and productive lives with most other people not knowing about their problem. For someone nearing the end of their lives, loving interactions with family and friends can help them put incontinence in to proper perspective. Dignity does not come from bladder control. Dignity is an inherent quality that says we have value and worth in our family and in our communities.

Bedpans and a commode by the bedside can help people go to the bathroom without having to leave their bedside. For incontinence in bed, special incontinence pads are available that are easy to use so that bed sheets do not have to be changed.

Catheters (a plastic or rubber tube placed into the bladder) may be used. These are often very comfortable and do not interfere with mobility.

Insomnia

Someone may have trouble sleeping for many reasons: they are cold or hot; they are afraid of the dark; their minds are rushing with information, ideas or concerns; they are afraid because someone told them that most people die in their sleep; they are bored; they are 'achy' from lack of activity; they hear too much noise or they enjoy the quiet time to think without interruption. Whatever the reasons, too little sleep is harmful to the body. Try to discover the cause and see if there is a simple remedy before trying medication.

Of all the possible causes listed, fear may be one of the most important and most difficult to address. While everyone else is sleeping (and we don't want to burden them by waking them up) we spend time worrying about our condition, our family's future, the meaning of our life and more. Addressing some of these concerns with trusted loved ones during the day will help us unburden our minds of some of our fears. If the person who is ill does not want to talk to a loved one, help them find a friend, neighbor, hospice volunteer or professional person (doctor, nurse, social worker, chaplain, spiritual leader) to talk to. Fear is decreased, when we share the fear; not by trying to conquer it on our own.

There are sleep disturbances, like mixing up days and nights that may be caused by the disease. These are not 'fixable' but can be explained and dealt with through emotional supports.

Mouth Problems

Can include thrush (Candidiasis), dryness or sores. Thrush are white patches on the inside of cheeks, roof of the mouth, on the tongue or on the back of the throat. It may also be on the esophagus where it cannot be seen. Medication can control thrush. Mouth ulcers are another common symptom requiring a physician or nurse's attention. Mouth care is very important when you are caring for someone who is dying. Here are a few tips:

- Clean teeth or dentures after each meal or snack.

- Use a soft, nylon toothbrush.

- Do not floss too forcefully as this can cause cuts and possible infections,

- Do not use mouthwashes with alcohol as these dry the mouth. Instead, rinse the mouth with 1/4 teaspoon of salt or baking soda in a glass of warm water, or mix baking soda with ginger ale (1 ounce ale with 2 teaspoons of baking soda). Spit out either mouthwash.

- Use lip balm to moisten the lips.

- Use special products designed for mouth care and recommended by the nurse or physician such as swab sticks or lubricating products.

- Offer sips of water or other liquids and ice chips often to keep the mouth moist. Keep them in easy reach so the person can choose when they want them.

If the person is bedridden and there is a lot of secretions from the mouth, lay the person on their side more often especially when they are sleeping. Medication may help reduce secretions. In rare cases, family members can be taught to suction if the secretions become troublesome.

Nausea

Can drain energy. The causes of nausea can be kitchen odors, certain medication, physical response to an illness, or smells and tastes that trigger a memory of past nausea. Frequent mouth care is very important. Encourage the person to eat often and in small amounts (day and night). Try not to do bowel care just before meals. Have the person change their body position slowly, especially if they are dizzy. Breathing exercises can give a sense of control and comfort back to the person. Too much wax in the ears may cause nausea. Help the person sit up more, especially after a meal. Cold foods may be easier to eat (less smell) e.g., sandwiches, salads, fruits. Some people find peppermint or ginger tea and other herbal remedies very helpful. Soda crackers, without salt, are also helpful.

Pressure/Bedsores (skin ulcers)

Pressure sores are areas of skin that open up to expose the nerves and surrounding tissue. They can be very painful and almost always preventable. They happen most often where the bones are close to the surface and on areas where you sit or lie. The buttocks, elbows, knees, hips, shoulders, ankles, heels and back are key areas. Pressure sores happen when someone does not move very much. Someone lying in bed, for example, must move at least every two hours or so to prevent sores. If they cannot move themselves, someone must help them. It is important not to slide the person up in bed but rather to use a draw-sheet to lift and move them as needed.

Proper skin care includes daily washing, skin cream treatments and the use of special supports on the mattress or chair. The person's skin may be dry and fragile so gentle and smooth movement during bathing and lifting help to protect their skin. Wet creams and lotions left on the skin may be quite uncomfortable. Get advice from the home care nurse about what is most appropriate in your situation. The key is to increase blood circulation to the danger spots through movement, less pressure and friction and keeping the area clean and dry. Avoid even gentle massage in reddened areas as it damages the skin further.

Other tips: make sure the bed sheets are dry and clean and smooth (sheet wrinkles can hurt the skin over time). Make sure the person's pajamas are also dry and clean. Use special devices like foot cradles and pillows to keep the weight of the sheets and blankets off the body if they cause reddening of the skin. Use pillows, foams or sponges to protect sensitive areas. For example, use pillows between the legs when the person lies on their side. A home care nurse can show you how to use pillows. Make sure that where the person sits is also comfortable, dry and clean.

A schedule to remind you when to ask someone to turn or to help them turn can be helpful. Modify the following example to the specific needs of the person.

12:00 a.m	on stomach	12:00 noon	on back
2:00	on left side	2:00	on right side
4:00	on back	4:00	on stomach
6:00	on right side	6:00	on left side
8:00	on stomache	8:00	on back
10:00	on left side	10:00	on right side

Restlessness

Can be caused by anxiety, boredom, confusion, lack of oxygen, a full bladder or other discomfort. Do not leave the person until you know what has caused the restlessness. Ask for a physician or nurses' advice. You may help the person to become more calm through talking, listening, walking with them, massage, music, dimming the lights, opening a window, using a fan near their face, removing distractions, offering a bed pan and following the person's lead.

Seizures

Are frightening for families to observe, especially the first time. It is important to find out the cause of a seizure. Medication is given to prevent further ones. The person going through a seizure may be aware of what is happening to them. Talk to them calmly during the seizure. Make sure the surrounding area is safe, do not try to hold the person down or force their tongue back into their mouths. Do not put anything into their mouth. Breathing may be labored but they will not choke on their tongue. Take a few deep breaths yourself to help you gain control if you are anxious. Reassure them. Try to get the person on their side. Call for help if the seizure is unexpected.

Swallowing Difficulties (dysphagia)

Swallowing or chewing difficulties can be helped by mincing food or using a blender. You can also moisten foods such as breads and cookies by dunking them into soup or a drink or using gravies or sauces with meats and vegetables. Discuss the specific situation with your physician, nurse or dietician. People with ALS, for example, may have trouble swallowing liquids (it may cause them to choke) so their drinks must be thickened first to help trigger their swallowing reflex.

Blended foods can be made more appetizing by using thickeners and moulds to recreate the appearance of the original. For example, chicken shaped like a chicken leg or carrots like the whole vegetable. Consider consistency, color and taste combinations to stimulate the appetite.

Food supplements may maintain the strength of someone with swallowing problems who can still enjoy eating. These are available through your physician, dietician or pharmacist.

Swelling (edema)

Caused by too much fluid in the tissues. If it is in the arms or hands, remove the jewelry. Provide good skin care and move and reposition the area frequently. Raise the part of the body that is swollen. As with other symptoms, follow the advice of your physician or nurse.

Taste Sensations

May be lost in some people. Add more flavorings and spices if the person enjoys them. Some people may also dislike certain foods that they once enjoyed. For example, if they no longer like red meats, they can still get their protein through cheese, eggs, fish, ham, milk, and poultry. If they no longer like sweet foods you can use unsweetened foods and drinks. Many people enjoy sucking on hard candy for the taste and to increase saliva production to keep the mouth moist. Too much candy, however, can make the mouth sore and one must be careful about choking. Smaller candies, especially if the person is lying down, may reduce choking. Sitting up is best. Popsicles are soothing and have a good aftertaste in the mouth especially if they are homemade with fruit juices and purees.

Vomiting

Vomiting is distressing and debilitating. Medications can help. A cool compress to the forehead and back of the neck can be comforting. Help the person clean their mouths after vomiting to keep the odor and taste away (these may cause more vomiting). Keep the person's head up or to the side. Breathing exercises can be very helpful both as a distraction and to regain control over the abdominal muscles. When the person wants to eat again, offer: clear fluids like consommé, broth, ginger ale, apple juice, or flat cola. They might also enjoy Jell-O or soda crackers. Avoid using perfume, colognes or perfumed deodorants as the smell may trigger more vomiting. Keep kitchen odors away.

Weakness

Weakness is a common symptom as one's illness progresses. The person's energy ebbs and flows during the day and night and so activities and personal care must be scheduled when a person can be most involved. Some simple exercises can help people regain some of their strength after a long period of inactivity. Follow the person's lead about what can be most helpful to them and when. Wheelchairs or walkers can help the person to save their energy for more important activities. Occupational therapists can teach patients and family how to save energy as well as "how to do things differently" but with the same results. For example, how someone brushes their hair may take too much energy and weaken the person. Using a different technique will still result in a nice hairdo but also more energy to do other things.

After all the studies have been read, the personal experiences related and the advice given, the underlying principle of total care of the person who has a terminal or life-threatening illness remains cooperation between patient, family and caregivers. A mutual respect and understanding of each other's feelings and needs result in a fuller life for the patient and personal satisfaction for family members and caregivers that they have helped the patient to the best of their abilities.

Chapter 9   What to Expect at the End of Life

Sudden Death
The Last Days or Few Weeks
At the Time of Death
After the Person Has Died

It can be traumatic waiting for someone to die if you don't know what to expect. When you understand what is likely to happen, there are fewer surprises and more comfort in knowing that you are doing everything you can to help a person die as comfortably as possible.

Someone who is dying may go through different physical changes. The more you know what to expect the more you will recognize how normal the process is for your loved one. Each person is different, of course, but there are some general trends. Talk to your physician and nurse. The person who is ill may only have some of the following signs.

Sudden Death

A person might die suddenly from a heart attack or stroke or stop breathing unexpectedly. If you were expecting the person to die soon but more slowly, this sudden death might make you want to try and help them to breathe or you might want to call 911. The person has died, quickly, without pain or suffering. It may be difficult to watch such a sudden death, but for the person who has died, it was quick and painless. It is best to take a few minutes to calm yourself. You might want to readjust your loved one's body into a more natural position. You might want to do some of the steps mentioned below to prepare yourself and the body for when the funeral home staff come to pick up your loved one's body.

If you do call emergency services (911) they are legally required in most provinces and states to try to have your loved one breathe again. This is rarely successful and painfully prolongs the person's death. They are rushed to the hospital where life support treatments start, unless you are their Power of Attorney for Personal Care and state they do not want life-support treatment. Once on life support, a decision has to be made about whether to continue the treatments or stop them. This situation can be prevented if you call your family physician or funeral director and avoid calling the emergency number.

In Quebec, many emergency services will honor a letter from the physician stating that your loved one has a terminal illness and that they should not be resuscitated if their heart stops.

Sudden death possibilities should be discussed with your loved one and your family physician in advance so that they can advise you on what they would like you to do in these circumstances.

The Last Days or Few Weeks

The following physical signs or specific needs are presented in the order they often follow in the last days or weeks of someone's life.

The person may **sleep longer** and may have trouble waking up. You may want to plan your short conversations for when the person is most awake. Ask visitors to stay for only short times and to sit quietly beside the person. Sleep or silence may also be a way that the person chooses to withdraw from their family and friends as they prepare for their death. It is quite natural to prepare for the next step after death by withdrawing a bit from the people and things around you.

The person may prefer dim lights in the room if their eyes are sensitive to light. Their vision may also be less clear.

The person may **eat and drink less** as their appetite decreases. Offer the person small amounts of their favorite light foods and drinks. At the end of life, they will probably have little or no fluids. You may wonder if using an intravenous line to give the person fluids might help the person be more comfortable. Probably not. The body is slowly shutting down and decreased fluid and food intake is a normal part of that. Check with your physician or nurse to make sure this is true for your loved one.

The person may have **trouble swallowing** or forgetting to swallow. Give them only what they want to eat or drink. You may remind them they need to swallow. Do not force food or drinks since this can easily lead to vomiting or choking. People near the end of life are just not that hungry or thirsty and that is normal.

The person may **become confused** as their body chemistry changes. They may not recognize everyone or everything and may be confused about time (day of week and time of day). They need your loving reassurance about who they are, who you are and where and when they are right now. These constant reminders plus familiar photos of you all together, calming familiar music, gentle massages and your peaceful presence will all add to their comfort and yours. When my mother and father experienced these periods of confusion, they never remembered afterwards what they did or said and were embarrassed when they found out. Periods of confusion are often harder on the family since the person experiencing them usually doesn't remember what happened.

Bed sheets should be loose for comfort. Tight sheets can feel quite frightening and make the person more restless or agitated.

The person may have **irregular or shallow breathing** in a distinct pattern of increasing and then decreasing respiration rates followed by periods of not breathing at all (also called Cheyne-Stoking). It is common for someone near the end of life to **not breathe** (sleep apnea) for 10-30 seconds at a time. It is difficult for a family to watch since they do not know if this is the last breath or not, but it is not uncomfortable for the patient. A person might breathe like this for several days before death.

The person may **make vocal sounds** as if they are in discomfort or pain. If their pain has been well managed, these sounds are probably just their unconscious use of their vocal chords. You can tell if the person is in great discomfort or pain by touching them gently where their pain is located. If there is no difference in their vocal sounds, their pain is probably well managed. If you are unsure, check with the nurse or physician.

The person may have an **irregular heartbeat.** Again it is quite normal for the person's heartbeat (or pulse) to change rhythm since the body is slowing down. This is not uncomfortable for them at all.

The person may have **'wet' sounding breathing.** This is not uncomfortable for the person but is difficult to listen to as a loved one. If saliva collects at the back of the throat and cannot be swallowed because of weak muscles, the breath may have a 'wet' sound to it. Turn the person on their side so that the saliva can rest in the side of the mouth or dribble out. If the breathing continues, it may be because moisture is in the lungs. Medication can help relieve some of this. Ask your doctor or nurse.

The person may **not react** to your voice or your touch. They may be sleeping very deeply or in a coma. Continue to talk in a calming, peaceful voice since they may be able to hear you. **Note:** many people remain conscious until just before death. Although they may appear to sleep longer periods, they are often still conscious.

They **may have less pain** as their awareness of pain decreases. Sudden, increased pain at the end of life is very rare.

The person's **eyes may remain open** even when they are sleeping. If possible, close them gently to prevent them from drying out.

The person may **lose control of their bladder and bowels** since their muscles are relaxing. The nurse can give you some tips on how to deal with incontinence. The amount of urine decreases near the end of life and is dark in color.

The person may have **cool arms and legs** as the blood circulation slows down. This does not usually mean that they feel cold, since their internal temperature can be high. In fact, they may become quite restless if they are too warm. Try removing a layer of blanket or comforter if the person is restless. They may also want lighter clothing. The skin may shows spots or streaks of blue or purple, along with bluish or grayish fingernails, toe nails and lips. Make sure there is fresh air and reduce odor as much as possible. If the person's knees are pink and their hands and feet are warm, the death will probably not occur for several days.

The person may turn to **face the wall** as a physical way of retreating from their world and drawing more inward. This is not a slight against their family but a necessary way for them to prepare to leave.

The person may go into a coma that can last for days. They will be unresponsive but may still be able to hear your voice or feel comforted by your touch.

Note: It is not uncommon that someone near the end of their life and having some of the above symptoms may improve again for several days or weeks. There is usually no explanation. It can be quite traumatic for a family expecting a death to occur soon to find out that the person is actually 'recuperating' for some time before their death.

Note: Just before a person dies, families sometimes wonder if it might not be better to call an ambulance and bring the person to hospital. If the person is comfortable, the symptoms are described as above and the visiting home nurse or your physician tell you that everything is going well in the circumstances, it is probably best to keep the person home for the last few hours or days. Calling 911 or rushing to the hospital can be traumatic at a time when you are trying to provide a peaceful and loving environment. Make sure you can reach your physician or nurse 24 hours a day to help you cope with changes in your loved one's condition. You may only help someone live at home until they die once or twice in your life. Nurses and physicians have done it many times and can offer you the comfort, information and understanding that you need.

At the Time of Death

The following signs will tell you the person has died:

The person is not breathing anymore.

The person has no pulse or heartbeat.

The person does not respond to sound, touch or movement.

The eyes stay in a fixed position either opened or closed (no blinking).

The person's bladder and bowels may empty.

The facial muscles and jaw relaxes and the mouth may open slightly.

With the muscles relaxing, the person's grayish face may have a calm, peaceful look to it.

There could be fluid coming out of the mouth.

After the Person Has Died

Do not call 911 (except in Quebec) or an ambulance.

Write down the time of death. This is needed later for legal purposes.
There is no rush to do anything. Take your time to say your good-byes, to cry, to talk to the person and to other family members and friends who are with you. There is no legal requirement for you to call your doctor or funeral director immediately. Follow whatever cultural and religious practices you are comfortable with.

When you are ready (and this could be several hours later) call your physician to tell them of the death. The doctor needs to declare officially that your loved one has died.

Call the funeral home where you have pre-planned the funeral. They, in fact, may call your doctor for you and do all the necessary arrangements if that is what you have pre-planned.

If you have not pre-planned a funeral, call your family doctor yourself.

Call your home care nurse or case manager to let them know of the death.

Take time with your family and friends over the next few hours. You may, or may not, be able to sleep or eat. You may need to go for a walk. After my grandfather's body was taken away by the funeral home people, those of us who cared for him went for a long walk in the woods. We remembered stories, we laughed, we cried, we hugged, and we prayed quietly. That memory brings me smiles and tears of love nearly 20 years later. Take the time.

Part 5: Emotional and Spiritual Needs

Chapter 10 Emotional Aspects of Dying and Death

To the Person who is Dying
To the Family and Friends Providing Care
Communication
Patient Needs
Their Fears
Labeling Feelings
Children and Dying
Family and Friends
Euthanasia and Assisted Suicide

There are three groups of people affected when someone is dying: the person who is dying, family and friends, and caregivers. Individuals react in different ways and for different reasons but there are common feelings.

Two of the most important things to remember about how different people react to emotional difficulties are:

- People's feelings of love, grief, frustration, joy, anger, compassion, and fear are real and unique to them. Something should be done with these feelings either through conversations or actions. These feelings and their reactions to them are similar to how they have dealt with difficult times before in their lives. The world does feel sometimes like it is coming apart but there are ways to deal with these feelings. There will also be times of happiness, laughter and joy, and these need to be shared as well. The most recommended process for dealing with your difficult feelings is to talk with family and friends and/or with professional people or volunteers who regularly deal with these situations. For personal, family or cultural reasons, people may feel uncomfortable talking openly about their feelings. They may be more comfortable with things like prayer, meditation, quiet walks alone or with loved ones, going fishing, writing, singing or listening to music, or concentrating on favorite activities to reflect their feelings.

• Sometimes people say or do things that unintentionally hurt the person they care about. If their concern and caring are real then their compassion and love overshadow any errors they make. There are specific things you can do to improve the life of someone who is dying, but few are greater than your expression of caring.

To the Person Who is Dying

Asking for help, and allowing people to help you, is the last gift you can give others. This is a time when everything you do or say that is kind and understanding is remembered. The people who care for you help you in intimate ways. Your patience as they try to do their best for you inspires them long after you have died. What you do now can provide decades of loving memories. It is not always easy but it is always remembered.

You may feel unhappy or sad about dying and leaving loved ones behind. You may get angry when the television breaks or furious at any injustices you have experienced. You will feel any, and all, of these emotions along with those of love, trust, laughter, joy, and pride in your family and friends.

There is no prescription for what you must or should feel. It means that you ask for help while offering help in return. It may sound like a cliché, but this time in your life can be one of the most rewarding as your body begins to wear down. There may be times when needing help going to the bathroom, changing your clothes, or eating your food feels undignified. In fact, these are just indications that your body is slowing down in preparation for death. Nothing more than that. It is exactly as these signs occur that you will be physically comforted and supported, hugged, have people's undivided attention, and be loved and cared for. Use these opportunities to look outward to strengthen your relationships with others and to enhance your bonds of love through memories that will last lifetimes.

You won't like everything that people say or do for you. Like all of us, you probably never have. That's natural. Pick the needs that are most important to you and talk to the person about what is most helpful to you and what you prefer they do not do or say. You have the right to ask for help and the right to agree on how it is provided. This is not about charity work for others; this is about mutually sharing the gift of time left to you.

Please read the suggestions offered to those caring for you as well and use them to talk as openly as possible about your love, your concerns and your needs.

To the Family and Friends Providing Care

When someone we love is dying, they may have body and emotional changes that may be difficult for them but also difficult for you to watch. At their most vulnerable moments, you have the opportunity, as never before, to demonstrate and feel unconditional love. No matter the positive or negative experiences you have shared together before, this period before death is remarkably filled with opportunities to evaluate what is truly important in your life, e.g., people, love, and the mutual benefits of caring for someone who is dying.

There may be times when you want to cry alone or in the supportive arms of someone you trust. Feel the feelings as fully as you can. They can be enormously healing even as you sob uncontrollably.

When you can't, or don't want to provide some physical, emotional or spiritual support, find someone who can. You can ask within your own circle of friends and neighbors or you can ask your home care case manager or local hospice program for help. See Chapter 19 on support circles to understand how immensely helpful they can be during these times.

The person who is dying may experience raw emotions of pure joy and pure fear. Your presence allows them to share their positive feelings and find support for their fears and anxieties. People need the time and space to go through these emotions and may not always be able to tell you so. Providing opportunities for them to share their thoughts, feelings or fears does not mean that they will take advantage of that opportunity. However without time together, they will not have that chance and may feel completely isolated at one of the most vulnerable times in their lives.

There will be moments when discussions of sports, weather, politics or gossip have no meaning at all compared to the bond of silence that exists between you, a look of unconditional love or a touch of complete trust. These are precious moments. Take the time to enjoy each of these moments fully and remember its significance for the years ahead.

It may sound like a list of platitudes but what I can tell you is that wisdom collected over thousands of years reaffirms people's basic needs to care and be cared for, to love and to be loved, and to experience life within a community of compassionate, thoughtful people. This is one of the times in our life when we can fulfil all of those needs together.

There will be difficult times physically and emotionally and, perhaps, spiritually. There may be times of exhaustion and frustration. There may be times of physical pain as your experience grief for someone who hasn't died yet (anticipatory grief). I hope this book will provide you with some of the information you need to help you through such times. I also hope this book encourages you to seize every moment, every glance and every touch of unconditional love, trust and gratitude that occurs.

With all the difficulties, suffering and frustrations with bureaucrats that I experienced caring for my parents, grandfather or other family and friends over the years, I can say that I am, without doubt, a better friend, spouse, parent and person because of these life-defining opportunities. I hope you are able to say the same and share your lessons with others too.

Please read the suggestions offered to your loved one who is dying. Use this opportunity to talk as openly as possible about your love, your concerns and your needs.

Communication

From the research done in this field, it is clear that the best thing that people can do during a difficult emotional time is to share their feelings and needs with others. Speaking with family and friends, a spiritual leader and/or professional counselors help people to air their feelings, look at their choices and understand more clearly what is happening to them. It is important to remember that, in the best of times, people **hear only 20% of what is said and forget 80% of that within 24 hours.** Therefore, much of what you say to someone else during these difficult times is forgotten. What people remember may not be what you thought was most important in what you said. Help them remember the important things through repetition, writing things down and asking them to repeat back, in their own words, important points.

The most powerful communication tool to help people say what is truly on their mind is to (1) ask a question that cannot be answered by one or two words, (2) remain silent while the person rehearses their answer in their head, and (3) listen intently to their answer. The less you talk, the more the other person can talk comfortably and safely.

For example, I asked my father's physician if I could be the one to tell my father that he was dying. I went to my father with these words:
"I have talked to your doctors and I have done some research on your condition. Would you like me to tell you what I have found out?" My father knew that if the news was "good" that I would have told him right away. Therefore, he knew my news would not be easy for him to take. My silence gave him three options: (1) yes I want to know, (2) no I don't want to know, or (3) yes I want to know but not right now. He chose the third option. For the first time in his medical history he had control over information.

When he was ready, he asked me short questions and I gave him short, clear answers. Over several days he learned everything he wanted to about his condition and his future. I never had to worry about when was the "right time to tell him the news" because he had control. It was very freeing for me and for him. It was the silence after the question that allowed him to control the information.

Communication is possible with all people including those who are confused and those who cannot speak anymore. Communication begins with the attitude that "I am here for you." It begins with the gift of your presence.

Some specific tips for communicating with people who are dying and who perhaps have dementia or are confused:

- Everyone, regardless of their mental or physical condition, need to be treated with the respect and care given to others of the same age. Even if they do not remember who you are, they do have emotional memories of being treated well, of love, of grief, of anger and of joy.

- Appropriate touch, holding hands or stroking their face are all ways to communicate our care for someone.

- As a person's language skills diminish, change your expectation of what kind of communication you can have with them. They may understand more than they can express. Provide them with the words and information and expect a shorter or non-verbal answer. There are many ways to communicate without using words. Hand movements, eyes, body language and sounds are all ways to express ideas and feelings. Concentrate on the present rather than asking them about their day, what they did last week, etc. Talk more than ask.

- Use any opportunities to help them connect to their past. For example, in my extended family it is quite common to prepare anniversary books or videotapes that highlight a couple's life together. In one case, the husband became increasingly confused in old age and began his day by going through his 40th anniversary 'book' complete with pictures of all his family members, his work history, where he lived, etc. It helped him to make sense out of his mental confusion.

- Any routines that you can establish that are comforting for both of you is very helpful. Perhaps you brush the person's hair at the beginning of each visit. One of my sister's youngest memories is of combing our grandmother's hair. You might always spend time listening to special music, reading from a special book, putting photos into an album, watching the birds outside the window or writing notes to family members who live far away.

- Have a visitor's guest book by the person's bedside so they can see who has come and who comes regularly. Sign in the book every time you come and write a word or two about what you did. The person may use the book to keep track of family and friends. This is also helpful for the caregivers as a confused patient may forget that someone has visited and may be very angry or hurt by this. A quick look at the book can point out who was last there for a visit.

- Use appropriate humor and tell funny stories about what the person has experienced in the past.

- Be patient. Conversations may take longer than normal. You may have to repeat yourself several times before you are understood. If you accept that things will take longer, your body language and the words you use will show that you are not in a rush.

- Although we try to 'lift someone's spirit' we must not avoid difficult conversations completely. If someone in the family has died or is going through a difficult time, sharing the information may help the person express, in some way, some of his or her own grief and sorrow. Such conversations can be powerful in how they return people to a previous level of intimacy in their thoughts and actions together.

- Silence and just being with someone are gifts. Many of our elders who have spent loving decades together find great comfort in sharing a room without having to talk all the time. For many baby boomers and their children, silence is quite discomforting. We are used to the television or music being on all the time in our homes, work places and cars. One of the gifts visitors can offer is the gift of shared silence. Quietly read, think, daydream or pray together. Sitting down near the person at eye level is less intimidating, more relaxing and gives the patient a sense that you are not in a rush to leave.

Patient Needs

No list can describe all the needs of each individual who has a terminal or life-threatening illness. Here are some of the most common ones:

- People need the hospice philosophy of care to meet their physical, emotional, spiritual and information needs. This care can be provided informally through one's family, physicians and community resources and/or through a formal palliative care program.

- People need to participate in their own care so they have a sense of control during a time when they may feel that they have little control. They need to make decisions, to actively help others to care for them, and to participate in relationships with those they love. Some people choose not to do these things. They need to know that they are, in fact, making a choice and that they can change their mind at any time.

- People who are constantly receiving care need opportunities to give back in some way. Imagine constantly receiving gifts from someone who does not allow you to give something back in return. Such one-sided giving leads to an enormous burden of gratitude on the part of the receiver. We all have gifts to share, no matter how small or how large.

When my mother was ill, a visiting home nurse who was usually full of energy and care arrived feeling somewhat troubled. My mother asked her what was wrong. After some persistent prodding, Mary told my mother about how a teacher's meeting she was having later that day about her 12-year old son's behavior made her a bit nervous. Over the following 10 minutes my mother and Mary spoke as mothers; not as patient and nurse. My mother was exhausted from talking so much, but exhilarated as well, because Mary saw her as a valued equal with information worth sharing. She slept more peacefully after that visit than after any other. Mary left with practical advice and encouragement from a person she had grown to respect and admire. She benefited as well and left smiling and energized. Mary saw the gifts my mother still had to offer and allowed her to share that gift. My mother died a few weeks later.

Other Needs and Feelings of Someone Who is Dying

People do not fundamentally change their character once they know they have a terminal illness. If they were happy and able to communicate openly before finding out that they have terminal illness, they will probably continue to do so. If they are quiet and reflective by nature, they will probably stay that way. If they were unpleasant and difficult to be with before, they could remain that way now.

Family and friends may treat someone who is dying differently unless they are made aware that the person has not changed dramatically. Because someone is terminally ill does not mean that she cannot work, play, talk, sing, tell jokes, laugh, swear, have sex, eat her favorite meals and be the person she has always been.

There is no reason to give up sex, socializing, and work unless physical conditions makes it impossible. Yet many people do give up many of these things because of social expectations that they should be resting in bed, conserving their energy or fighting depression. A person's abilities decrease as the illness progresses but there are often years or months of life before overall lifestyle is drastically reduced. Open communication will let others know what the person can do, wants to do and still enjoys doing.

Other needs include what Robert E. Kavanaugh and others describe as:

- The need to be accepted and respected as the unique people they are rather than the dying person other people see.

- Permission to die, from all the important people in their lives. People who are dying do not want their loved ones to be angry or deny that they are dying because it makes their illness and saying goodbye too hard. Loved ones need to accept the truth that the person is dying. Pretending otherwise puts up barriers to communication. People end up isolating each other because they cannot talk about their loneliness, hopes, fear and feelings of love.

- A need to voluntarily let go of every person and possession that they hold dear. People need to say goodbye to their families, their friends, and their material possessions (photos, hobbies, books).

Fear of an afterlife can make accepting death hard. People may ask questions like: "What happens to me when I die? Is there a heaven? Is there a hell? Will my spirit leave my body?"

One doesn't need a specific religion to think about an afterlife. If people are concerned about this, they need to talk to someone who accepts their view of God and can help them develop their concept of God and the world that may exist after death. A chaplain, a social worker, a psychologist or a very close friend can listen and give comfort that people may not be able to give themselves.

People who have written about their experiences before their death have given us a better understanding of what might be going on in their minds and hearts. It is common to read about people who are dying finding that their five senses come alive. They see more clearly: the colors of autumn, the snow fall on an evergreen tree or a flower grow over several weeks. They hear sounds of birds and leaves falling that we regularly miss. They smell fresh-baked bread, feel a cool summer night's breeze and the traffic noises of a busy street. They turn the stress of dying into an opportunity to live.

Others who are bedridden and near death feel purpose in simply receiving other people's love and prayers. These people who are dying encourage so many others to take time to talk, touch, laugh and love. They can bind a family together and leave memories that give their loved ones great strength during a difficult time of mourning. It is a wonderful gift and a purposeful one.

For people who are dying it is often very hard to tell their family and friends what they need and want. It may be difficult to discuss such matters as family conflicts or going on a vacation together. Patience is needed to encourage discussion. Telling a friend that they need a hug or asking a family member to go for a long walk to talk about "the good old days" are just two examples of asking to have their needs fulfilled.

Sex depends on the patient's previous experience of having sex during stressful times, the presence of pain and medication, the perception of their ability to live a full and meaningful life, if they have privacy, and how other people treat them. If their physical or mental condition precludes intercourse, a fulfilling and caring intimacy can still happen. A snuggle on the couch, watching a sunset or listening to classical music together can be very intimate and loving.

Patients can choose to make decisions and take control of their lives by finding out more about their illness, how it progresses, what pain and symptom control techniques are available, alternatives to traditional medicine and other relevant information. They should not be afraid to ask for help from a family member or friend.

Patients also need:

- To belong to a compassionate family and/or community. When this does not exist, others can help create it in the time left through a support circle or personal friendship.

- To have opportunities and encouragement to practice their spirituality.

- To have honest and open communication between themselves and their caregivers. They need to express their thoughts, in their ways, be listened to and supported.

- Financial security and a safe place to live until their death (preferably in their own home or someone else's home).

- Meaningful activities, stimulation, fun, enjoyment, laughter, time with people, meaningful conversations, in typical and familiar settings.

- Hope maintained, at all times including encouraging patients to talk about their hopes for their families, work and the world in the future after they have died. They need to have hope about today as they learn to let go of hope for a cure, one more treatment or for a longer life. They need their hope for a peaceful death supported through palliative care so that it is fulfilled as best as possible.

- Their differences and similarities addressed including culture, age, gender, history and family background, religion, their experiences with death, social roles, unfinished business, other losses, and personal beliefs and wants.

Their Fears

People may have any of the following fears. These fears may be expressed out loud or thought about quietly in their minds with sentences like:

- How will I die? Will there be pain? Will I suffer unbearably? Will I look terrifying to my loved ones?

- Will I lose control over my body and my feelings? How will I cope with not knowing what is going to happen to me? I can't stand the pain. I am afraid I am going to be a bad patient. Will I be a coward and disgrace my family and myself?

- I don't want to leave the people I love. I don't want them to suffer when I am gone I don't know how to help them cope with their fears.

- I don't want to be a burden to anyone.

- I am afraid of dying alone.

- I've lived a whole life now. Did my life have any meaning? I was just a mother and secretary all my life or just a father and a carpenter all my life. Was that enough?

- Is there a heaven or hell? What happens to my soul after death? I've done bad things -- what will happen to me?

- I can't talk to my family or friends about my dying or death because they won't accept that I am dying. What can I do?

These fears are real and common. People who are afraid have more physical and emotional pain so their fears must be dealt with as early as possible. Dealing with fear is time consuming and energy draining for everyone but is very important. The following are just a few thoughts on dealing with fear. Whatever one does, one must address the fears and try to comfort those who never quite give up those fears.

- How someone lives until they die depends on many things, especially their disease and overall physical, emotional and spiritual health. Information about what is typical is very comforting. People do not have to suffer unbearable pain. We have the knowledge and skills to make sure people life relatively comfortably until they die.

Body image is very important because our society values how someone looks. It is not frivolous or 'crazy' to want clean and well groomed hair, makeup, etc. There may be modifications but the old saying that "if you look good, you feel better" is true for most of us.

- Losing control over one's body is a natural consequence of the body slowly stopping its many functions. It happens to all of us when an illness or condition takes time to come to a natural end. Coping with those changes requires a great deal of physical, emotional and spiritual support. Seeing one's own deterioration as a natural consequence helps put it into perspective. Knowing in advance, what may happen will help for some people. The 'signposts' point to the end we will all experience.

Fear of not being able to deal well with the illness and the pain, frightens people. They do not want to disgrace themselves or their families. They need constant reassurance that their illness, their pain and their emotional and spiritual needs will be taken care of quickly and effectively. When this is not possible, they need help in putting their typical reactions into perspective so that they can feel some comfort and pride in how they are dealing with their condition.

Grieving one's own death is natural. There is the fear of the unknown. The worry about people left behind. Most people have had difficult times in their lives before. Encourage them to use the strengths gained from those experiences to help their loved ones. Talking, holding each other, and looking outward in ways to help others are all proven ways of dealing with the unknown. Whether in war, famine, poverty or death, for centuries, people have returned to these proven techniques.

- The concept of being a burden to one's family and society because one is ill and dying is only about 50 years old. After World War II North America and Europe had great wealth and expanded health care services so that most people died in hospitals cared for by people outside the family. Before the war people died at home. Their care was not always perfect and their pain was not managed as well as it can be done today. However, there was a natural cycle of care from birth to death within families and communities. Many people who have cared for someone near the end of life understand the difficulties and frustrations involved but will also tell you about the joy, laughter, intimate love and caring that was shared with their loved ones. These gifts are often not possible in a hospital or institution because of all the rules and false beliefs about what is important. What one may perceive as a burden now, can in fact, be a life-defining gift for your loved ones if only you, and they, will work towards that goal. That said, the fear of being a burden to one's family is real and must be dealt with to minimize some patients desire to die quickly through euthanasia or suicide.

• Many people, especially older women, live alone with family either too busy or too far away to be of much comfort. The fear of dying alone is real because it happens so often. This must be addressed head on with the only answer possible -- there must be people present at all times when the person who is dying wants them there. It takes planning, asking others for some of their time, and a commitment to meet this fear head on. Support teams or circles (see Chapter 19) are one way of doing that.

At the same time, some people, consciously or unconsciously, prefer to die when their loved ones have left the room. Professionals and volunteers with many years of experience have seen this over and over again. A family may be with the patient, around the clock, for days on end. They leave briefly to shower, get a bite to eat or stretch and while they are away, their loved one dies. The person is usually not alone but with a professional or volunteer or a friend. Their death can be devastating to the family who believes that it is wrong for a person to die 'alone'.

I remind family members how difficult it might be to say goodbye to the people you love most. Sometimes people need to be 'alone' to die. My mother was in a semi-coma during her last two weeks. We had been with her for many weeks at home and finally needed a nurse to come and be with her during the night. During her last few weeks, she experienced her 29th wedding anniversary and my sister's birthday. Shortly after midnight on the day after my sister's birthday, and after I had said goodnight, my father went to my mother to say goodbye and that, if she was ready, she could leave us as we were now ready (unlike four months previously when she was in a coma in the hospital). She died ten minutes after he left her. We spent the following hours with her in her room until her body was taken by the funeral directors.

• Whether someone's life has meaning or not is dependent on how we value them when they are dying. Isolated, lonely people, no matter how productive in their lives may find little meaning in their personal history. Someone loved, cared for, respected and listened to can come to understand that each person's life has meaning because each of us has affected the lives of others.

Helping people record their life stories earlier in their illness can be a wonderful heirloom for one's family and friends. Concentrating on the lessons learned through hardships, and the value of relationships in one's life helps family members rejoice in their heritage and cope with their grief.

- A fear of the unknown, after death, can be crippling. One's religious and spiritual beliefs are powerful. Sometimes these beliefs are comforting and sometimes they just make the person more frightened. (See Chapter 12 on spirituality for concrete ideas of how you can help.)

- Patients, even young children, may accept their death much sooner than their family and friends. This can be very isolating and frightening. Someone in that patient's life needs to ensure that a few accepting people (either other family and friends or professional or volunteer caregivers) are in regular contact with the patient so that they can share in conversations, prayer or activities that provide understanding to the patient. Patients may not have the energy to find such people themselves. Through example, the family and friends who have not accepted that their loved one is dying may slowly come to terms with their own fears and grief.

Labeling Feelings

In order to understand what a patient is going through, doctors, psychologists and others have tried to label our feelings. They have come up with theories and terms like denial, bargaining with God, reconnecting with loved ones, depression, isolation and others. Few discuss the joys and intimate love shared during periods of difficulty.

Labeling feelings can help all of us face the truth about dying. Labels are just words that give us common language. But the words we use may not describe the same feelings. For example, 'denial' of our upcoming death is often defined as bad. Denying our death can make it hard to deal with many of the other fears and feelings we have as well as the fears and feelings of those who love us. On the other hand, denial can be something very powerful in prolonging our lives. Take the example of a woman riddled with cancer who refused to die until her daughter reached 18 years of age. She went against all medical odds and accomplished her goal, living five years longer than anyone expected. Knowing the strength of denial or anger or acceptance can help us talk about what we are doing and why we are doing it. When we discuss our feelings, we need to make sure that the person we are talking to has the same definition of what the words mean otherwise the conversation can be misunderstood.

There is a similar danger in labeling stages of how we are supposed to feel. There has been a popular belief that when someone finds out they are dying that they go through the emotional stages of denial, anger, bargaining with God for a longer life, depression and finally, acceptance. **These stages are not true.** People do not go from one emotion to the next in a predictable sequence. Nor do they have just negative feelings. They still experience love, joy and hope.

When people believe in stages, they assume that all the patients' emotions stem from the knowledge of their impending death. For example, they may be in a hospital and be very angry that a family member hasn't visited as promised or that the doctor failed to see them today. They may be depressed because a friend at work has had a heart attack. If their television is broken and the repair person doesn't come on time their anger is not because of their illness; they are angry because they can't watch the hockey game.

These emotions are related to the things that they normally react to.

A person's reaction when they find out they are dying or a person's reaction when they find out a loved one is dying is based on how they have dealt with difficult situations in the past. The only predictable theory that fits each individual case is that they will go through three specific time periods where their reactions are quite similar to past reactions:

At the time they find out the news. Some people deny the news and say there must be a mistake. Others welcome the news as a definite answer to the questions they have had for months about their condition. Others are relieved that their long life is nearly over and they are "going home to God."

The period of time between finding out about the terminal illness to just before the person's death. During this period, people experience all of their typical positive and negative emotions. They feel love, anger, happiness, fear, closeness and isolation. It may be a roller coaster changing from moment to moment or their emotions may change gradually. Whatever their feelings, they are real and in need of support through physical, emotional, spiritual and information comforts.

Just before someone's death, perhaps only minutes, days or weeks, there may be an acceptance of all of their past, an acceptance of their death and a feeling of connection with all the people they love. Other people may die with feelings of anger, injustice and a complete sense of failure. The range is as endless as is the human population. The only thing that is certain is that people choose how they face death (especially if they have had some time to prepare) and we cannot make them feel a certain way just to please us. Death is not always a peaceful leaving of this life for an adventure in another world. This is hard for loved ones to watch. The best we can do is to be as comforting as possible and to comfort each other during such difficult times.

Children and Dying

This book is too short to allow a detailed account of how children view their own death or the death of a parent, grandparent, sibling or friend. Very young children don't understand what death is about, therefore we need to answer their questions honestly, concisely, and when they come up. Not exposing children to the natural occurrence of death around them will only make it more difficult for them to understand it later.

Children's reaction to death depends on their intellectual and emotional maturity as well as their age level. They need different types of resources to help them than adults do. (Check the References). Obviously a four-year-old child has different concepts of death than a ten-year-old child. Like adults, each child is different and understands and accepts death differently. The younger the child, the more likely she is to take our explanations literally. Imagine the image a child might have when we talk about someone who is dead as "sleeping," or that we have "lost them," or that "Daddy is in heaven looking at us," or that "God has taken her away." These words are meant to comfort a child but they often frighten the child instead.

Rather, honest answers to questions of "Where is Mommy?" such as "I sometimes wonder about that myself," are better. If you have a religious belief in an afterlife, explain it clearly. If you are not sure of your own feelings say: "I'm not sure but I believe...."

Children are more often concerned about being abandoned. Will their parents die and if so, what will happen to them? They need reassurance and love rather than a quick reply not to worry. We can help our children by using the example of the death of a pet or a plant to discuss feelings. Many North American children were introduced to death through public expressions of grief. In the 1960s it was President Kennedy's death. In the 1970s, it was the ongoing death and grief shown on the nightly news during the Vietnam war. In the 1980s it was the crash of the space shuttle Challenger with a teacher on board. In the 1990s the public grief over the death of Mother Teresa and Princess Diana was visible on every television and newspaper front page. These experiences are opportunities to discuss death generally and within one's own family and community.

It is all right to cry with your children and to express your grief. It allows them to share their grief with you. Touching and honest talking can make a real difference. Very intense grief can be frightening to children and must be explained to them. Let them know that you have experienced death and grief before and that the hurt and pain of grieving lessen with time even though the memories of their loved one will not. Explain your feelings. Expect your children to ask the same questions over and over again as they come to understand what death and grief are. Your reassurance and your patience help them see death and grief as natural parts of our lives. If you are uncomfortable talking about these things with your children, find someone else for them to talk with such as an elder, spiritual leader or professional counselor.

For a child who is dying, the suggestions are much the same. Children at a young age are more aware of what is going on around them than we acknowledge. When children are dying at a young age their maturity increases more rapidly. They watch and learn from their parents' and doctors' body language and they also learn from other children who are dying. They need to talk about dying just as adults do.

A three-year old girl with leukemia spent the last year of her life at a children's hospital for treatment. When no further treatment was possible, she was allowed to go home. During that last year at the hospital, she physically clung to her mother who was with her most of the time. After several days at home, the little girl asked her mother to 'pack her bags.' "Where are you going, dear?" asked the mother. "I'm going to Sesame Street and you can't come," was her daughter's answer. This little girl knew she was dying even though she didn't have the words or concepts to express it.

Check with your doctor, support groups and professional counselors to help you and your children understand what is happening and how you can turn the months or years to follow into a memorable time. Children, even when they are dying, need the same things as all children: friends, connection with school, play time, vacations, the occasional junk food, to get into trouble and to be scolded like everyone else. They need to feel normal just as an adult who is dying needs to feel normal and needed. They need respect, their dignity maintained and valued, and they need information suitable to their age. They do not need to be patronized or elevated to sainthood as this takes away from their most valued role -- a child within their family and community.

You will find from the books in the References that parents often make similar mistakes when their child is dying: spoiling the child, not talking openly enough with their child and their other children, assuming the child thinks a certain way, or trying to protect their children from the truth. When a child is dying, the child, the parents and other family members and friends need to talk about their thoughts, fears and feelings.

Family and Friends

What can I do to help someone who is dying? How do I overcome my fear of saying the wrong thing? Does someone who is dying want to talk about dying? They aren't interested in hearing about my job, the kids and our vacation are they? I'm scared. What do I do? Death is a topic that few people can talk about openly except in a general philosophical sense during a card game, a fishing trip or after a news story about a terrorist act. People often find it very difficult to talk about dying when they actually know someone who is dying. It has been a social taboo to talk honestly with someone who is dying.

Most of the literature written about death and dying concentrates on the person who is dying. Very little is written about what practical things you can do to help the person dying while helping yourself to feel useful.

The "right" attitude toward people who are dying is neither that of an indulgent grandmother nor of a detached observer. The best that anyone can do is to care sincerely, be respectful and offer to listen. Sometimes it is the very simple things that make such a difference: a wave from the sidewalk to a person sitting by the window; dropping over an article you thought might be interesting; calling someone up to say there is a good show on the radio right now -- any expression of concern and support.

Sometimes people say or do things that unintentionally hurt the person they care about. If their concern and caring are real then their compassion and love overshadow any errors they make. There are specific things you can do to improve the life of someone who is dying but few are greater than your expression of caring. If you can openly tell the person who is dying that you too, are afraid sometimes and feel angry or lonely, then you open the door to honest communication. You allow the person to choose how much he wants to talk and what he wants to talk about.

A simple example of how two caring people can help each other is to continue to do things you used to do together. You might have to adapt your favorite past times. For example, if the two of you used to go to movies together, you might bring in a home video instead. Such social events provide people with an opportunity to talk about themselves, about their feelings toward movie characters or specific events in the film. They may then feel more comfortable talking about their feelings about illness, dying and death.

Another example is the story of how one person who was dying of cancer had her friend come to visit. The friend was unable to talk about the patient's illness but did express his own fear of cancer. Some people would consider this unsympathetic. After all, the visitor wasn't dying. Yet his need to talk about cancer and his own possible death, allowed the patient to console him, offer him insight and most important, feel useful herself. This was the type of relationship they had always had. Her comforting him, in effect, reinforced her invaluable role as confidant and friend rather than the role of dying patient that other people imposed on her.

One of the rules we think we should follow is that when someone is sick we must talk quietly and solemnly. Others think that only a long list of bad jokes will help the person out of a slump. What is probably best is to combine many emotions together. People need to laugh, to cry, to love, to hope, to express faith but also to be angry. That is the beauty of friendship and companionship; you can listen, without judgment, and let the person express his own needs while you express yours.

See Chapter 14 on home care tips for other specific ideas and examples.

Euthanasia and Assisted Suicide

When most people want to talk about euthanasia, suicide or assisted-suicide, they want people to listen and to understand the reasons for their interest. Like all of us, they want to be loved, supported, listened to, and respected. They may want to discuss euthanasia or assisted suicide because of their fears of the unknown future or how they might die. They may have terrible experiences of watching loved ones suffer horribly before their death and they do not want to have the same experience. When the question comes up, it must be discussed openly and honestly. The request to die should never be answered with, "Oh let's not talk about that" or "I don't believe in euthanasia!"

One of the greatest fears of North Americans is that they will have unbearable pain before they die. Enough health care providers still do not practice modern pain and symptom control. People's experience with other loved ones may be that death is painful. They may also believe that taking narcotics is dangerous or will lead to immediate death or addiction. **Pain control techniques today are so advanced that no one has to die in unbearable pain. Proper pain control can reduce or eliminate pain.** In extreme cases, a person may need medication for a short, drug-induced sleep to help their body relax. Whatever it takes, no one needs to suffer unbearable, untreated pain. Proper pain control also lets patients remain alert and as active as their physical abilities allow. The more pain control techniques are understood by physicians, the less the cry for euthanasia on these grounds. (See Chapter 8 on pain and symptom control.)

Another real consideration for people who may choose euthanasia is their worry about being an emotional and financial burden to their loved ones. People who are dying worry a great deal about their families. The cost of dying in North America can be very high indeed. Studies have concluded that seventy-five percent of our life-time medical costs are spent in the last year of our life. In Canada, many of these costs are covered, but not all of them. People caring for loved ones at home may have to quit their jobs or juggle several part-time jobs to fulfil their wish to care for someone at home. Many home care supplies are not covered by insurance. Some people argue that euthanasia allows someone to die before the heavy emotional and financial costs of 'prolonging life' bankrupts their families. This argument reflects our society's inability to deal with this very real problem, and as such, it is one of the saddest arguments for euthanasia It is, nonetheless, a reason why people have suicidal thoughts and must be addressed.

Some people actually plan for this event by saving prescription medication. These people plan to use these drugs to commit suicide if they ever became terminally ill. This practice gives a false confidence in their ability to maintain control over their own lives and deaths. There are no studies to show how many of these people actually try to commit suicide later on. The important fact is that these people want control over their deaths.

The danger in using drugs and other methods to commit suicide is that many people fail in their suicide attempts and are worse off for the effort. Hangings can cause paralysis; failed shootings can cause brain or heart injuries; too little or old medication can cause an irreversible coma; carbon monoxide poisoning can inflict brain damage, and chemical poisoning can ruin internal organs without causing death.

Euthanasia is a subject that can never receive unanimous support either for or against it. People who wish to legalize euthanasia are, on the whole, as respectful of life as those who oppose it. The philosophies on both sides of the debate are very different but there is a common ground; most people involved in this debate want to improve the lives of people who have a terminal illness. The hope is that the debate is helping us to examine our own beliefs while also encouraging us to improve present services for people who have a terminal or life threatening illness.

Chapter 11   Understanding and Dealing With Grief

Thoughts about Grieving
Children's Grief
Elders' Grief
Special Events

We all experience grief from the time we are young children. We all learn from grief. We all help, or hurt, others with their grief depending on how we deal with our own. Grieving is a spiritual and emotional journey that both patients and families experience. How you dealt with past grief is a strong predictor of how you deal with this one.

Simply put, grieving is emotionally, physically and spiritually painful. It opens us up to our deepest feelings of love, anger, joy, rejection, compassion, loneliness, wholeness and fear. We might grieve intensely for weeks, months or for years. Over time our days of grieving turn into hours of grieving and then, perhaps, only minutes of grieving. However, no matter how long our periods of grief, it can be just as intense as the day the person we love died. A song on the radio, a smell of familiar perfume on the street, a dream or a special anniversary can all bring back intense grief. The difference is that it might only last a few seconds or minutes rather than days.

Grieving is a natural process. It is the price we pay for deep love. Sometime the price feels overwhelming. We may have physical symptoms like a tightness in our chest or our throats, trouble breathing or a choking sensation. We may feel empty in our stomach and heart. We may want to sleep for days or we cannot sleep well at all. We may not want to eat, become easily distracted and forgetful, feel anxious or irritable. Some people become depressed, feel isolated or feel overwhelming guilt. These are all fairly typical feelings.

As overwhelming as it may seem, we survive, heal somewhat and continue to live. At first it may be very hard just to get out of bed and have breakfast. Over time, we can do more and feel the hurt for shorter periods of time.

With effort over many months, and perhaps years, we become stronger for the experience. Later in the chapter, I present some specific ideas that have helped many other people deal with their grief.

We do not wish grief on anyone, yet we all learn from our grief. Grief can make us stronger and can make us better children, spouses, parents, friends and neighbors. Grief can also make us weaker when it overpowers our ability to cope with day-to-day activities over long periods of time.

There is no right or wrong way to grieve unless your grief continues to harm you, and others, long after a loved one has died.

How we grieve depends on our cultural and personal experiences with other grief. Grief may come to us after we lose a job, move to a new home, break up with our first boyfriend or girlfriend. Each time we experience grief we set a pattern of how we deal with future grief. We can change how we grieve over time but it takes a conscious and ongoing effort.

Grieving is often called 'work' and a 'journey'. It takes effort and time to move from the initial grief after someone's death to when the grief is something you can live with in a healthy way; finding new ways to live without the person we miss. At some unique point for you, you can have a new relationship with the person who has died, make new commitments to others and enjoy love in new ways.

You know when your grieving journey is at a more comfortable point when you can miss someone without being sad that they are not there. When we are in the middle of intense grief there is no difference between missing someone and being sad. At some point, you can wish that someone was here with you at a wedding, birth, or special family dinner without feeling sad that they are not there. The memories of them are more comforting than sad. For some people this point comes after several months of grieving. For many of us, however, this point might take a few years. There will probably, always be some times when missing someone and being sad they are not here become one feeling again. At these times, the intensity of grief might be the same as when the person died, but the duration of that intense grief lasts for minutes rather than days.

People who die continue to help the living. Not in material or even mystical ways but because they influenced our lives through the life they lived. The lessons and example given to us by them influence our thoughts and the way we view the world. When we have a hard decision to make we think how they might have handled it. If our relationship with them was mostly positive, we try to do things in similar ways as they did. If our experiences were mostly negative, we use their lessons as examples of what we will not do. No matter our history with the person, they continue to teach us.

To reach that place of greater comfort we must go through difficult and painful events like funeral preparations, cleaning out closets, finding and reading old letters, getting through the bureaucratic paper work of settling the estate and more. Each painful event is part of the healing process although it might not feel very healing at the time.

Thoughts about Grieving

Grieving is a difficult subject to write about in such a short space. In the References there are books listed that deal more specifically with grieving. As well, check with your family physician, hospice or home care program about bereavement support groups and resource centers in your area. Some are offered through hospitals, social work programs, private bereavement counsellors, funeral homes or volunteer organizations. Here are just a few points I think are worth mentioning.

There are basically three main phases that one goes through with their grief. There is the time just before and after a death. There is a time at the other end of the line when you can re-invest your energy, love and commitment to others. The time in between can be the longest as you deal with all the ups and downs of starting a new life without a loved one present.

Grieving may begin weeks or months before someone dies. This is called **anticipatory grief** because we anticipate a life without our loved one. This grief may have its ups and downs as you experience the ups and downs of someone's illness. One day the person may feel quite good and energized so anticipatory grief may be less. If there is a sudden deterioration in their condition, your grief might be greater.

A common occurrence in anticipatory grief happens when a person is near the end of their life and death is expected soon. My mother had cancer throughout her body. One day she went into an unexpected coma from which she was not expected to wake up. For several days, we all prayed for a peaceful end to her life. During this time I went to a funeral home to arrange her funeral so that we would not have to make rush decisions after her death. When I returned from the funeral home I was told that my mother had woken up and wanted to see me. One minute I was praying for her peaceful death and grieving my upcoming loss; the next minute I was praying for her to live longer. Such a roller coaster is painful as it calls into question what we should be praying for and how best we can help each other during such difficult times. My mother lived another three months.

The following tips may help:

Feel your hurt rather than fighting it or masking it with medication or alcohol. If you don't take the time to experience the pain of grief now it will remain inside you until, perhaps, another tragedy overwhelms you. You may see people grieve over the death of a pet with such force and drama that you wonder if they are sane. It may be that they are reliving previous, unresolved grief. Grief needs to be experienced but some people can live their whole lives without going through the complete grief process. Their ability, however, to love fully and live enthusiastically may also be affected.

Experiencing grief may feel like the world is coming to an end. It is physically and emotionally painful. Sharing this feeling with others who understand grief can be helpful but it will not instantly take the pain away. Only time, supportive family and friends and lots of time spent thinking, feeling, talking and reflecting on experiences will work. Some people look inward through prayer or meditation for peace and a bigger perspective of how grief can help them. Others look outward to see how they might help others in the neighborhood, in their spiritual community or through volunteer work.

Knowing that this debilitating sense of loss is normal and that it becomes less difficult to deal with over time, may help you to make it through this process as a whole person.

It is not easy for most of us. Some people may harbor real, intense grief for decades. Some people do die of a 'broken heart' after someone they loved beyond words has died. I suspect that my father died of a broken heart even though the death certificate says emphysema and cancer.

The death of a child or the death of a loved one who died because of violence can be the most difficult to deal with for some people. Others may see these people as 'coping very well with day-to-day life'. They may, however, never be able to love and commit themselves to others in the same way as they did before. If they accept help through professional counseling or through their spiritual leaders, they may heal part of this deep wound. Sharing their stories with people who have had similar situations can also be very helpful.

Your emotions may include feelings that you think are unhealthy or abnormal. Some people feel a strong relief that the person has died. If the person had wanted to die or if the family has provided care for a long time, relief is quite a typical feeling. Your life has been on hold for a time and now it can continue in new ways.

Regret and guilt are also common feelings. You wish that you had said or done something before the person died or feel guilty that you did something wrong. Regret and guilt are powerful emotions that take time to heal, if they ever do. The healing comes through understanding that all of us have regrets and feelings of guilt. We can either do something about our feelings or let them simmer. Some people, for example, wished that they had expressed their love more to someone who died. They might express that love at a graveside or through art or music. Or they might use the experience to express their feelings more often with the people still in their lives now.

There may be times, such as at a funeral, a social gathering, or at work when you get a sense of the world being unreal -- almost as if you were watching yourself in a film. The experience of death and dying can be so intense that the only way to cope is to, quite naturally, distance yourself from the feelings for a time. A young boy whose father died in a corporate jet refused to admit that his father had died. Instead, he told people that his father was a spy and was just on a secret mission. Through the prodding of a counselor who was trying to help him understand 'the truth' he finally burst out with: "I know he's dead. I'm just not ready yet." The story/fantasy was his way of making his world unreal for a time until he was ready to deal with his father's death. He was taking care of himself in the best way he knew how. He needed support more than confrontation -- acceptance more than well-intended truth.

Face the reality of the death. Begin by continuing small daily activities, return to work when you feel ready (although employers and society may only give you five days of bereavement leave -- we must change this!), continue your relationships with people you are close to, and talk about your feelings when you can.

The reality of death may hit hardest when you begin to clean out the person's closet, collect their things and perhaps, give some of them away. There is no need to do this within the first few days or weeks after someone's death. Take your time. People who have rushed through their home to clear out the person's effects days after a death have told me years later that they wished they had taken more time. Death seems so unreal around the time of a funeral and the days right afterwards. Wait before hurrying to 'tidy things up'. The same advice is true for moving away from a home shared with the person who has died. Again, there is no hurry. If you plan to move, take some time to say goodbye to the memories of that home before creating new memories in a new home.

Remember the good and the bad. The person who died was not an angel or a devil. They were human. Talk to someone about these memories. You may want to repeat over and over again what your feelings are and what memories you have that are important. Find some friends to talk or write to about these feelings. Repetition is important to make your loss real. Tell them what you need and ask if they will help you.

Seek spiritual help. If you rely on books for comfort, then begin to read again. If travel or work are therapeutic then do that. If you need to hide away for a few days to allow yourself to feel depressed, then give yourself that time. Playing a musical instrument or singing vigorously may be therapeutic.

When you feel ready, begin to invest your emotional energy in new relationships or stronger relationships with old friends. It is not a betrayal of the person who has died or an effort to forget him. It is sharing your love again as you did with the person who has died.

Note: Some people talk about different stages of grieving just as they do about stages of dying. People **do not go through various "stages" after any loss.** Whether a loved one has died, or people have lost a job or become unable to fulfil a dream, their reactions to each loss are surprisingly alike; the degree of the reaction is different. People do not go through denial, anger, bargaining with God, depression and acceptance as we once believed. People experience a range of negative and positive emotions. Sometimes these emotions happen all at once, like when you lose a child in a grocery store. You are in a panic running every which way to find them. When you do, your emotions range from anger that they ran away to complete love that they are safe. Grieving is like that--a range of emotions that can move from one to another quickly and back and forth. The only true predictor of how you deal with grief is how you have done it before. If you have learned from previous grief you might do it 'better' this time, but your instincts will be the same.

Write a journal of your feelings or write letters to the person who has died with any thoughts and feelings you feel were not said to the person when they were alive. Writing or recording one's feelings and ideas can be very healing. Writing to a close friend is another wonderful way to get the jumble of thoughts out of your head and onto paper. It helps people to think more clearly.

We all experience grief. For most of us, we have memories of going through very difficult situations and coming out of that experience to continue to enjoy our lives. Even when your body and heart do not feel like those good feelings will return, allow your mind to remember past experiences with grief and the joys and love you have experienced since then. This won't speed up your grieving or relieve the pain. Overcoming past grief, however, will provide that light at the end of the tunnel. There is much love, gratitude and service ahead of you when you are ready.

People who are dying may have different emotions or they may keep denying their illness to the end. People who are grieving may do the same by denying their need to experience grief. At the same time, not all of their anger or depression is caused by their grief. Their life continues and so do normal frustrations with plumbing, rude drivers, and job tensions. If you understand whether your own feelings are from grief or from normal living you can accept the reality of your situation and deal with your stresses more realistically.

When trying to help a friend or family member deal with their grief, it is important to listen to their stories, their feelings and their concerns. You may hear these ideas from them over and over again during months of conversations. At some point, however, perhaps many months after a person's death, just listening to a grieving friend's stories is not enough. People must move beyond their feelings. Sometimes they use us to postpone their inevitable need to move on. We can hold them back by being too supportive. This is a hard distinction to make but it is important. If a friend cannot move on with their life and continues to hurt themselves by wallowing in grief, then, as a friend, you need to help them see what is happening. The only way it may work is to refuse to listen to the old stories without the person also talking about what they are going to do to help themselves work through the grief. This is a most difficult situation to be in but as a friend, you must be the stronger character rather than the excuse. How to know when the time has come to change the type of support you offer? You might ask yourself, "How has my friend's grief changed in six months, if at all? How must it change so that I can continue to be supportive?"

Children's Grief

A child's first experience with the death of a loved one is very difficult. They have no real comparison to make with previous grief. The death of a gold fish or other pet may help them draw some comparisons but the intensity is quite different.

We do not know how to deal with children's grief. It is not part of our education. We are often uncomfortable just talking about death generally, never mind helping a child who has lost someone very important in their lives. There are books, videos and organizations such as The Childhood Cancer Foundation -- Candlelighters Canada and Bereaved Families of Ontario that have a vast store of information and services that can help. The following information barely touches on some of the major issues.

We often underestimate a child's grief because they do not easily talk about their confusing feelings. They do not know what 'normal' is and may be afraid to admit to feelings of real fear of abandonment, despair, anger, guilt, loss or confusion. Death is difficult to understand at any age. It is about 'forever' and the person never coming back to us. Children need to understand these concepts but that takes time and experience. Talking is not always the way they will learn these ideas. They may lack the maturity or concentration to understand fully what the death of a loved one means to them. Younger children are in the 'here and now' in most of their activities while adults tend to focus 'way back' and 'far ahead'.

Children need your example to understand what are typical feelings and how to deal with them. They need to see the adults in their lives expressing sadness, confusion and uncertainty. They also need to see adults go on with their lives in ways that encourage the child to understand that even in tragedy, one can move forward.

One way to prepare for the death of a loved one is to encourage a child to do special things with that person or to create something special to give to the person. Any positive memories of time spent together or time spent making something for the person can add courage and strength during the grieving process. After a death, a memory book or collection of items can be made to celebrate the life shared with the loved one. For some children, making or choosing something special to include in the casket or to give other family members at the funeral can be comforting.

Many children need the reassurance that they are not at fault for the death. They may remember saying something, like "I wish you were dead," or "I'm going to kill you" as part of a game they were playing or out of anger to the person who died. They may feel that if they had done or said something they could have prevented the death. Understanding how the person really died reassures them that they are not responsible.

Children also worry about themselves. If Grandma or Dad have died, what will happen if the other adults taking care of them die. They may worry about being abandoned and need reassurance that they will always be well cared for in any circumstance. Again, helping them see what really caused the death and that other adults in their life right now do not have a similar disease or condition can help. Reassurance and love are always better than a quick "You don't have to worry dear."

It is not helpful insisting that a child talk about death. However, every question should be answered. Take advantage of opportunities to talk about death. For example, news reports of a death, a neighbor's death, an event at school or on television may help you discuss the child's feelings. We cannot make it 'okay' for children within days of a death in the family. It will take them many months and years, just as for their parents, to come to terms with all the aspects of someone's death. Do not rush them.

Children are not adults. They need to be children. If a parent has died, the child should not be expected to become the 'man' or 'woman' of the house. The remaining adults may need extra supports, but it should not be the children who provide that adult support. Children can be wonderfully supportive as children but they should not fulfil the role of the adult who has died.

When children ask questions that you have no answer for, say so. "I don't know" is a wonderful phrase because it means that the adult and child can look for answers together. Some questions, of course, have no answers and that is part of life too. Children can often tell when someone has told them something that is untrue, too simplistic or gives a quick answer to keep them from asking more questions. If children feel this happening often, they will shut out the adults and withdraw or act out in frustration or anger.

Children need the security that comes from rituals, rules and structure. They need limits and consistent discipline that tells them they are loved, safe and part of a family that works things out together. If parents are having trouble providing these things during difficult times, they must look for outside help to give their children and themselves comfort and support.

Children have wisdom that is often overlooked. They may want to save items of personal importance from the person who has died. They may want to create a scrap book of pictures, art work, poems and thoughts. They recognize, intuitively, that collecting memories is a way to deal with grief. Encourage their natural tendencies and ask them to explain why they have chosen certain items over other ones. You may be surprised by the depth of their thinking and comforted by their genuine love.

Children may have temporary periods of needing to hold onto to their parents or a trusted adult for comfort. They might have nightmares or wet their beds. These 'regressions' are just a sign that they need extra caring and time with trusted adults. My grandfather was 91 when he was dying and he spoke of wishing that his mother was there to hold him. We never lose that desire to be safely in the arms of someone we trust. Children express this need more through actions than words and we must pay attention. They also have short attention spans so you may see them laughing and playing soon after a death or at the funeral. Young children may appear to forget that someone they love has died but they are actually just being children. They will come back to their feelings and questions over the months and years ahead. We must be patient and understanding of their different ways of coping with difficult, emotional times.

Elders' Grief

Our elders have experienced grief many times. If they experienced the horrors of war, the depression years, or the death of a child, grandchild or spouse, they have dealt with grief in ways that many people cannot imagine. Their longevity probably means that they also have dealt with the grief of losing some of their physical and mental abilities. Grief is a constant companion for many of them. As they anticipate their own deaths, they deal with the grief of saying goodbye to loved ones left behind.

At the same time, their experiences have given many of them an understanding of grief, of their own responses to grief and how best they can be supported and supportive. Elders have, through longevity and experience, much to teach younger people about coping with the difficulties of life. They can show great empathy to a young mother whose husband has died.

They can understand the trauma of their grandchildren as they begin to explore the world of relationships, study and work. That same empathy is possible in reverse as grandchildren, family and friends can empathize with part of their elders' grief when a spouse, friend or family member dies. When my grandfather was dying, he spoke about feeling like an orphan without his mother there to comfort him. He was 91 years old and he missed his mother as I did mine. We have much more in common with our elders than we sometimes realize.

Elders are no more perfect or ideal than younger people. They can be angry, lonely or unkind at times like everyone else. They do, however, offer a wealth of knowledge and skills. This offer is not always accepted by those around them and in North America, we have tended to isolate them from their communities.

In helping an elder deal with grief, it might be best to allow them to 'teach' us about grief from their perspective. In listening to their lessons we might find ways to be most helpful. It is also important to recognize that the person within an older body still feels many of the same emotions that younger people do. A friend of mine was once talking about the old people in the seniors' home where she lived. I asked her how old those people were. "Oh in their seventies or early eighties, I guess," she replied. "Are you old," I asked her. "Heavens no, dear." She was 86 and felt much younger because her interests had not changed very much over the decades. My grandfather still had a glint in his eye when he told us about putting a girl's ponytail in the ink well in 1899. He still had some of the mischievous personality of a 10-year-old boy at 91 years of age.

Special Events

Special holidays or events may trigger difficult emotions. After my mother died I often wished that she was there for Christmas, holidays, birthdays and other special events. It was not until my father died four years later that I understood that my spending so much time wishing my mother was at certain events, meant I did not pay enough attention to my father who was there.

Many people have more difficulty in the days before a special event than the day itself. In our anticipation of a difficult day we actually lessen the effect of the day itself.

Here are a few tips for dealing with special days:

• Get extra support from family and friends. If you choose to be alone for that day, purposefully mix feelings of happy memories with sad ones. We need to remember the good and the bad of such events and use these lessons to help us cope. If you over-indulge in food or drink, recognize that you don't want to do that every day or else you will hurt yourself. Feel the emotions that are there. Sob if you need to. Laugh if you want to. There are no rules about what you MUST do, only suggestions about what you might do to help yourself and others that are grieving too.

• Make lists if you have trouble around such events remembering simple chores, gifts to buy, places to be on certain days, or cards to mail. On the list, mark off any items that are important to do first. Lists give us some sense of control and satisfaction as well tick off items that we complete.

• Some traditions you will want to keep and others you may want to change. You will get lots of free advice from caring family and friends. Go with your instincts as long as they do not hurt others. For example, you may not have liked a certain dish that was prepared for every formal family event. You will not dishonor the person's memory by choosing to cook something else.

• Some people spend money to 'take the pain away'. An elaborate vacation, too much shopping or too many dinners away from home will hurt you financially. Don't spend your way through grief as it only adds the grief of financial troubles. You may inherit money after the death of a loved one. Take some time before spending any of it. You have a whole life ahead of you and your loved one is trying to help you by easing your financial burdens.

• You may get many invitations to parties, get-togethers, and special events. People may want you to attend to "take your mind of things" when that is not what you want to do. They may worry that you are too isolated on your own. You need to judge at what point you are ready to socialize. These events are usually not the time or place to talk about your grief so you may not want to attend soon after a death. Instead, you might invite people over for informal visits to chat or ask someone to go for a walk with you. People mean well but you must decide when the time is right. On the other hand, do not isolate yourself from those who care about you. Find other ways to spend time with them. If you do not, they may well stop asking to be with you and your isolation from people who care about you may become permanent.

- New rituals can help ease grief. Lighting a candle to honor the life of a loved one is an age-old tradition. Playing favorite music or watching a favorite film can bring back happy memories. These memories may also bring sadness. Feel the emotions that come. Purposely balance the happy and sad feelings you have.

- On the anniversary date of the person's death, you might decide to create a new ritual of celebration to honor the person's life and their importance in your life. It might be as simple as a visit to the cemetery or going for a walk in your favorite spot together. It might be reading a special book or writing to loved ones to share the love you had with the person who died.

Feel the feelings at appropriate times. Remember the good and the bad memories. Use what you have learned to help others. At least, that is what so many others do, with perfectly human, mixed results. We can only do the best we can do, day-to-day, month-to-month and year-to-year. What a gift our experiences can be to others.

Chapter 12   Spiritual Aspects of Dying and Death

Definition
How to Support Each Other Spiritually

Whether facing a terminal or life-threatening illness or dealing with grief, spirituality has been a comfort to people for thousands of years. The belief that we are not alone give us a sense of reassurance that things will turn out okay. Prayer and meditation give us rituals, routines and strength to face difficult situations. Religious practices give us a sense of belonging to a spiritual community that stands by us.

Spirituality can also be difficult for people who believe that they are unworthy of a peaceful afterlife. Their religious beliefs, or lack of them, may lead them to believe that their death is the beginning of a terrible experience or no experience at all. They need opportunities to share these feelings, fears and beliefs with others who can listen, comfort and share in peaceful prayer or meditation.

It is often hard to put into words what spirituality can and cannot do for people. Sometimes reading biographies of people who have gone through similar situations is helpful and inspiring. Your local library has a collection of these books.

Definition

Spirituality is about the human spirit and our interconnectedness with each other and with God, however we define the creator. Faith describes our specific religious beliefs usually learned in childhood and refined as we continue to try to find the answers to 'what do I believe?' Religion is a particular system of faith and worship usually organized by a formal authority such as a church or holy book.

Spirituality is at the heart of the hospice movement. One does not have to have a specific faith to be spiritual. One does have to believe in the connection between all people at all times. There is often a blurring between meeting people's emotional and spiritual needs. Emotions are personal and individual experiences. Spirituality is the connection of all experience based on a faith in God, however one defines God.

A spiritual foundation can lead to even greater emotional support and comfort for people who have a terminal or life-threatening illness. Spirituality and faith can help to answer some difficult questions: "Do I matter?" "Does anyone love me?" "What is my role and purpose in my family, my community and my world?" At other times, spiritual beliefs can help us deal with questions for which there are no 'scientific' answers: "What will happen to me after death?" "Why me?"

Hospice care is about meeting the physical, emotional, spiritual and information needs of people who have a terminal or life-threatening illness. I believe it can only be accomplished to its fullest potential from a spiritual foundation. Dr. Dorothy Ley, a pioneer in Canadian palliative care put it this way:

Spiritual care lies at the heart of hospice. It says we are here. We will be with you in your living and your dying. We will free you from pain and give you the freedom to find your meaning in your life -- your way. We will comfort you and those you love -- not always with words, often with a touch or a glance. We will bring you hope -- not for tomorrow but for this day. We will not leave you. We will watch with you. We will be there.

Spirituality has to do with who we are as people. Religion has to do with how we practice our spirituality, if at all, through various religious beliefs, practices and rituals. I believe we are all spiritual people in the sense that we all have a need to know our lives have value and meaning. We are connected to each other as members of a living community. Most of us share a belief in a power or force greater than ourselves. We may define that force as nature, God or gods, collective human spirit, the Creator or a higher power. The only thing that separates us spiritually is our belief that separateness is possible. Our spirituality is often best developed and expressed in times of great joy or distress.

The following quote from Ram Dass and Paul Gorman's book *How Can I Help?* is about helping each of us to see the "whole" person. Not the diseased person, the dying person, or the disabled person. The whole person. The person who has exactly the same physical, emotional and spiritual needs as everyone else.

*I've been chronically ill for twelve years. Stroke. Paralysis. That's what I'm dealing with now. I've gone to rehab program after rehab program. I may be one of the most rehabilitated people on the face of the earth. I should be President. I've worked with a lot of people, and I've seen many types and attitudes. People try very hard to help me do my best on my own. They understand the importance of that self-sufficiency, and so do I. They're positive and optimistic. I admire them for their perseverance. My body is broken, but they still work very hard with it. They're very dedicated. I have nothing but respect for them. But I must say this: **I have never, ever, met someone who sees me as a whole**... Can you understand this? Can you? No one sees me and helps me see myself as being complete, as is. No one really sees how that's true, at the deepest level. Everything else is Band-Aids, you know.*

By seeing each other and ourselves as whole, we start to recognize the spiritual connection between us and the care, love and respect we all deserve and need. (See "Mr. G's Story" in Chapter 4 as an example of this.)

How to Support Each Other Spiritually

Spirituality is not separate from emotional support. They are connected even when we separate them by chapters in a book. The following suggestions incorporate some emotional supports with spiritual supports. The main difference is the underlying attitude that we are all members of the human family. Patients and families have complex relationships. There is not always a strong bond of love. There may be years of conflict, abuse or trauma that separate the person who is dying from some of the people caring for him. Whether our spiritual support of a loved one comes from a sense of love or a sense of service and duty, our support can make a positive difference in the last weeks and months of someone's life.

The following story by a non-religious person may help explain how spirituality can help us see the power within the idea that we are members of the human family:

I never had any real relation to Christ at all, and I can't say that I did at that moment (of visiting dying father). But what came through to me was a feeling for my father's identity as...like a child of God. That was who he really was, behind the 'distressing disguise'. And it was my real identity too, I felt. I felt a great bond with him that wasn't anything like I'd felt as father and daughter. In a way, this was my father's final gift to me: the chance to see him as something more than my father; the chance to see the common identity of spirit we both shared; the chance to see just how much that makes possible in the way of love and comfort. And I feel I can call on it now with anyone else.

Ram Dass & Paul Gorman in *How Can I Help?*

Some tips:

Recognize that you are directly connected to everyone you meet; even people you do not like.

No one can like everyone; everyone can be treated with respect, compassion, excellent medical care, love and a common spirituality.

Help create memories, using humor and creativity and a 'conspiracy of well-meaning' people to help each other. These memories serve people well as they go through the process of living fully until death. For families, these memories are an anchor of love as they go through their grieving process.

For example, a young woman recently married who was nearing the end of her life. She wanted to have one more special dinner with her husband at her favorite restaurant but could not leave her home. Several friends arranged to pick up her favorite meal from the restaurant and serve the couple in their home. The friends dressed up formally, served the meal quietly as would be done in a fancy restaurant, cleared and washed the dishes and left the couple alone for the rest of the evening. The young woman had a memory of intense love for her husband and for her friends before she died. The husband and friends carry that special evening with them for the rest of their lives.

Relationships are more important than things, work or health. When you feel hurt, joy, anger, happiness, grief or love -- share these feelings to allow others to help you and maybe to help themselves as well. Sharing your feelings through prayer and meditation is also very comforting.

Near the end of life many people look back and understand that it was the people and relationships in their lives that were most satisfying. It was not the material things they collected or the amount of work they got done. It was the relationships with family, friends, colleagues at work, neighbors and caregivers that were truly important. It is a perceptive family who learns this lesson from someone who is dying to use as new beginning in their own lives -- lives dedicated to building and strengthening their own relationships with others.

Prayer, meditation or a spiritual bond shared in silence are powerful tools to help us feel connected with each other and to a higher power. Whether one believes in God, in a creator, in the cosmic energy of love or however one describes one's belief in a high order, that belief can provide strength, direction, love and hope. Sharing one's belief with others of similar beliefs can be a powerful source of comfort.

We can express our spirituality through traditional forms like meditation, prayer, religious rituals and sacraments, and through connection with a member of the clergy. Rev. Douglas Graydon of Toronto's Casey House Hospice explains that non-traditional forms of expressing one's spirituality can also be very powerful and comforting. For example, creating personal rituals by bringing together people, places, things and symbols of personal significance is very moving now and as a memory to look back on for strength and comfort. Just as non-traditional weddings may occur at a park's water falls or in one's back yard, personal rituals around dying, death and bereavement can be held anywhere and include almost anything of personal significance.

Other forms of non-traditional spiritual expression are seen in people who remember and think about their dreams to search for spiritual meanings, clarity or comforting thoughts. (Note that some medications suppress dreams.)

Sharing one's life story and experiences with those who are interested is also a meaningful way to share one's spirituality. Sometimes this is done through one-to-one conversations and other times through peer support groups.

Rituals from one's faith are a way to dramatize the importance of a moment or event. Shared meals, holiday festivities, wedding and funerals are all rituals that help us celebrate life, love and faith. Using them when someone is dying or after their death can structure time and activity during periods of intense emotion and, possibly, chaos. This may also be a time to create new rituals that reflect one's evolving beliefs.

Books, audio, and videotapes can be very spiritually comforting. People's stories of going through similar circumstances can be very helpful and enlightening. Sacred religious books have provided people with perspective, peace and comfort. They may enjoy reading these books or having someone read favorite passages to them.

Providing physical and emotional support from a spiritual perspective means that a massage turns into an intimate sharing of love and faith; a walk in the park becomes a sharing of God's many gifts of beauty and peacefulness. A silent prayer shared together becomes a moment of lasting memories of time spent together.

Dr. Larry Dossey describes in his book *Healing Words* how prayer and spiritual practices act to influence physical health. His summary of possibilities include:

Adopting health-related behaviors by modifying one's lifestyle to the specific circumstances.

Increasing our social support through participation in spiritually-based community rituals.

Encouraging the process of emotional and spiritual expressions and resolutions.

Using faith to change a belief that you are blessed into the comfort of knowing you blessed.

Experiencing the presence of healers and healing fosters a sense of belonging and support that is healthful (even for people with a terminal or life-threatening illness).

Being the receiver of people's prayers or laying on of hands or other rituals may stimulate an endocrine or immune response that can help you feel better and reduce pain and symptoms.

Preparing physically for special spiritual rituals and events such as feast, meditation or abstentions, may promote your feeling better.

When someone's faith, religious beliefs and rituals are frightening, such fears are not easily reduced or erased. My grandfather's strong religious convictions led him to believe that he would go to hell for swearing, for his unkindnesses and for his "bad" thoughts. Prayer and faith were not comforting to him. The following thoughts helped him a bit but could not completely erase 90 years of firmly held beliefs.

Talking about my own faith and beliefs, which were more comforting than his own, calmed him at times. It opened up an intellectual discussion that led to prayers that addressed his specific concerns.

Talking about research into near death experiences helped identify what other people's experiences were and how this confirmed the most positive and loving images of what happens to people when they die. His own daughter, my mother, had such an experience. He found it was a powerful, comforting image to concentrate on.

Reminding him of the good he had done through his life, the love of the people around him who were caring for him day and night, helped him remember that his life had meaning and value to both himself and to others. The world was better for his life and that gave him some comfort as well.

The spiritual support of the hospice philosophy of care reminds us all that being there, even from a great distance in prayer and thoughtfulness, is the root of spiritual support that binds us all.

Part 6: Information Needs

Chapter 13   Medical Questions To Ask and Answer

Introduction to Information Needs

Some people like to know everything about their medical, legal and financial situations. Others do not. Adapt the following five chapters to meet your own needs as either the patient or the family caregiver. If you are not interested, try to find someone who is and who can help you understand those portions of medical, legal and financial information that is important for patient and family support and comfort.

Forms

The following forms and lists of questions can become the patient's personal medical file. Records kept by physicians, hospital and insurance companies are difficult to get, therefore, they are little use in a medical emergency. Photocopy the forms you wish to use.

Note: The 'you' I address in these chapters can be either the person who is ill if you have the energy and concentration to work with these forms or 'you' as the family member or friend acting on the patient's behalf.

Having your own medical file allows easy access to information for new physicians and others who need it quickly and accurately. Even if you have been a patient at a hospital before, it may take hours before your record reaches a physician and he can use it to help make decisions. As it is, maintaining and storing medical records is low on the funding list of our medical system and we belong to a very mobile society where it is difficult to get records transferred from one facility to another. Therefore, maintaining your own records can save valuable time in emergency situations.

Depending on a physician's style, medical records and taking a medical history provide the information for up to 85% of a diagnosis. The other 15% comes from a physical examination and tests. An updated medical record is very important when you see a new physician but even more important during an emergency situation.

I suggest you use a black pen to fill in the sections of the forms that are unlikely to change (your name, birth date, childhood illnesses). For information such as addresses and telephone numbers use a dark pencil so that you can easily change the information when it is necessary. Fill in only the information you want to. Information that you consider too personal can be left blank. Remember this is your medical file and you choose what goes in it. If there is information you do not know (e.g., when you had the mumps), put in a question mark and your best recollection (e.g., about 1943?). Have these forms with you whenever you go to a hospital, other medical care facility or a new physician.

Filling in forms is boring and it may also make someone feel less comfortable about her or his medical situation. Always keep in mind the uniqueness of this situation. We are dealing with someone who has a terminal or life-threatening illness. The forms are meant to be helpful but too much emphasis on them can make living until death a "big production". These forms (and the list of questions) have different uses depending on how long someone has been ill. If they have just been diagnosed as having a terminal or life-threatening illness, then these forms can be very useful. If the person has been ill for a long time and under the care of the same physicians, then filling in some of the forms in great detail is not necessary. In any case, it is up to the patient and family to decide how much effort is put into filling in these forms. If patients want the forms used but cannot fill them out themselves, a family member or friend can help them.

There are many suggested questions in the following pages. These questions are not meant to second guess the caregivers but rather help the patient and family who want to take an active role in their medical treatment to understand what is happening. These questions are a way to develop a trusting, working relationship. You will not be able to ask all the questions listed because many will be answered for you or because there are time constraints. You can ask some of these questions of physicians while some of the other questions are best reserved for other professionals: nurses, pharmacists, therapists and others. Also the references at the end of this book provide you with information on tests and procedures, illnesses, medications and more.

Each individual has specific needs but also individual responsibilities. The purpose of getting medical information is to better inform yourself before you have to make medical decisions about medical treatment.

Physicians and other caregivers can use the following forms and questions to encourage participation by their patients and to minimize wasted time. For example, if a patient completes a medication chart and then brings a copy of the chart and their medications to a new physician, there is little time wasted in examining and listing the drugs in the physician's file. Time can be better spent talking with the patient.

Chapter 16 on Financial Planning includes a Personal Information Record that can be photocopied and included with the medical records. It provides information that might be required by hospital/hospice administrators.

Questions Physicians Need Answered

Depending on how often your various physicians see you, they require the answers to some or all of the following questions. If you or a family member or friend can, write down the answers for the physician. Some physicians prefer to receive verbal answers to their questions but you can still use the written answers as a reminder of important points.

- What specifically concerns you about your condition today?

- What is the history of this condition? (Your Medical Record can add to the verbal information your new physicians will require.)

- Where in the body did the pain or symptom begin?

- When did it start (date and time)?

- On a scale of 1-10 with 10 the worst pain you have ever had (e.g., broken arm, and appendicitis) how would you measure your pain?

- Describe any other symptoms you have had?

- What were you doing at the time of the pain or symptom?

- To what degree does your pain or symptom limit your normal activities?

- How long does the pain or symptom last? (an hour, all day)

- Is the pain or symptom constant or does it change?

- Does the pain or symptom stay in one place or spread out to other parts of your body?

- What makes the pain or symptom worse?

- What makes the pain or symptom better?

- How do the following things affect your symptoms: bowel movements, urination, coughing, sneezing, breathing, swallowing, menstruation, exercise, walking and eating?

- What do you intuitively feel is wrong?

- Do you have any other information that might help me?

Questions About Tests

Studies have shown that patients who know the physical effects of a test or treatment are less afraid and recover more quickly from the procedure than patients with little or no advanced information. Although caregivers may not have had a particular test themselves, they can usually provide fairly detailed information based on other patients' experiences and the medical literature on the specific test or treatment. It is important for a patient to understand why a physician has recommended a test and how the test is done. The following questions can be asked of a physician, nurse or technician to help the patient decide whether or not he will consent to the test.

- What is the purpose of this/these test(s)?

- What do you expect to learn from these tests? Will the results change my treatment in any way?

- What will happen to me if I choose not to take these tests?

- What will the test feel like (any pain or discomfort)?

- What are the common risks involved in these tests?

- Are there any after effects of these tests?

- Can my spouse/child/friend come with me? If not, why not? (The medical world is slowly changing to allow someone to be with the patient during tests. This change is similar to how fathers now come into the delivery room.)

- Can I return home/to work after the test?

- When will I get the results of these tests? Can I see you to go over them with you?

- What are the chances of error or false positive/negative results? (Some tests have a high incidence of "false positives". Often tests are not definite but can help physicians know if they are on the right track.)

- What are the costs involved, if any?

- Other questions:

Questions About Medications

You may ask your pharmacist or physician the following questions. Some of the information, however, is listed on the medication or included with it. Patients are responsible for thinking about these questions before they start new medication. Keep in mind that people react in different ways to medications or may not follow the instructions carefully. If you have many medications, take the time to fill in a medication timetable (see Medication Timetable form).

Some of the answers to the following questions can be found in the pharmaceutical textbooks listed in the References. If your pharmacist or physician cannot answer your questions with enough detail, check with one of these texts.

- What do the drugs actually do inside my body?

- What is the name and purpose of these drugs?

- How often do I take them each day and for how many days?

- What food, liquids, activities and other medications should I avoid when taking these drugs?

- What are the effects of mixing these drugs together?

- What are the common and less common side effects of these drugs?

- How can these side effects be controlled?

- When should I return to give you feedback about the drugs?

- What happens if I choose not to take these drugs?

- What are some alternatives to taking drugs for my condition?

- Is there a less expensive generic version of these drugs?

- What special storage instructions should I follow? (Pharmacists usually label medication with specific instructions but you should be sure that the labels are present.)

- Can this prescription be repeated without coming to see you again?

- What are the costs involved? (Many prescriptions are never filled because patients do not tell their physicians that they cannot afford the medication.)

- Do you know if my medical insurance covers any of these costs? (Ask your pharmacist or insurance agent).

- Other questions:

Questions to Your Physicians About Your Condition

Once you are examined and appropriate tests are done you talk with your physician about your condition. Your family physician, as your advocate and mediator in the medical world, should help you understand the medical system. Why and how are tests done? What do the results tell you?. What are the treatment alternatives? What is the prognosis (prediction of the probable course of a disease) for your condition? What types of support (financial, physical, emotional, spiritual and informational) are available?

Try to get your family physician actively involved if you have trouble understanding or talking to your specialists. Always make sure that you understand what your physicians are saying. It is common for them to use terms you may not understand. Physicians had to learn what these terms meant, so they can discuss them with you and help you understand them too.

In order not to waste your physician's time, it is important to ask specific questions. If you know your family physician well, you might give him a copy of the following checklist of items that you want answered, especially if your situation has changed since your last visit.

Fill in the answers to your questions so you do not have to repeat the questions later on. Also ask for reference material that might answer some of the questions for you. This reduces the time commitment of your physician and allows you to return later with even more specific questions and concerns. There are times, of course, when your physician cannot give you specific answers because your disease may not be predictable. However, your physician can offer some educated guesses with recommendations of where you can go to get further information.

The following are some questions that might help you understand your condition better. You already know your diagnosis but you may want to know more.

- Based on your experience and the medical literature, what is the usual progress of this disease?

- What can I expect next?

_____

- What other parts of my physical and mental abilities will be affected?

_____

- What happens if I choose not to treat this illness through medication, surgery or other treatments?

_____

- What are the long-term effects of this illness?

_____

- Will I have pain and/or other symptoms as the disease develops?

_____

If yes,

- What treatment do you suggest?

_____

- How does the treatment work?

_____

- How will I evaluate its success or failure?

_____

- How long after I begin the treatment should I see you again to report any progress?

_____

- How often will I need the treatment?

_____

- What are the side effects to this treatment?

_____

- What are some of the medical and non-medical alternatives of these treatments?

_____

- What is an educated guess as to how long I have to live?

_____

- Other questions:

_____

_____

Questions When Entering A Hospital/Hospice/Other Facility

When patients enter a hospital, hospice or other care facility, it is important to remember that they are there to receive a service. They remain in control of that service by consenting to, or refusing, the tests and treatments offered them.

- If English is not your first language, ask if there is anyone who can speak to you in your own language and help you understand your medical care. Make sure you have a family member or friend present during all conversations that require consent.

- What is the name of the admitting physician?

_____

- Who is the physician in charge of my case and how can I reach him or her?

_____

- Is the physician in charge of my case a specialist, intern or resident?

_____

- Does the facility have special rules and regulations I should know about?

_____

- What is the discharge procedure for leaving this facility?

  _____

- Is this a teaching hospital, and if it is, will anyone request that I participate in a research or education program? (You have the right to consent
  or refuse to be part of any research or education program.)

  _____

- Does the hospital have a patient advocate office or social worker who can
  answer my questions about hospital procedures?

  _____

- What costs are involved in my hospital stay, if any?

  _____

- If I have chosen someone as my Power of Attorney for health care decisions, how do I make sure they are accepted as my legal spokesperson if
  I cannot speak for myself?

  _____

- Other questions:

  _____

  _____

Personal Medical Record

Name _____

Sex _____

Health insurance _____

    Type _____

    Policy number _____

    Policy owner _____

    Name/telephone number of agent (if applicable) _____

Date of birth _____

Blood type _____

Rh factor _____

Language spoken _____

Language preferred for reading and writing _____

Name and telephone number of biological father and/or
mother (this information can provide necessary genetic history)

_____

Height _____

Weight _____

Immunizations _____

Allergies

    Medication _____

    Food _____

    Chemicals/cleaners _____

    Substances (e.g., dust, grass) _____

    Other _____

For smokers

    How many years have you smoked _____

    Average daily amount (e.g., 20 cigarettes/day) _____

    If you quit smoking give date _____

Alcohol/non-prescribed drug use _____

    Type(s) of alcohol/drugs _____

    Amount a day or week _____

Do you exercise regularly? If so, what activity and how often? _____

Average number of hours you sleep every night _____

Religious affiliation, if any? Any religious or cultural limitations to care,

(e.g., Jehovah Witnesses cannot have blood transfusions, some Jewish people require kosher meals, etc.)

Next-of-kin (name) _____

    Address _____

    Phone _____

    Daytime _____

    Evening _____

    Relationship _____

Family physician (name) _____

    Address _____

    Telephone _____

    Hospital affiliation _____

Specialist physicians (name of principal specialist; for other specialists, use a separate page) _____

    Address _____

    Telephone _____

    Hospital affiliation _____

Spiritual leader _____

    Address _____

    Telephone _____

Optometrist (regarding lens prescriptions) _____

    Name _____

    Address _____

    Telephone _____

Dentist (name) _____

    Address _____

    Telephone _____

Pharmacist (name) _____

    Address _____

    Telephone _____

Any physical limitation due to an injury or disease, e.g., arthritis, paraplegia, loss of limb or other limitation _____

Difficulty with vision? (give details) _____

    Left eye _____

    Right eye _____

Do you wear contact lenses or glasses? _____

Difficulty with hearing? (give details) _____

    Left ear _____

    Right ear _____

Do you wear a hearing aid? _____

Do you wear false teeth? _____

The following charts are guides so you can create your own with enough space for the answers.

Childhood Diseases

Condition	Date	Complications
Chicken pox		
Whooping cough		
Meningitis		
Mumps		
Rheumatic fever		
Rubella (German measles)		
Rubeola (measles)		
Scarlet fever		
Strep throat		
Others:		

Adult Illnesses

Condition	Date	Details
Alzheimer Disease		
Arthritis		
Bronchitis		
Cancer		
Diabetes		
Emphysema		
Epilepsy		
Gynecological problems		
Heart condition		
Migraines		
Mononucleosis		
Multiple sclerosis		
Parkinson's		
Pneumonia		
Past operations		
Others		

Recent Medical History

This file keeps your Personal Medical Record history up-to-date.

Visits to Physicians	Lab Test Results
Date	Date
Physician's Diagnosis	Test
Treatment	Physician
Results	Result & Suggested Treatment

Medication Timetable

If you are taking various medications, a Medication Timetable is very useful in helping you to remember what medications to take at what time during the day. Use a pencil to fill in the medication names, because your prescriptions will probably change over time. This timetable is for your personal use and not meant as a detailed list of your prescriptions (see Prescription Drug Record form).

Medication Timetable

Time (a.m.)	Medication(s)	Time(p.m.)	Medication(s)
1:00		1:00	
2:00		2:00	
3:00		3:00	
4:00		4:00	
5:00		5:00	
6:00		6:00	
7:00		7:00	
8:00		8:00	
9:00		9:00	
10:00		10:00	
11:00		11:00	
Noon		Midnight	

Prescription Drug Record

During treatment for a terminal illness, it is quite common to have your prescriptions changed from time to time. The following record allows you to record the kind and dose of medications you have been prescribed, how often you were to take them and the overall result of the treatment. The date and physician's name is useful in emergency situations when your regular physician is not available to help you.

Prescription Drug Record

For example:

Date	Drug	Dose	Result/Side Effects	Physician
8/1	Tylenol #3	10 mg 4/day	pain relieved after 5 hours but returned 3 weeks later	Dr. Kildair
8/23	Tylenol #3	20 mg 4/day	pain relieved after 6 hours	Dr. Kildair

Medical Expense Record

Financial records are important to keep even if your costs are covered by insurance policies. Computer mix-ups are common and without adequate record keeping you may have to pay an unexpected bill. Keep all receipts plus records of other costs like travelling, eating out, etc., as some of these may be tax deductible (e.g., mileage to and from treatment, parking at treatment centers). Keep them in a file, box or envelope. Photocopy the form below or use a simple scribbler or note pad to keep a record.

Medical Expense Record

Date	Treatment	Dr/Hospital	Paid to	Insurance Paid or I Paid

Chapter 14   Home Care Tips

Preparing for Someone at Home
Visiting Someone at Home
Friends and Families: Other Things You Can Do
Patients: Letters Written to Your Family, Friends and Colleagues

Preparing for Someone at Home

There are many books on the subject of home care and what family members can do and learn to make the situation more comfortable for everyone involved including the companion book to this one, *Caring for Loved Ones at Home*. The following are a few suggestions:

• Remember that people do not change much in character because of their illness. If they were easy going, caring and enjoyed a good joke before their illness they are probably the same now. If they were unsatisfied with their lives, not easy to please and uncommunicative, they will probably not change a great deal because they are dying. Therefore treat them with respect and give them the opportunity to direct your involvement in their care.

• Do not try to force someone to eat. People need control over their lives and should be encouraged to make their own decisions. Patients know that food is important to living. Their diet may be prescribed but a hot plate, small cooler or refrigerator by the bed allows them to eat small meals when they are hungry. Have lots of liquids available. The person, at some point, may only eat what they want or nothing at all as their body no longer needs the nutrition. This is perfectly natural. One day they may not want anything, and the next day they do. Allow for this flexibility.

• Daily baths, massages and general hygiene are important for comfort but also to prevent bed sores for bedridden patients. Bedsores are very painful and almost always avoidable.

• If conditions permit, encourage patients to decide if they wish to smoke, drink, walk around and have visitors. Even if these activities are tiring or unhealthy, the decision must rest with the person who is dying unless it harms someone else.

- Although family members often want to do what is best for their loved one, they must not forget about themselves. If you feel like you are being used, say so. If you are uncomfortable with decisions that the ill person has made, be honest about your feelings and arrange for someone else to help.

- Have a bedside bell or other device available so that the person in bed feels they have direct access to you. An ability to make contact, at their discretion, is crucial for the emotional confidence of people who are ill.

- Have music and television available. People who are great sports fans, for example, may enjoy watching a game on television that allows them to be involved in something totally different from their own situation.

- Plastic bed pans and vomit trays are not as cold as metal ones.

- Perhaps you can move the bed to the living room, den or other area where the person who is ill feels more a part of the family and every day activities. If you live in a multi-level home you might relocate the patient to a ground floor room. If the bed is near a window the person can see what is going on outside.

- Either get a hospital-style bed or raise the one you have so that the people helping do not hurt their backs.

- For the caregivers at home, get all the help you need from family, friends and professionals. Most people do not know what to do under these circumstances so they need to know how they can be helpful. Ask for specific help (e.g., grocery shopping, walking the dog or reading to the patient).

- Borrow *Caring for Loved Ones at Home* which gives you suggestions about how to change beds when someone is still in it, how to move someone, how to bath a person in bed, how to provide good meals that discourage constipation or nausea, and other useful tips.

Visiting Someone at Home

(Feel free to copy this section to give to visitors.)

Many family members and friends find it difficult to visit someone who is very ill. If the person is in the hospital or other facility, it may be more difficult for some family members and friends to visit because of past negative experiences they have had in a hospital.

It is natural to hesitate in seeing someone you love or care about who is in pain or is seriously ill. Here are some suggestions that may help:

- If you care about the person then go and visit, even if you are not great friends (e.g., a colleague from work). The gift of your presence is as important as anything you might say or do. Your presence gives the patient a sense of belonging -- of being part of a group and community. This helps the person remember that their life matters to others.

- Check with the patient, the family or nurses' station to see when the best time is to visit. You don't want 20 people arriving one day and no one coming the next.

- Remember that the person you care about has not changed. She may be your parent, your child or a dear friend. Her personality, the qualities you admire and love, has not changed because she is ill or tired. Respect her rather than baby her. Include her in decisions. Ask her advice. She will probably change less than you will. There is nothing as comforting as a touch. If the person gives you permission (not everyone likes to be touched) and if you feel comfortable yourself, sit close to the person, hold her hand or give her a hug. Your touch and the caring in your eyes express more than words ever can.

- Use open-ended questions to help the patient decide what he wants to talk about (if he wants to talk at all). Questions like: "How are you feeling today?" "Are you comfortable?" "I love you so much. Is there anything I can do or say that would help?" Try to be at the same eye level as you talk, or if the person is lying down, it may be easier for them to look up at you.

- Perhaps you can show or give this book to a family member or friend to help them understand what is happening to them and to the people around them. A small section of the book may open up the discussion in a non-threatening way. A book like this may or may not be read but it gives information to people who are naturally curious.

- Don't prepare a speech. Admit your fear of hospitals or sick people. The patient needs to feel useful and if you are honest she can help you overcome some of your fear so that you can have a really good talk.

- Be yourself. Act as you always do with the person. If you are naturally quiet then avoid telling all the latest jokes from work. If you normally chat about old friends then continue to do so. If you are naturally outgoing don't become somber and serious. People need stability in their lives and family and friends can offer the greatest emotional stability.

- Let the patients vent their anger, frustration and despair. Their feelings are real and they need to get them out. It may have nothing to do with their illness but could be their treatment, their employer's attitude, old friends who no longer visit, or an acquaintance who owes them money but is nowhere to be seen. Offer to help if you can help improve the situation. Beware of getting too involved in an 'unfixable' situation -- not all conflicts can be resolved before a person dies. Try not to become part of the conflict by choosing sides.

- It is often not helpful to compare the patient with other people who have gone through similar things. It minimizes his or her own feelings. Some examples of other people's successes in similar situations may be helpful at times when the person is looking for inspiration rather than just the comfort of someone to listen to them.

- It is all right to cry and show your own feelings. You don't have to be strong all the time, for that makes the patient dependent on your strength. If you cry and allow him to be strong it is a normal relationship and one that benefits both of you.

- Don't hide behind a gift or card for it is your presence that is the gift. You can send a card or gift if you are unable to visit, or between visits, to let the person know you are thinking of her.

- Try not to stay too long. Two short visits are better than one long one. This is especially true if the person tires easily.

- Remember the other family members. They need your emotional support, too, and practical things like driving, food, baby-sitting, staying with the patient for a while, and running errands can reduce their stress and provide them with the precious gift of time.

- The gift of just being with someone, often in silence, may be difficult at first but offers you and the person you are visiting the comfort of companionship and the opportunity to think quietly and peacefully about what is truly important.

- Remember that the person's sense of time is different than yours. While we visit someone, we are likely also thinking about what to cook for our supper, how to get the kids to the hockey practice on the weekend and our vacation next summer. The person we visit has a much more intense sense of the present time. If you appear rushed or distracted, it is a sign that your sense of time is not the same as theirs.

- Before entering their room, make a conscious effort to join them in their sense of the importance of right now.

- If you get permission to bring children with you, prepare them for what they are likely going to see, hear, and smell. Children are wonderfully curious and ask a lot of questions. This can be a great gift when their curiosity is met with honest answers. If they are hesitant to visit, ask them why and try to truly understand their perspective. If you believe that they would benefit from the visit, have them stay for a short while for the first few times until they get used to the new situation. Again, answer their questions and concerns as honestly and completely as they want or need.

Family and Friends: Other Things You Can Do

Before the Person Dies

If you are a close family member or friend, offer to help with estate and funeral planning if you feel this is appropriate.

Encourage the person to resolve any unfinished business, including family or friendship conflicts that may exist. If such resolution is possible, it is a powerful completion to one's life and a legacy of fond memories for grieving family and friends.

If appropriate, help the person plan the surrounding environment e.g., have music/food/ films/videos handy that the person enjoys, arrange to have visitors arrive in smaller numbers, move the person to a more comfortable room or to where there is more activity they can join in. These little things give a person a sense of control, peace and comfort.

After the Person Dies

Attend the funeral. Again a hug can mean more than standard comments like: "He lived a long life." (Not long enough for me.) "It is better this way." (Not for me!) "She would want you to be happy." (I can't be happy now.) "You did everything you could." (Maybe I did, but she is still gone and it hurts.)

The family will have lots of visitors for the first week or two. Plan to be there near the month anniversary and after that too. Offer to listen.

Do not expect the pain of losing someone dear to end after a few months. It can easily take one or more years before anniversaries, birthdays, songs, smells, faces in a crowd, favorite foods, found letters, clothes, photos, gifts and so many other things no longer bring tears of sorrow and loneliness. Be patient with yourself and others.

Let the grieving person talk repetitively about the person who has died, their illness, their life story and the person's own grief. People often need to repeat over and over again the sequence of events leading to a death or repeat memories that are especially important. Talking relieves anxiety and the inner pressure to not forget the person. It makes the situation real when they wish it wasn't. Try an open-ended question to encourage such communication.

Do not be afraid to mention the dead person's name. People need to remember and don't want to go through life as if the person never lived. Even if the mention of the name brings tears it is a most valuable gift.

If you know of support groups that might help, provide the information without forcing the people to go. Information is useful and allows people to decide what needs they have. (See the appendix with a list of possible support groups.) However, if you are very close to the person, no support group is more important than your friendship. You have an ongoing relationship and history with the person that is vitally important. Nurture that relationship any way you can that benefits you both.

Patients: Letters Written to Your Family, Friends and Colleagues

One of the very special gifts someone who is dying can give to her or his family, friends and colleagues is to write a note or letter to them. It could be read before or after the death.

You know all too well the stress and grief that your family and friends will have when you die. You also know how cherished a note or letter would be as a gift to them. Words of encouragement, understanding, friendship and love can help them through a difficult time of grieving.

For those of you with children a letter, cassette or videotape filled with your love, thoughts, hopes and dreams for your children is a life-long expression of parental faith and love. These are not easy to do, especially for those very close to you. You do not need to write a long letter or a diary. My mother gave my father a book of Norman Rockwell prints and signed it: "All my love." It said it all perfectly. It was the last thing she wrote.

When my father was dying, he had my sister write out numerous cards for him that he signed. It was a goodbye to his family and friends. It drained him but he wanted people to know he was thinking of them; just as they were thinking of him. He asked my sister to write a special wedding card for my fiancée and me that I received seven months later on the night before my wedding. The card brought sobs of sadness, tears of joy and great love and pride. It helped me deal with all my emotions about not having my parents and grandfather at my wedding the next day. My father's card was a special gift shared between my father, my sister, my wife and myself. The next day was glorious and filled with great love, laughter and happy memories.

Chapter 15 Legal and Moral
Rights and Responsibilities

Definition of Legal and Moral Rights

There is a difference between the legal and moral rights of patients, family members and caregivers. Legal rights have their source in law. Moral rights have their source in generally accepted principles of care and respect which may, or may not, be enforceable by law.

Legal rights are constantly changing through legislation and case law. Legal rights are interpreted differently in each province and territory in Canada and each state in the United States for each specific case and, therefore, I cannot list your specific rights. I will give you some general concepts of your rights but you will have to verify the specifics within your province, territory or state.

Moral rights are very subjective and cannot always be argued in courts. When issues are brought to court, the resulting decisions about what is acceptable care and respect of patients depend on the laws of that specific jurisdiction as well as the details of each particular case.

To make sure of the legal rights within your jurisdiction check with: 1) your family physician or local hospital; 2) the provincial/state medical licensing and regulatory bodies (in Canada, with the provincial College of Physicians and Surgeons or in the U.S., the state medical boards); 3) relevant medical, professional and consumer groups listed at the back of this book; or 4) for more complex issues, with a lawyer specializing in your area of concern.

Since the person with a terminal or life-threatening illness is the only person involved in all aspects of their medical care (tests, examinations, operations, etc.) they must take the responsibility for making sure they receive the care and respect they deserve. Where they cannot act for themselves, a family member or close friend can act as their advocate.

American and Canadian laws stem mostly from the same English Common Law, except in Quebec, Arizona, California and Florida, and have many points in common. However, the specific provincial, state and national laws and procedures have developed differently. Although I will present some of these differences, it remains up to individuals to determine if these rights and responsibilities are applicable to their own situation.

Patients' Rights and Responsibilities

Patients' Legal Rights

- The right to be adequately informed about their illness so that mutually agreeable decisions can be made.

- The right to consent or refuse any treatment as long as the consequences of this action are not harmful to others (e.g., authorities must treat some contagious diseases). This consent is based on an understanding of the nature and risks of the treatment and any alternatives to it. The patient must be told if a treatment is experimental and the consequences of such treatment. The patient can always refuse to participate in experimental treatments and still expect good treatment and respect. This right is taken away if a patient is assessed as incompetent. Patients should have a Power of Attorney for Personal Care so that someone you trust will consent or refuse treatment on your behalf when you cannot decide for yourself.

- The right to consent or refuse treatment and to know that your consent or refusal will be followed even if you become incompetent.

- The right to change consent forms to include specific treatments you will or will not consent to and to have a list of the specific caregivers who provide the treatment. Sometimes physicians allow medical students to perform the treatment without a patient's knowledge. Your physician may accept or reject your changes.

- The right to receive adequate medical care under the circumstances. Although we all want to receive the best medical care available there is no working definition for "best medical care" so the courts rely on minimum standards of care to make their decisions.

- The right to choose one's physician if that physician agrees. Patients do not have to accept a specific physician and a physician does not have to accept someone as a patient.

- The right to not take part in research or teaching procedures (including refusing to be examined and treated by students in teaching facilities).

- The right to delegate decision making for personal health care, and for financial and legal decisions.

Patients' Moral Rights

Moral rights have some foundation in law but may prove difficult to argue in a court of law. Moral rights are a reasonable expectation of the kind of care and treatment a patient should receive.

- To be treated as a whole person rather than as a body with a disease.

- To be fully informed about your condition, prognosis and treatment alternatives, unless you wish a family member or friend to represent you.

- To be actively involved in making decisions at all times and having control over those decisions, unless you wish a family member or friend to make them for you.

- To be respected so that your descriptions of pain and symptoms are treated seriously.

- To be spared unnecessary tests, examinations, and treatments.

- To be fully informed of all direct and indirect costs.

- To be treated free of discrimination.

- To have a second opinion on request.

- To have one's family and friends treated with consideration and respect.

- To have one's information kept confidential unless doing so will harm the patient.

It can be difficult to translate rights into appropriate actions. As I mentioned earlier, definitions of terms like: reasonable standard of care, informed consent, and respectful care depend a great deal on who defines the term. If a court of law defined these terms in each specific patient-caregiver relationship you would find as many different definitions as situations.

More specifically worded rights are difficult to enforce as well. Although it is wise to know a hospital's admission, treatment and discharge policies it is impossible to list all the policies of any institution or to expect that they are always followed.

The demand for confidentiality or privacy of medical information is difficult to enforce. Although the medical records are considered confidential they can be examined by other caregivers involved in the patient's care, and perhaps medical students, insurance companies and administrators. Patients' medical records are owned by the physician or hospital; not the patients. Patients may request to see their records and can expect cooperation.

Patients' Responsibilities

Just as people have rights, they also have responsibilities. Without responsibilities, we cannot expect cooperation and honest communication with our caregivers. Some responsibilities are:

- To honestly communicate your symptoms, past medical history and your own idea of what is wrong.

- To take an active role in your own health. It is difficult to expect reasonable care if you leave all the decisions to the caregivers, because they cannot know what is going on inside you. It is not helpful to lessen the effects of treatment by abusing cigarettes, drugs and alcohol.

- To follow your caregiver's instructions carefully after you have both agreed to a treatment or procedure.

- To treat your caregivers with the same respect and consideration you expect from them.

- To understand and respect the time constraints and other professional stresses that may affect the patient-caregiver relationship.

- To request only tests and treatments that the physician agrees may improve your physical and emotional comfort.

Caregivers' Rights and Responsibilities

Rarely are caregivers' legal rights mentioned. Physicians, for example, do not have to accept a person as a patient nor do they generally have to provide patients with a copy of their medical record. The record is legally held by the physician or hospital although you can get copies (often for a fee).

Caregivers, physicians in particular, are given protection under the law for their medical judgment. If in their opinion a comatose patient requires life-support systems their opinion can overrule the family's wishes, unless the family has a legal Power of Attorney for Personal Care. However, in emergency situations when patients cannot speak for themselves and there is no time to read through forms, emergency physicians and nurses have a responsibility to treat patients with, or without, the consent of their family. The law still assumes that in emergency situations, physicians know what is best. Most physicians will, if there is time, consult with the family to talk about the options and to come to mutual decisions about care.

When someone has a terminal or life-threatening illness, there is usually time to notify physicians and other caregivers, in advance, of your concerns and wishes. Written confirmation of what you have told them will encourage acceptance of your wishes. As in all medical situations, patients must give consent to have any tests or treatments or to withdraw any treatments.

Caregivers are given a great responsibility by society and in return, their judgments are not considered legally negligent unless minimum standards of care are not followed. Extreme cases of negligence occur and should be prosecuted, however, a physician, nurse or therapist must sometimes make life-and-death decisions without the help of hindsight. Their legal rights help protect them from criminal and civil convictions.

There are codes of ethics for all professional caregivers including physicians, nurses, therapists, chaplains and psychologists to guide them in making decisions. These codes describe a professional's responsibilities to act in the best interest of the patient, to respect their professional and to acknowledge their limitations.

Families' Rights and Responsibilities

Generally speaking, the family cannot go against a patient's expressed wishes. In fact, a primary purpose of this book is to stress our need to respect a patient's wishes. The greatest difficulties for family members arise when they wish to make decisions on behalf of loved ones that cannot speak for themselves. Physicians should listen to a family's wishes but are not bound by them. The physician may ask the family for their opinion about life-support systems and other treatment but their opinions do not have to be followed. Even if the patient has shared his wishes with his family, physicians do not have to listen or act on these preferences if in their medical judgment there is a better way. Legal forms such as Powers of Attorney or Living Wills can help families speak on behalf of their loved ones.

Many of the above moral rights and responsibilities apply to family members or close friends.

Powers of Attorney and Living Wills

Powers of Attorney and Living Wills give written directions about what a person may want in different situations. As legal tools they leave many unanswered questions. As communication tools, they encourage people to talk about what they want and still leave enough room for flexibility as situations change.

For example, a woman brought into the emergency department for respiratory arrest was about to receive help when her husband produced the woman's Living Will. The document clearly stated that the woman did not want life support treatment during an emergency. The doctors immediately stopped the treatment. The woman was conscious. An emergency nurse, at some risk to her career, asked the woman if she wanted help breathing. The woman's body language clearly indicated she did. With some hesitation she was helped to breathe with a ventilator. The woman was grateful that her written instructions were ignored because she had not thought of this particular situation. Were it not for the nurse, this woman would be dead. After the medical emergency was over, she was taken off the ventilator and went home without other treatments or problems.

A **Power of Attorney** document gives a designated family member or another trusted person the right to make legal decisions in situations where the patient cannot decide for themselves.

There are generally two types of Power of Attorney forms: (1) dealing with **personal care** concerns including health care decisions, home care decisions, life and death decisions, and (2) dealing with **financial, banking, insurance and other legal issues.** An ordinary power of attorney ends when the person making the document becomes mentally incompetent, therefore, it is suggested you also have an 'enduring or continuing power of attorney'. It is also often suggested that one person should not have authority over both these general categories as there may be a conflict of interest. For example, one might be less likely to demand certain medical interventions if they know it will deplete a person's financial savings. By splitting up the two categories, there are at least two people who can speak up for the person who is ill. This may not always be practical when the person has only a spouse, child or friend to act in both capacities. It is especially important in this circumstance to have honest and open communication about what the person does, and does not, want done in various situations.

A **Living Will** is another form that helps speak up for the person who is ill. This document is very different from a Last Will and Testament that tells people, after a death, what is to be done with someone's property and assets. A Living Will puts in writing what medical interventions someone does or does not want under certain situations and the will may designate someone to speak on behalf of the person, similar to a power of attorney.

Each province and state has different rules in place about Powers of Attorney and Living Wills. Rather than provide a sample from only one province, it is important for you to get the forms specific to where you live. Forms are available from bookstores, government, libraries, software packages, and through your lawyer.

Resuscitation

Do not resuscitate orders (DNR) are instructions that must be written in a patient's medical record by the physician saying that the patient should not be treated if they stop breathing. This order is meant to prevent heroic efforts to help prolong someone's life who is actually dying a natural death. The order is usually written in the chart after discussion with the patient and/or family speaking on behalf of the patient. **The order can be changed at any time the patient wants** although it is not always as easy as it sounds, especially if the professionals disagree with the patient's decision.

Patient's Caution: As with any policy in health care, the original intent of the policy is sometimes lost in the day-to-day work of professional caregivers. Sometimes it is assumed that disabled people, our elders or poor people do not want to be resuscitated. This false assumption may put about one-third of our population who are not valued in our society at greater risk for a premature death. To safeguard yourself, make sure that you understand DNR orders and when you do or do not want it used in your case or the case of a loved one. Legally designate someone to speak for you through a Power of Attorney so that you are protected as much as possible.

Withdrawing or Preventing Life Supports

Withdrawing or never beginning life-support systems or treatment (which is not euthanasia or assisted suicide) may be allowed when:

- The patient refuses the treatment.

- The patient is believed to be permanently comatose and the physicians and family agree that life support systems and treatments are no longer helping the patient to improve.

- The patient is considered legally dead. It is also allowed under certain specific circumstances to not resuscitate a terminally ill patient who is near death and who has stopped breathing through a 'do not resuscitate' order (DNR). These orders are intended to prevent the horrible situations where families watch a loved one go through tortuous efforts to stay alive rather than die a natural death.

The problem is deciding when a person can no longer be helped by life-supports. One person with a life-threatening illness may want to die after months on a ventilator while another person wants even more life-support treatment. The value of one's life is extremely difficult to assess, on your own or with the help of others. Caution and taking one's time to decide can encourage thoughtfulness and questions about one's assumptions about what is right. Keep the person's cultural and religious beliefs in mind when making decisions on their behalf.

Talking about these decisions beforehand with the health care professionals most involved in the case can help avoid the trauma that may come when you second guess any decisions you make. "Did we treat too long?" "Should we have tried other life-support treatments before giving up?" "What was the right thing to do?" The more you can minimize the second guessing by making decisions openly and honestly beforehand, the better.

Negotiated Death

Negotiated death is when the patient (when able), the family, physicians and perhaps nurses, hospital administrators, lawyers etc., discuss and record what treatment is best suited for situations when a person is near death. The documents I have suggested provide more help with this. Once decisions are made, they are recorded and reviewed as the patient's condition changes. At any point the patient may unilaterally cancel any of these decisions although, in practical terms, it may be difficult to do if the professionals and/or family disagree.

Legal Definition of Death

Medical technology has progressed to the point where laws have been passed or are being examined to define when death occurs. The definition of death is very important in cases of terminal or life-threatening illness. Without a definition it is difficult to know when life-support systems can be legally removed. It is also crucial when considering donation of organs. The time of death is important for deciding when a legal will or insurance policy comes into effect, or in considering the facts during a criminal procedure.

There is no ultimate definition of death as different jurisdictions have different definitions. For some, death occurs when the heart and breathing stop. For others, it is when there is no brain activity. To date, the criteria used most often (but not always the legal definition) is one developed by the Ad Hoc Committee of the Harvard Medical School to Examine the Definition of Brain Death, 1968.

This criteria for a definition of death is:

- no responsiveness,

- no movements or breathing,

- no reflexes,

- flat electroencephalogram (EEG) except, for example, if the body teperature was lowered by freezing lake water or the person has poison in his body.

The debate on the definition continues but it is important for you to know that in cases of terminal or life-threatening illness, or when a life-support system is used, that the definition is blurred. If a person in an irreversible coma, is breathing by artificial means, is he still alive? Is a person alive if she has no brain activity but her body is kept alive with intravenous feedings and medication?

These are not easy questions, nor is there any unanimous agreement on the answers. Knowing about these difficulties can help you to discuss them with the other people empowered to make decisions with you. These types of decisions rarely have to be made quickly. Do not rush into a decision. Take the time to feel comfortable with your choice.

If a person is able to live and die at home, most of these issues do not come up as there are no life-support machines nearby and death is more natural.

Legal Concerns After Death

People generally have no right to will their body away. They can direct that it is used for organ donation, education or research. If a person dies at home, the body needs to go directly to the hospital. Only some organ donations are possible if a person dies at home.

Survivors cannot be forced to consent to an autopsy unless the death falls within the power of medical examiners or coroners (e.g., if they suspect the death was not by natural causes).

Complaints and Lawsuits

The increase in medical malpractice lawsuits in North America has increased insurance rates dramatically. Unfortunately, a concern about legal problems can make open communication and cooperation difficult. As a result, patients and caregivers may become defensive and the patient-caregiver relationship breaks down, leading to a lawsuit. It is a vicious circle.

Other reasons for lawsuits include caregiver negligence or the malicious prosecution of caregivers by patients or family members. People sometimes need to blame someone else for the illness or pain and suffering, and physicians and other caregivers are often the people singled out for such lawsuits. At other times patients or families want a caregiver or institution to apologize for a serious error and when an apology isn't made they file a lawsuit to demand an apology.

There is rarely a need for lawsuits if patients, families and caregivers work together. Hospice care in Canada has no examples of lawsuits.

In situations where problems occur, a lawsuit does little to help someone who is terminally ill because it usually takes years for it to reach the courts. Lawsuits may improve the treatment of future patients but they rarely benefit the people for whom the lawsuit was filed.

Concern must remain with the person who is dying. If caregivers are not cooperative and communicative, then speak to their superior or hospital administrator. The option of changing doctors is often available to you. Bringing in a go-between like a doctor, social worker, nurse or other caregiver is an option. If you wish to complain constructively, speak to the person with whom you have the difficulty, to see if the problem is simply a communication problem. If that isn't effective:

- Put your complaint in writing and send it to the person you have the difficulty with and his immediate supervisor. Request their reply by a certain date including what you want to have happen as a result of your complaint.

- List all the facts of your complaint including dates, peoples' names and important conversations.

- Keep a copy of all letters and a diary of all communication including person-to-person conversations, telephone calls, etc.

- Be assertive without being aggressive. Mutual respect goes farther in helping someone with a terminal illness than confrontation between patients, family and caregivers.

- If you do not get satisfactory results, you may make a formal complaint to the physician's licensing and regulatory body. In Canada, you could contact the provincial College of Physicians and Surgeons. In the U.S., you could contact the state medical board (usually located in each state capital).

Medical and Hospital Insurance

The cost of medical and hospital/hospice care is often very high. Certain government programs in Canada and the United States offer help, but many direct and indirect medical costs (loss of salary, transportation, medications, personal medical equipment and homecare) are not always covered. To understand what medical insurance (e.g., government and/or employment plans) you are entitled to and what insurance you must pay for requires patience. **Whenever you get information on insurance by phone, write down the date, the person you spoke to, your questions and the answers you receive. You may be passed from one person to another before getting the answers you require, but be persistent.**

In various jurisdictions you have a legal right to medical insurance. In Canada there are provincial government medical plans, usually with set premiums, that cover basic medical and hospital care. Extra insurance for things like private hospital rooms, special nursing care and medication is available, often through employment benefit packages.

Note: Some private life insurance policies allow you to cash in part of the benefit before you die to cover some of the costs of caring for you in your last months. Check with your insurance company to see if this is true in your case. If not, ask why not and request an appeal to allow you to get some of the money, if you need it. There are also new insurance policies that cover long-term care of patients at home. Check with your agent.

The purpose of understanding legal and moral rights and responsibilities is simply to encourage cooperation between the patient, family and caregivers. In many situations, mutual respect and understanding prevents the need to argue the letter of the law. Knowing the ground rules of the patient-family-caregiver relationship, however, allows people to understand what their roles are, how their roles can be improved and how, together, they can provide the total care needed by someone who has a terminal illness.

Chapter 16   Preparing Legal and Financial Affairs

Preparing a Legal Will
Organ Donation
Estate and Financial Planning
Personal Information Record
Documents and Property Checklist
Personal Financial Status

Chapter 2 has useful checklists to use with the information in this chapter.

Preparing a Legal Will

Each jurisdiction in Canada and the United States has rules about what to do with a person's estate after death and what types of wills are acceptable.

The purpose of the will is very simple. It states what you want done with your assets; who gets what and how much. It may also include funeral instructions, your request that a family member or friend be the guardian of your children, and sometimes a last word to specific family members and friends. These funeral instructions should also be filed as notes elsewhere, as the will is not always available to the family before funeral preparations are made.

Some jurisdictions limit the power of your will. For example, a jurisdiction may have regulations requiring division of the estate to include former spouses and dependent children by a former marriage. Your request to leave your children under the care of another family member or friend may not be followed in some jurisdictions where it is up to the court to determine who can best care for the children.

It is important to realize that each jurisdiction has its own regulations about wills and estates, therefore, you should get professional advice to make sure your wishes are followed as much as possible and that estate taxes are kept to a minimum.

Every adult member of a family should have a will and have it renewed at least every five years. A new will is often legally required after a marriage, divorce or death of a beneficiary.

Organ Donation

Most jurisdictions have their own Anatomical Gift Act. Check with your home care case manager to see what your local laws are to make sure your wishes can be carried out properly.

Some general information about organ/body donations:

- Some medical schools need bodies for study; transportation costs are generally not paid for by these schools.

- The body can be present for funeral or memorial services whether an organ or the whole body is donated.

- The ideal people for organ and body donation are less than 60 years old. Their weight is not a factor but generally cancer patients (except in some cases of brain cancer) are not acceptable for organ donations.

- The common organ donations are skin, heart, liver, kidney, lung, cornea, pancreas, certain bones, and middle ear.

- The time factor is crucial in most organ transplants, therefore, hospital deaths are most suitable for transplants except for cornea and skin.

- Some organs (eye, skin and some bones) may be "banked" for up to 48 hours.

- Organ or body donations do not have to be accepted by a medical team so make other plans.

- There are many organizations in North America which coordinate organ donation. Donor cards may be part of a driver's license, or you can become of a member of an international organization such as the Living Bank.

Although a person's consent to donate organs is binding on the family, in reality, most hospitals will not accept an organ donation if family members are opposed. If a person has not authorized organ donation upon their death, family members (in the following order) can consent on their behalf:

- the spouse (if there is one)
- if no spouse, an adult child
- if no adult child, a parent
- if no parent, an adult sibling
- if no adult sibling, any adult next-of-kin

Estate and Financial Planning

Estate and financial planning can help an executor/executrix and family administer the estate. There are many tax and legal considerations. In some cases it may be wise to transfer bank accounts and other assets before your death to save on possible inheritance taxes and probate costs.

Check with the local government or a lawyer about legal and tax considerations for the estate. If the estate is complex, or if there are real estate and other major investments, it is wise to get the advice of an accountant and/or lawyer.

Note: *Check with Canada Pension Plan, Veterans Benefits, the life insurance company and other associations, unions or groups that may provide the family with benefits.*

Where possible, change certain documents into joint custody so that bank accounts, home mortgage and other assets do not become part of the estate. This permits a spouse, for example, access to money quickly and reduces the value of the estate for tax purposes. It is also best to have a single person named as the life insurance and RRSP beneficiary rather than the estate. In this way, the money is paid out right away rather than waiting for the estate to be legally processed.

Make sure there is a current legal will to settle the estate. This is often a tricky question that family members do not want to bring up with someone who is dying. However, the legal nightmare and bureaucratic frustrations involved in settling a disorganized estate is not a last testament the person would want to burden the family with.

The Financial Status form in this chapter records the financial affairs. The forms record the extent of the estate. Many people who say they have nothing may be amazed at how much net worth they have.

I suggest you use a black pen to fill in the sections of the forms that will not change (e.g., names, past events). For information that will change (e.g., financial data, addresses), use a dark pencil. Read all of the sections within a form first before writing in any information. This familiarizes you with the forms and prevents you from repeating information within the same form.

The patient should be encouraged to sign a Power of Attorney for Financial and Legal Matters to give a family member, friend, lawyer or accountant the power to handle the financial affairs in case the patient is unable to do so for themselves. This permits someone to do the banking, pay the bills, look after investments and minimize any taxes or probate costs.

A Power of Attorney, easily drawn up in most jurisdictions, simply states that the patient gives a named person the right to handle the financial affairs and that the Power of Attorney can be revoked at any time. It should be witnessed and, in certain circumstances, notarized to make sure the patient is signing away these rights voluntarily. (See Chapter 15 on Legal and Moral Rights and Responsibilities.)

Personal Information Record

Full legal name _____

Previous surname if any _____

Sex _____

Telephone _____

    Daytime _____

    Evening _____

Legal residence address _____

Mailing address if different _____

Year you moved into your residence _____

Other residences: (e.g., summer home) _____

Work address _____

Social Insurance Number (Canadian) or
Social Security Number (USA) _____

Date of birth _____

Place of birth _____

Citizenship _____

Marital status (circle answer) single, married, widowed, divorced.

If married or widowed give person's full name, including any previous surname (if more than one, use a separate page) _____

Date and place of marriage _____

If widowed give date and place of death _____

If previously married give name of former spouse(s) and date(s) marriage ended _____

Father's full legal name _____

    Birth date and birthplace _____

    Address and phone number if still living or date and place of death

_____

Mother's full legal (maiden) name _____

    Birth date and birthplace _____
    Address and phone number if still living or date and place of death

_____

Occupation _____

Employer name and address _____

Religious affiliation
(including name of your cleric and place of worship) _____

    Important dates and locations of significant religious
    ceremonies (e.g., baptism, confirmation, bar mitzvah)
_____

Veterans

    Date and place of enlistment _____
    Date and place of discharge _____
    Service number _____
    Organization or outfit _____
    Rank or rating _____
    Commendations received _____
    Location of discharge papers _____
    Should flag drape casket _____

Name, address, telephone and relationship of important relatives and
friends (or give location of where these addresses can be found)

Name _____ Address _____
Phone _____ Relationship _____

Executor/Executrix (name)

    Address _____
    Telephone _____
    Daytime _____
    Evening _____

Family physician (name) _____

    Address _____
    Telephone _____

Lawyer (name) _____

Address _____

Accountant (name) _____

Address _____

Telephone _____

Documents and Property Checklist

Documents

Name	Location
Passport no	
Medical Insurance	
Driver's license	
Birth Certificate	
Marriage Certificate(s)	
Separation/Divorce papers	
Children's Birth Certificate(s)	
Last Will and Testament	
Living Will	
Powers of Attorney (Personal Care, Financial)	
Military Discharge	
Income Tax Records	
Mortgages and Notes	
Deeds and Titles	
Address book	
Other documents	

Credit Card Name_____ No. _____

Expiry Date _____

Property

Safety Deposit Box(es)
Location
Box number
Key number
Key location
Principal Financial Institution (e.g., bank)
Address
Telephone
Type of account(s)
Account number(s)
Secondary Financial Institution (e.g., trust company)
Address
Telephone
Type of account(s)
Account number(s)
Location of Bank books, records
Insurance policies (if more than one, use a separate page)
Name of company
Address
Telephone

Type of insurance(s)
Insurance Policy number(s)
Name of insured
Beneficiary
Agent's name
Address
Telephone
Location of policy(ies)
Real Estate (if more than one property, use separate page)
Location
Assessed value $
Mortgage(s) $
Mortgaged with
Mortgage number
Name on Deed Title
Property insured with
Address
Telephone
Agent's name
Address
Telephone
Policy number and amount
Home contents insured with
Agent's name
Addres
Telephone
Policy number and amount

Government Bonds	
Value $	
Location	
Corporation Bonds	
Value $	
Location	
Guaranteed Investments	
Value $	
Stocks, Shares and other Securities (if you require more space, use a separate page)	
Company	
Type & Number of Shares	
Employee Benefits	

Family Heirlooms List

Item	Where it is located
Furniture (list)	
Wedding Ring(s)	
Jewelry/Medals: (list)	
Photos	
Letters	
Diaries	
Cassette tapes/CD ROMS	
Home movies/videos	
Career papers/awards (list)	
Family tree	
Books (list)	
Others	

Personal Financial Status

(To be completed before death if possible, and reviewed by the executor/executrix after death. For each major section below e.g., retirement savings or bank loans, make a separate list. For complicated estates, I suggest you get the advice of an estate accountant and ask her to prepare your financial records and provide you with extra photocopies.)

Estimated Assets

Cash _____

Insurance policies _____

Retirement savings _____

Business interests _____

Total securities _____

Money owed by others _____

Real estate _____

Pensions _____

Annuities _____

Trusts _____

Household effects _____

Cars _____

Boat, snowmobile & others _____

Collections (coins, art, etc.) _____

Other assets: (list)

_____

_____

Total Estimated Assets _____

As of this date _____

Estimated Liabilities

Mortgages _____

Real estate contracts _____

Bank loans _____

Personal loans _____

Credit card, charge accounts _____

Personal bills (telephone, gas, hydro, TV)

_____

Pending lawsuits _____

Unsettled claims _____

Outstanding taxes _____

Back alimony and child support _____

Other debts (list) _____

Total Liabilities _____

As of this date _____

Note to Patient: If you have liabilities that your family doesn't know about (e.g., gambling or personal business debts,) keep a record with your lawyer, executor or friend. Otherwise your next-of-kin might be surprised by unexpected demands on the estate and this could be emotionally and financially hurtful to them after your death.

Chapter 17　Preparing Funeral Arrangements

Pre-planning a funeral and the disposition of the body (e.g., burial, cremation or donation) can save a lot of emotional strain for survivors. After a
death the survivors have limited physical and emotional energy so advanced
planning saves money and also helps the family. If possible shop around for
the kind of service you want at the most reasonable costs. It is a serious mistake to leave the arrangements for such major investments till the last
minute. If the funeral and disposition of the body are not pre-planned, use
the forms at the end of this chapter to help you make some of the decisions.

That said, funeral preparation can be a useful diversion for family members
looking for something concrete to do after a death. Discuss with your family how much of the funeral should be pre-planned and how much should
be left for the family to do after the death.

The first rule of planning a funeral service is not to feel rushed. If a person
has died at a hospital there is no need to rush him or her to a funeral home.
The hospital has facilities to keep the body for a time to let family members or friends make the proper arrangements. If the person died at home,
you can keep him there until you are ready for him to go to the funeral
home of your choice.

There are basically two types of general funeral services available to the
public:

- Traditional funeral services

- Services arranged through a Memorial Society or 'simple alternative',
  usually at reduced costs.

Neither service is better than the other. Just as some people prefer large weddings over smaller, less expensive weddings, there are others who prefer more elaborate funerals over less expensive ones. Always get a list of all the costs and taxes before agreeing to any type of funeral service.

Let us begin with some definitions of terms used by funeral professionals to help you understand the choices available to you.

Definitions of Funeral Terms

Conventional Funerals

Funerals organized through a licensed funeral home probably cost thousands of dollars. The more elaborate the funeral the higher the cost. This figure does not include costs for cemeteries, flowers and headstones/monuments.

For-Profit and Not-for-Profit Alternative Funerals

These funerals have similar services but at different costs.

Memorial Society Funerals

Memorial Societies are non-profit, non-sectarian consumer organizations that deal directly with select funeral homes to promote simple and dignified funerals at reduced costs. For a nominal fee (e.g., $10.00-20.00) members of these societies receive the latest information on low-cost yet dignified funerals. These societies also act as consumer watchdogs on legislation regarding funerals. They do not arrange funerals themselves.

Non-Professional Funeral

A funeral arranged privately without the help of a funeral home. The family or friends prepare and transport the body, provide the casket and obtain the legal documents. This option requires the family or friends to understand the local laws to make sure no violations are made. The family physician or a cemetery official may be able to provide the information about legal requirements. This process involves a lot of effort for people not used to these procedures but it is possible.

Funeral Director

Also called a Mortician (avoid the title Undertaker as it is disliked by most funeral directors). Most funeral directors must be licensed. They make all of the funeral arrangements including pre-paid services, the funeral itself, getting legal documents and handling the family's questions.

Funeral

Usually implies that the body is present for post-death services. A funeral usually includes a religious ceremony in a church/synagogue/temple, at one's home or in the funeral home chapel. A "wake" or "visitation" may precede the funeral where people can pay their respects to the deceased and immediate family. The casket may be open or closed.

Memorial Service

Usually implies that the body is not present for any post-death services. This service may be held in a church, funeral home chapel, at someone's home or another location (not to be confused with a Memorial Society Funeral).

Body Donation

Although people may donate their body to a medical school, the school does not have to accept the donation. It is important to make these arrangements before death and have other plans made.

Funeral Costs

Memorial Societies have set fees in agreement with specific funeral homes. The various "plans" encourage low-cost caskets, few extra services such as visitations, no embalming etc. Conventional funerals vary greatly in price as each funeral is based on service-used fees. Some of the services that are available (but not always necessary) include: removal of the body from the place of death; the care and preparation of the body (embalming is optional in most cases); coordination between family and clergy for religious service; preparation and filing of legal documents; writing the obituary; use of the facilities and equipment; use of the chapel; visitations; the casket; transportation to the cemetery or crematorium.

Other Costs

The burial or cremation charges; fee to clerics; use of the place of worship; organist; flowers; and transportation of the body from another town/city. In cases of body donation to a medical school, the cost of transportation and other costs may be involved.

Embalming

Disinfecting the body by replacing body fluids with chemicals. Prevents quick deterioration of the body and the odors that occur. Generally not required except in certain circumstances, e.g., if the body is to be transported between states/provinces. Embalming does not preserve the body indefinitely.

Pre-planning

Saves the survivors many decisions but should provide flexibility for them to change parts of the plan to meet unexpected circumstances. Memorial Societies encourage pre-arranging your funerals and disposition of bodies. They keep a record of your wishes on file and transfer the file to any area in the country you move to. This arrangement is also possible with some funeral homes.

Pre-financing

For funerals, burials and cremations, pre-financing can permit you to pay today's prices for tomorrow's services. Be sure that your funds are put in trust and cannot be used for any purpose other than the services you have paid for. Ask if you can withdraw your money (ask if there is an administrative fee charged), or transfer them to another funeral home or cemetery, at a later date. Ask for a detailed list of services and costs before agreeing to purchase anything. Try to include other members of the family in the decisions.

Questions About Conventional Funerals

Is the funeral home and funeral director licensed? Licensed businesses ensures some minimal standards of practice as well as being part of a system that has a complaint procedure if you are unhappy with the service you received.

Will the funeral home provide a written report of the decisions you made including all direct and indirect costs?

If you are pre-arranging and pre-financing your own funeral will the funeral home keep your funds in trust? Can you withdraw or transfer your funds and if so at what cost?

If the funeral has been pre-financed will the funds cover all direct and indirect costs at the time of death?

What complaint system is in force in cases of disagreement on services and costs?

If you have selected a Memorial Society-style funeral, will the funeral home accept it and at Memorial Society costs?

Disposition of the Body

Just as funerals can be quite expensive, the disposition of the body can also be expensive. Again, pre-planning can save the survivors' physical and emotional energy. However, if you know what you want and how to get it, disposition of the body does not have to be difficult.

Earth Burial/Internment

Burial can be in a municipal, church, veteran or other non-profit cemetery, or in a privately owned fraternal or corporate cemetery. Provincial/State jurisdictions may regulate cemeteries including whether they must have an endowment or perpetual care fund to make sure the cemetery grounds and individual graves are properly maintained. A point to remember is that some cemeteries are non-profit and others are owned for profit. Prices do not vary greatly but the services and care offered may be different.

Cremation

Is a process of combustion and evaporation that reduces human remains to charred fragments. These cremated remains may be stored in a container (urn) and kept anywhere you wish or buried in a cemetery plot or placed in a columbarium. Cremated remains are sometimes scattered but local laws should be checked to insure the legality of scattering. **Note:** some religions do not permit some of these practices. Check with your cleric or funeral director.

Entombment

The casket is placed into a mausoleum crypt (above-ground structure) and sealed by a marble or granite face. Mausoleums are usually on cemetery grounds.

Vault or Lawn Crypt

A concrete box in the ground where a casket is placed and then sealed with a lid. This prevents the ground from caving in around the casket. Elaborate vaults are available.

Columbarium

A structure where urns of cremated remains are placed into one of many spaces or niches. This structure may be part of a mausoleum.

Headstones/Monuments

Some cemeteries have limits about the size, shape, material (granite versus concrete) or whether the marker must be flush with the ground or stand up.

Traditional Cemetery versus Memorial Park/Garden

Traditional cemeteries permit upright monuments, usually made of stone. Memorial Parks/Gardens have bronze or granite memorials level with the ground to blend in with the landscape of lawns, trees, flowers and gardens. Either can be publicly or privately owned, for profit or non-profit.

Pre-planning

Does not involve a cost reduction (considered unfair business practice) but does permit shopping around, making a choice you prefer regarding location, services and costs, avoiding estate problems and giving peace of mind. Many cemeteries allow you to withdraw your pre-paid funds with little or no charge. Cemeteries may also belong to the National Exchange Trust which can credit your account to another cemetery.

Relationship with Funeral Homes

In some jurisdictions funeral homes own their own cemetery that may mean a cost reduction. When the cemetery is not affiliated with a funeral home, it is best to go to the cemetery yourself to make your own choices because in most cases, the cemetery staff will have more information available than the funeral home staff.

Questions About Cemeteries

Is this cemetery or memorial park/garden licensed? As with funeral homes, licensed cemeteries have some minimal standards of practice as well as being part of a system that includes a complaint procedure if you are unhappy with the service you received.

_____

With which authority?

_____

Who owns this cemetery or memorial park/garden and how long has it been in existence?

_____

According to local laws how many days do I have to cancel this agreement without penalty? (Check with your local government agency, Better Business Bureau or consumer organization to make sure you are getting what you pay for.)

_____

What is the size of the plots available?

_____

Do you have any restrictions about the type of monument or marker I wish to use?

_____

Can I buy one separately or must I buy one from the cemetery?

_____

Does the marker or monument have to be made out of granite or bronze? (Granite and bronze last longest.)

_____

Are there any restrictions on religious or cultural observances, like using lighted candles at the grave or having a survivor sit with a chair on the plot?

_____

Can you supply me with a list of the various options and services available plus their costs, e.g., burial, a crypt in a mausoleum, a niche, opening and closing the grave/crypt, and installing a memorial?

_____

Can I pre-pay through time-payments?

_____

Do you have a perpetual care fund so that I do not have to pay maintenance costs each year?

_____

Can I cancel any pre-arranged plans and get back any pre-paid funds?

_____

Are there any administrative penalties for this service?

_____

Can I transfer my pre-arranged plan and pre-paid funds to another cemetery or memorial park/garden?

_____

Are you a member of the National Exchange Trust or similar organization?

Is this cemetery or memorial park/garden a member of any local, regional or national associations? If so, which ones?

What *Code of Ethics* or *Creed of Ideals* do you abide by?

Can you handle some of our preferences that are different from other people (e.g., planting a small garden on the plot)?

Questions About Cremation

Cremation may be arranged through a funeral home or cemetery or separate company depending on local regulations.

How long after death can cremation occur? (a time limit is set to prevent cremation in cases when the cause of death is uncertain.)

Must we have a casket for cremation?

What are the local regulations about scattering cremated remains?

Can you provide me with a list of options and services you offer plus a complete list of direct and indirect costs?

Arrangements for Monuments and Markers

It is important to consider what type of monument you wish to purchase before you buy a cemetery plot. Cemeteries may restrict the kind of monuments placed on plots in different areas on the grounds so it is important to know what you want before committing to a specific plot.

You may buy a monument or marker through a special dealership or perhaps the cemetery itself. Make sure you are dealing with a reputable group and that all direct and indirect costs are made clear. Also make sure that any monument or marker you buy meets the regulations of the cemetery or memorial park/garden.

Funeral and Cemetery Service Instructions

If you want to be involved in the planning of your own funeral, it is important to leave instructions for your family and/or executor. Use the following form to help make your ideas plain. It can be very helpful to one's family to pre-arrange a funeral. However, making all the decisions in advance leaves little room for your family to be actively involved in honoring you. Having family make some of the decisions about funeral arrangements after your death can also help them through their grieving process. Time may go very slowly for family members right after a death. Having to make some of the arrangements gives them something concrete and valuable to do.

Have you pre-arranged your funeral?

If yes, is it with a funeral director or memorial society?

Name _____

Address _____

Telephone _____

Contact person _____

Location of contract _____

Have you purchased a cemetery plot? _____

If yes, where _____

Name _____

Address _____

Telephone _____

Plot number and site _____

Location of contract _____

Are you a member of a Memorial Society? _____

    If yes, name _____

    Address _____

    Telephone _____

    Contact person _____

If you have not pre-arranged your funeral and the disposition of your body, answer the following questions. If you have made arrangements, read the following questions and fill in any of your wishes that are not recorded elsewhere.

_____

Do you wish your body to be embalmed?

_____

Do you wish to be buried or cremated?

_____

Do you have a preference for a particular funeral home? _____

    If yes, name _____

    Address _____

    Telephone _____

    Contact person _____

Clothes you wish used

_____

Jewelry you wish used, if any

_____

Religious items to be included in coffin (e.g., prayer book and religious jewelry).

_____

What type of casket would you like: wood, fiberglass, metal?

_____

Do you have a color preference for the inside and outside of the casket?

_____

Do you wish an open or closed casket?

_____

If you are a veteran and entitled to a flag draped casket, do you want the appropriate authorities notified?

_____

Do you wish visitation rights for your family and friends?

_____

If yes, how often? _____

Would you like your cleric (e.g., minister, rabbi and priest) to officiate at a funeral service? _____

    If yes, name _____

    Address _____

    Telephone _____

    Contact person _____

Do you want a funeral service in your own place of worship or do you prefer to use the funeral chapel?

_____

Do you have any preferences for pallbearers? _____

    If yes, _____

    Name _____   Name _____

    Name _____   Name _____

    Name _____   Name _____

Do you wish an organist? _____

    If yes, do you have a favorite piece(s) you wish played?

_____

Do you wish a soloist or choir? _____

    If yes, do you have a favorite song(s) you wish sung?

_____

Do you have a favorite passage you wish read during the service?

_____

Do you wish flowers or do you prefer donations to your favorite charity?

_____

    If a charity, which one(s) _____

Disposition of the Body

Are you donating your whole body right after death?

_____

Are you donating any part of your body upon death?

_____

If yes, which parts?

_____

Have you filled out an organ donor card?

    If yes, where is the card located, and who should be notified?

    Card location _____

    Contact person's name _____

    Address _____

    Telephone _____

(If you do not have a card, please arrange to sign one and keep a copy in your wallet.)

    Do you wish to be buried or cremated? _____

For Burials

Do you have a cemetery preference? _____

    If yes, name _____

    Address _____

    Telephone _____

What type of grave monument or marker do you wish?

_____

Do have a preferred inscription? _____

    If yes, what it is? _____

For Cremations

Do you have a crematorium preference?

_____

    If yes, name _____

    Address _____

    Telephone _____

Do you wish the ashes deposited in a mausoleum or buried?

_____

Do you wish the ashes given to a specific person? _____

    If yes, name _____

    Address _____

    Telephone _____

Do you wish the ashes scattered? _____

    If yes, by whom _____

    Where _____

    (Make sure that your wish to scatter the ashes does not go against any local laws.)

Obituaries

Do you wish a newspaper obituary notice? _____

    If yes, name of newspaper(s) _____

What do you want mentioned in your obituary? _____

_____

_____

If you are a citizen or past citizen of another country do you wish that country's embassy to be notified of your death? _____

    If yes, name of Country Embassy _____

    Address _____

    Telephone _____

Other special instructions or information not covered by this checklist _____

_____

_____

_____

_____

List of people to notify

_____   _____   _____

_____   _____   _____

_____   _____   _____

_____   _____   _____

Part 7:   Community Resources

Chapter 18   Finding Support In Your Community

There are many community resources available to help people with a terminal or life-threatening illness and their families. The difficulty is knowing who to ask and what to ask for. One of the fastest ways to get the information you need is to talk to people who have gone through a similar situation recently.

The following organizations also have many services to offer and information to give you. Your local home care, hospice care and disease-specific organizations (e.g., Cancer Society, Heart and Stroke, public health department) are the best places to start. Listed are their names, telephone number and Web addresses.

If you receive information by phone always have a list of questions written out and write any answers on the same sheet of paper including the name of the person providing the information.

Home Care

Almost all communities in Canada have access to home care services through the local or provincial health boards or ministries. These programs may have various names (e.g., Community Care Access Centers) but most health care professionals still use the term 'home care'.

Home care programs offer home nursing, homemakers and home care supplies free of charge plus other services. In small communities where there is no access to home care services, residents may find help through a local physician and/or nurses. Contact your provincial or territorial health ministry or the Canadian Home Care Association if you cannot find anything locally. Their number is in the Blue pages of your telephone book.

The Canadian Home Care Association
(613) 569-1585
www.travel-net.com/~chca

National Association for Home Care
(202) 547-7424
www.nahc.org

Hospice Care

To locate hospice or palliative care groups in your community, check your telephone book first or your home care case manager. If you have trouble finding a group you can check with the national palliative/hospice care associations.

Canadian Palliative Care Association
1 (800) 668-2785

National Hospice Organization
(703) 243-5900
www.nho.org

Legal and Financial Aid

To help you with your legal and financial affairs you can hire your own lawyer or check into Legal Aid Clinics or Lawyer Referral Services in your community. Also, many not-for-profit organizations provide free or low cost income tax services.

National Organizations

The following list of health information organizations and consumer organizations does not include all the available groups. There are hundreds of smaller organizations that may suit your specific needs. To find their address and telephone number, check with your local telephone book, library, family physician or community health information centers.

If you live outside of an urban center you can call the Area Code + 555-1212 to get the branch office in the city nearest you. If you have access to the Internet, use www.canada411.ca to help locate the services nearest you.

Whenever you are in a hurry to get information, I advise calling these organizations directly and asking for information to be mailed, faxed or e-mailed.

You can also check at a main library for organizations in other parts of Canada and the U.S. through the latest edition of the following directories:

In Canada: Directory of Associations in Canada by Micromedia.
In the United States: The Encyclopedia of Associations

AIDS Committees
(check your local telephone directory) or nearest urban center.

Amyotrophic Lateral Sclerosis (ALS) Society of Canada
1 (800) 267-4257
www.als.ca

Alzheimer Society of Canada (and related Dementias)
1 (800) 616-8816
www.alzheimer.ca

Arthritis Society
1 (800) 321-1433
www.arthritis.ca

Local **bereavement support services** (grief counseling) in your telephone book or local hospice office.

Brain Tumour Foundation
(519) 642-7755
www.btfc.org

Canadian **Cancer** Society (Cancer Information Services)
1 (888) 939-3333
www.cancer.ca

Childhood Cancer Foundation--Candlelighters Canada
1 (800) 363-1062
www.candlelighters.ca

Canadian **Diabetes** Association
1 (800) 226-8464
www.diabetes.ca

Distress Lines
(check your local telephone book inside cover for numbers)

Epilepsy Canada
(514) 845-7855

The **Heart and Stroke** Foundation of Canada
1 (888) 473-4636
www.hsf.ca

Canadian **Hemophilia** Society
1 (800) 668-2686
e-mail = chs@odyssee.net

Canadian Continence Foundation (**Incontinence**)
1 (800) 265-9575
www.continence-fnd.ca

Kidney Foundation of Canada
1 (800) 361-7494
www.kidney.ca

Kids Help Line
1 (800) 668-6868

Lifeline (electronic alert system)
1 (800) 543 3546

Canadian Lung Association
1 (888) 566-LUNG
www.lung.ca

Lupus Canada
1 (800) 668-1507
www.lupuscanada.org

Canadian Medic Alert Foundation
1 (800) 668-1507
www.medicalert.ca

Medical/Physical Aids
(e.g., wheelchairs, bathtub chairs, elevated beds).
Check with your home care service, medical supply stores and/or family doctor.

Canadian Association of Retired Persons
1 (800) 363-9736
www.fifty-plus.net

Social Assistance
(check the Blue government pages in your telephone book).

Stroke (See Heart)

Chapter 19   Creating Your Own Support Circle/Team

June Callwood's book *Twelve Weeks in Spring* tells the story of Margaret Frazer. In 1985 Margaret was dying of cancer and did not want to go into hospital or become involved in a formal palliative care program. June Callwood and other friends recruited close to 60 friends, acquaintances from Margaret's volunteer work, church, and other volunteers to help her stay at home until her death. They provided practical help as well as physical and emotional comforts. Margaret's doctor, Linda Rapson, was part of this "support team" and provided the others with information to help Margaret stay as comfortable as possible. Near the end of Margaret's life this support team gave round-the-clock care and support.

From that experience several of Margaret's friends from the church of the Holy Trinity and other volunteers established Trinity Home Hospice in Toronto to help people who wanted to keep as much control over their lives as possible through an informal hospice program. The volunteers at Trinity Home Hospice provide practical care and supports during weekly four-hour visits with someone who has a terminal or life-threatening illness. These volunteers are not trained medical staff (although some volunteers have professional backgrounds) nor is their purpose to replace homecare and homemaker supports available through government health care. Their purpose is to provide the kind of practical help and emotional support that friends and good neighbors have provided for each other for generations.

Over the years, several Trinity Home Hospice staff have helped in preparing this information on support circles/teams. Beth Pelton, Elaine Hall, Blair Henry and June Galbraith have been particularly helpful about how people could design their own support teams to allow them the most control and flexibility when they had a terminal or life-threatening illness. Not everyone wants to receive care through a formal hospice program and others do not have hospice care programs available to them. Developing a support team may be one alternative open to such people.

The following ideas are not in any specific order. You might use some or all of the following ideas to develop a support team. Take only those ideas that apply to you and change or add ideas that meet the specific needs of the person who is ill. Remember that a support team is only effective when the person with a terminal or life-threatening illness agrees with the idea and participates in making decisions.

Keep in mind that the support team idea can be used in many different ways. In this book I look at how to help someone with a terminal or life-threatening illness. It can also be used for someone who has a chronic illness; for someone (old or young) living at home alone and needing extra help to stay in their own home; for a parent who wants some time away from the children once or twice a week; and for people who want to increase their circle of friends. In other words, do not be limited by the ideas presented here. Let your imagination run wild with potential rather than with limitations.

I use the word friends to include family members and friends who do not live with the person who is ill, as well as volunteers who over time will probably become friends of the person.

It helps to have one or two friends act as the coordinator(s) of the support team. This person is generally not the spouse or closest loved one. The coordinator is responsible for organizing everyone's schedule for visiting the person who has a terminal or life-threatening illness. Freeing this responsibility from the closest loved one allows that loved one to concentrate on the person who is ill rather than on the day-to-day details of scheduling and answering phone calls. It also gives the person who is ill and loved ones more time to relax, go out for walks, eat together quietly, and make plans for themselves and their family.

How do you recruit enough friends? How many do you need? Beth and Elaine suggested that a coordinator ask other friends for their help in visiting the client. As a coordinator (and not the patient or immediate family) people may feel freer to say no if they do not want to participate. In this way there are no hard feelings. People can be recruited from the family, friends and work colleagues who live in the area; people from clubs and organizations that the person belongs to (e.g., service clubs, volunteer work, veterans groups), and where the person worships. Another group that is often overlooked is neighbors. Neighbors are often willing to drop by with some food, help with running errands, cleaning up the outside (e.g., shoveling snow, mowing the lawn), or popping in early in the morning or late at night to help the person with getting up or going to bed. Friends, family and neighbors may also help with basic child care, help people get to appointments, bring someone over to their house for a change of pace and more. The more specific and time-limited the request, the more likely someone will say, "Oh sure. I can do that."

The number of friends one person might need depends completely on the client and family's needs. Some people only want and need the help of a few close people. Other people may need more help, especially near the end of an illness. Trinity Home Hospice often schedules people in the following way if a person needs round-the-clock care – in weekly four-hour shifts. They find that this fits in well with other community supports to ensure seamless, 24-hour care for the person who is ill. The following is a general schedule .The shifts can actually be slightly longer or shorter depending on the circumstances and needs.

   8 a.m. - 12 p.m.

12 p.m. - 4 p.m.

   4 p.m. - 8 p.m.

   8 p.m. - 8 a.m. (night visit by a friend if possible and necessary)

If a friend wishes to stay overnight, it works best if the friend brings their own linen or sleeping bag and often a change of clothes so that they can leave directly from the person's home to go to work or back to their own home to start the day.

If this schedule is followed it requires four people a day (other than the immediate family that lives with the person) or 28 people a week. Except for the night person, everyone commits to only a four-hour visit once every week. Of course, some people want to participate more often which cuts down on the number of people you need.

It is helpful for everyone on the team to have the monthly schedule and a list of all team members and their telephone numbers. Encourage team members to find their own replacements if they cannot make an appointment and let the coordinator know about any changes to the schedule. Such thoughtfulness can save hours of frustrating telephone calls and communication problems.

As well as visiting the person at home, friends often meet once a month, or more often depending on the illness, to compare notes and feelings. Often the person who is ill participates in these meetings or they may ask one of their family members to go. These meetings are held in the person's home or elsewhere depending on the person's wishes and the space available.

What qualifications must a friend have? A friend is there to provide emotional support, practical help and companionship and to lessen the fear and isolation of the person who is ill and their family. Trinity Home Hospice states some of their qualifications as follows: motivated to help without interfering; emotional maturity; tolerance for different social, cultural and religious beliefs; warmth, empathy, tact and discretion; flexibility; dependability; good listening skills; ability to work with others as a team member; different talents and skills (e.g., from past work experiences and hobbies); and a sense of humor (it is helpful not to take yourself too seriously). The key is to be there for the person and not to fulfil your own, unspoken needs--to provide unconditional support and compassion.

Trinity Home Hospice recommends that clients use the services offered through the Home Care Program and homemaking services where available. These services depend on the area you live in and may include: visits by nurses, physio/occupational therapists, social workers; homemaker help (e.g., to cook some meals, do dishes, do shopping and some light cleaning); and overnight nursing if available.

A logbook is a helpful communication tool when more than a few people are involved in providing support at home. In this log book volunteers, professional caregivers (family doctor, visiting nurses) and family members write notes about the likes and dislikes of the patient and other information that needs to be passed on to different people. The person who is ill often reads the comments and adds comments of her own. Some people who are ill like the idea of a logbook and others do not, so check before hand. The book should also include information about what to do in an emergency, the person's provincial health care number, next of kin, medications, name and number of the coordinator, and name and number of family physician. If for some reason the person needs to go to the hospital the logbook can provide up-to-date information. The book must be kept in a very visible and easy to find place in the house. There should be a checklist of what to do in emergencies and at the time of death and who to call first, second, etc.

People writing in the book should begin with their name, date, time, and length of visit. In point form, you might write the person's activity level (conscious, unconscious); communication ability (recognizing, understanding, speaking coherently or not); eating during the visit; any pain or symptoms; their emotional state or mood (restless, peaceful, worried about....), any activities you did together or discussions you think others would benefit hearing about. Family members can add their own notes about what they heard the doctor or nurse say during their visit. The logbook is also used to write questions that someone else can answer during a later visit as well as questions you want someone to ask the doctor or nurse during their next visit. There can also be questions or comments to people you know who will visit later such as, "Please make sure that Mom gets the herbal tea rather than the plain one." or "Please check the electric box to see if we need a new fuse for the kitchen," or "Please add the following items to the grocery list." You might also include a "guest book" portion of the book where guests write in inspirational, spiritual, or funny thoughts or memories of times spent together, etc.

The logbook has another purpose. Even if only a few people write in it, it serves as a 'history' of the last weeks and months of someone's life. It can provide a history of the person's medical condition in the last months for new caregivers, family members or visitors who come often in the last days or weeks. After the death, parts of the logbook can become a family treasure to help them remember events, people, kindness and compassion.

The logbook belongs to the patient and their family. Anyone may read it, so make your writing legible. Do not include confidential information or discussions that others do not need to see. If you include specifics of a conversation, ask the person for permission first.

Recognize that not everyone who wants to help the person will be accepted, for various reasons. If the person prefers not to have someone come to their home, the coordinator tells the person that the person's wishes are paramount and should not be taken personally. Some people do not "click" and that is all right. That person might still participate indirectly by cooking some meals, answering phones, etc.

Recognize those whenever a few people get together there are tensions, misunderstandings and mistakes. People are doing their best but may do little things that annoy each other. Recognize these stresses and discuss them with others on a one-to-one basis or at general meetings if the problem goes beyond a few people. An example is people who enter the person's home without taking off their shoes. This custom is perfectly acceptable in most people's homes but unacceptable in other homes. Knowing these little things help make the experience more positive for everyone. The key is to remember that you are visiting someone's home where they are used to certain routines and behaviors. It is quite different from visiting that person in a hospital where their routines must blend in with the hospital's routines. You are a guest in the home.

It is sometimes difficult to draw the line between giving support and making decisions for the person. We all have opinions and feelings about what a "dignified death" is. Some people believe that people should be at home, classical music playing in the background, quilt on the bed, a dog or cat nearby, fresh flowers everywhere and the family and closest friends at the bedside. Other people prefer to go into hospital near the end of their lives to receive all the technological and emotional supports that round-the-clock hospital care can provide. Some people want to be alone while others want to have many people nearby. Regardless of your views and wishes, you must, as a friend, follow the wishes of the person as best you can. If you strongly disagree with a decision the person has made (on ethical or personal grounds) try to get another friend to be with the person. Call the coordinator to make different arrangements so that you do not have do to something against your strongly held beliefs. At the same time, the person does not have to give up control over their life to make you happy. This line between providing support and making decisions should be discussed at most general meetings to help remind people of this gentle, yet vital, balance.

If the person is ill for a long time there will be friends who come and go because of other commitments. When new people come it is difficult at first for them to fit into what has probably become a tightly knit group. For the person who may be more ill than when the team began, it is one more person coming into their life and home. Recognize some of the difficulties and provide extra support to both the person and new visitor.

Friends hear confidential information from the person who is ill and their family members. All this information is confidential and must not be repeated to anyone without permission. This includes one's own family and curious neighbors. The smaller one's community, the harder it is to keep information confidential. Confidentiality is a useful topic to discuss at a group meeting to ensure the patient's privacy.

Use the talents you have rather than try to learn many new ones. Find people who have the skills and interests you miss so that you can concentrate on giving your talents to the person. For example, you may enjoy reading and writing and can help the person with their mail or read a book with them. Someone else may help without being with the person who is ill. They may enjoy cooking, cleaning, gardening, walking the dog, or running errands without having to spend time with the person. Other people may enjoy helping the person eat their food, doing arts and crafts together, or doing bookkeeping, financial or legal work together (or alone). Still others may enjoy helping the person bathe or go to the bathroom. "Being there" is also a wonderful gift. Sometimes people don't want to talk, listen or do things. They want to rest, think, pray or daydream. Being there means that you do not interrupt but give the privacy or companionship the person wants.

If you are interested in this kind of friendship you may want to read some of the books or articles in the field of palliative care (see Reference section), attend some volunteer training workshops and talk to other people. Active participation is the best teacher but other ways of learning can also help you.

People who have a cold, flu or infection should not visit the person until they feel better themselves. You do not want to pass on an illness to the person.

At the first meeting of a Trinity Home Hospice Care Team, several key points are highlighted for team members, including:

- Remember that your purpose is to meet the needs of the person who is ill—not your own needs.

- It is important to remember that the person who is ill needs to be able to give as well as receive.

- Continuity of care is very important in functioning teams. We need to act as a team, not a group of individuals. To lessen the disruption to the person who is ill and their household, the delivery and standard of care should be as even as possible. We can bring our individuality to the team while acting as a single unit.

- If in your professional life you are a nurse or health care provider, you need to be aware that in this volunteer situation you have a different role to play. Your skills (personal and professional) are an asset to the team but they need to be complimentary to your role as a volunteer.

- A care team requires committed and responsible team members to make it work.

  - Incorporate this into your life and give it priority in a way that fits in with your other priorities, e.g., family and work.

  - When you make a commitment, stick to it.

  - Know your capabilities and respect your limits.

  - Use others on the team for support.

  - Confidentiality is critical.

- Respect the person's home. It is not just a place of caregiving but their home. This experience is disruptive enough without turning their home into a hospital.

- The coordinator of a team is the focal point for a smooth running team. They act as the center point for information from the person who is ill and all the care providers. This person is the key contact to relieve the burden from the person who is ill and their immediate family. If the team needs to know something quickly, the person only needs to call the coordinator. Team members needing help or advice can look to the team coordinator for this support.

- Care team member roles may include:

  - Remind the person to take their medication.

  - Assist with meals.

  - Be a good listener (non-judgmental and patient).

  - Understand the difference between being a friend versus a caregiver—as a friend you may challenge your friend about specific issues or concerns; as a caregiver you need to be there as a helper and supporter.

  - Help to keep the household running smoothly.

  - Help with taking care of young children.

  - Help with running errands.

  - Take the person to appointments.

  - Respect the privacy of, and give support to, the primary caregiver.

  - Make sure the person is safe.

  - Provide care and comfort.

- In the event that you need emergency support while you are on your shift, a list of telephone numbers are supplied to each team member (see the logbook). Remember that you are not alone. You are part of a team; help and support are often just a phone call away.

- To minimize caregiver stress:

  - Be realistic about your time commitments.

  - Use the logbook, phone contacts and attendance at meetings to feel supported and improve communication.

  - Attend training programs in your community that may help now and in the future.

  - Discuss and deal with your own difficult issues, such as coping with your anticipatory grief, examining past issues in your relationship with the person who is ill, dealing with anger or answering ethical questions.

- Be mindful of basic infection control to protect the person who is ill and yourself. Wash your hands thoroughly. Do not visit when you have a contagious flu, cold or other illness. The person's immune system makes them more prone to infection than you are.

- It is important to keep your commitment to do a shift. Arriving 10 minutes early will enable you to overlap with the previous caregiver. Try to stay 10 minutes longer at the end of your visit. If you need to change your shift, arrange a swap with another team member. Once the swap is arranged, call and have it noted in the logbook at the person's home. Make sure the person and the team coordinator know about the swap. If you cannot arrange a swap, contact the team coordinator for help.

- Unplanned visits, drop-ins and frequent phone calls can make the home environment seem very chaotic. Energy conservation is an important consideration when someone is seriously ill. If the situation at the home becomes too hectic, suggest scheduling visits from family and friends and encourage people to have shorter visits when necessary.

- Consider specific training in areas where you feel less comfortable. This is especially helpful when assisting someone to move about, transferring them from their bed to a chair, or with personal care. Your local home or hospice care organization can give you information on training opportunities.

Spending time with someone who has a terminal or life-threatening illness is very rewarding and very traumatic. Friends must take care of themselves and each other as much as they try to help the client. People need to talk about their experiences. People need time to think about what they are experiencing. Take the time and make the efforts. Having helped my parents and my grandfather live at home until their deaths are some of my richest experiences. I learned so much about them and so much about myself. I took the time to try to understand what I was thinking and feeling. There were many happy moments and many sad ones. The wealth of that experience will sustain me for the rest of my life. Enjoy the learning. Enjoy the giving. Enjoy the receiving.

For more information on palliative care support teams write or call Trinity Home Hospice: 25 King Street West, Commerce Court North, Suite 1102, Box 324, Commerce Court Postal Station, Toronto, Ontario, M5L 1G3. (416) 364-1666. Their web site: www.interlog.com/~thh

If you want to offer support to people who may, or may not, have a terminal or life-threatening illness you can check your phone book to see if you have a local Citizen Advocacy organization in your area.

According to Cecile Lynes, Coordinator of Toronto Citizen Advocacy, "citizen advocates are ordinary community people who are recruited specifically for a person we know who is isolated, marginalized and vulnerable for any number of reasons. Citizen advocates learn by listening to the stories of their vulnerable friends, by walking in their shoes, by experiencing for a time what life is like where their friends live or work or spend time.

"Sometimes, in Citizen Advocacy, an advocate brings a group of people together [similar to Trinity Home Hospice's support circles but not limited to people who are dying] around an individual who has a disability, and together they decide what needs to be done. Some groups or 'circles' as they are sometimes called, are very focused around a specific goal such as getting a person out of an institution or working to include a child in his or her neighborhood school in a regular classroom, or helping a person to find a job.

"People within the group may have different responsibilities which they undertake at particular times. The idea of 'circles' extends beyond people with disabilities. It may have evolved from simpler times when a neighbor could be counted on to look after your children when you needed a break or got sick, or when you talked to friends about a possible career change. Some people are still able to draw on personal, informal supports. Others may choose to use a professional service for such support, while others may be forced through lack of options into the service world. If people can draw on their own natural supports, they may be able to stay out of the service world and thus maintain control over their lives."

For more information about Citizen Advocacy you may contact this author.

Chapter 20   Using Your Experience to Become A Neighborhood Resource

At some point after you have cared for someone with a terminal or life-threatening illness, you might think about how you can help other people going through the same thing. There are several options:

Volunteer with a local hospice or hospital group that provides free help to patients at home, in hospital, in a freestanding hospice, in a long-term care facility or other institutions.

Become a neighborhood resource in caring for people at home. Use books such as this one and *Caring for Loved Ones at Home*, to provide your neighbors, families and friends with contact sheets of telephone numbers of local service providers. Encourage them to prepare for an upcoming illness or death by taking a home nursing course or similar program. Help them set up a neighborhood support team, if needed, for the person who is ill.

Your example helps neighbors and their families feel less intimidated by all the medical, social service and bureaucratic goings on that happen when someone is ill. The more educated you become the more your own family, friends and neighbors benefit. Knowing how to provide physical, emotional, spiritual and information support to people who have a terminal or life-threatening illness and their families is an invaluable gift you give to those around you.

As a neighborhood resource you are not trying to replace doctors, nurses, social workers, pharmacists or your community spiritual leaders. You are helping people work together to provide the best possible care in a specific situation.

Any and all of these activities help humanize dying within our communities. We help take away the emphasis that dying is as a medical failure to be dealt with in acute care hospitals. We return the emphasis to the hospice philosophy of care no matter where the care is provided. We re-introduce children and adolescents to the natural caring of their family, friends and neighbors. Everyone benefits from your leadership.

The skills you have developed together with information you will continue to learn can provide your neighbors, family and friends with the information and support they need regardless of the homecare situation. For example, your information can help women just home from the hospital with their new baby. You can help people recovering from surgery. You can provide ideas to someone caring for a loved one with a chronic illness. Just offering to be a sounding board for questions can help you and your neighborhood develop even more into the kind of community you want to live in.

Glossary

Never be afraid to ask a medical caregiver for the definition of a term. They learned what the word meant when they studied so they can easily explain it to you too.

The following list includes medical and legal definitions, descriptions of various medical specialists, and common abbreviations used on medical charts and prescriptions. For a complete definition use a more extensive standard medical or legal dictionary.

abnormal Something is not considered 'normal'. For example, a temperature is abnormal if it below or above the typical level.

abscess A sac of pus formed by the breakdown of infected or inflamed tissue.

a.c. abbrev. = before meals.

acupressure A method of pain relief using finger pressure on the same points used in acupuncture.

acupuncture Chinese medical practice of inserting needles through the skin in specific points to restore the balance of a body's energy flow.

acute Condition with symptoms that develop quickly, are severe, but do not last long. Opposite to chronic condition.

acute care facility Hospitals and medical centers where patients come for relatively quick care for sudden illness, surgery, testing or treatment. Opposite is chronic or long-term care or hospice facilities.

addiction Uncontrollable craving for a substance with an increasing tolerance and physical dependence on it.

adjuvant treatment An added treatment to what is already being done.

advance directives One of two types of legal documents that either give specific instructions or name a substitute decision maker. They may describe what medical treatments a person does, or does not, want under certain circumstances.

adverse effect Negative side effects of a treatment or medication.

allergist A doctor who also specializes in the treatment of allergies.

allergy A reaction substances that may cause a rash, swelling or more serious physical response.

alopecia Temporary or permanent loss of hair (may occur as a side effect of chemotherapy).

ambulatory The ability of someone to walk. Ambulatory centers refer to health care facilities where people go for part of a day for treatment.

amyotrophic lateral sclerosis (ALS) A deterioration of the spinal cord that results in the wasting away of muscles. Also called Lou Gerhig's Disease.

analgesic A pain-relieving drug.

anaphylaxis An exaggerated, often serious, allergic reaction to proteins and other substances.

anemia A decrease in red blood cells or in the hemoglobin content of the red corpuscles. The normal count is 4.0 to 6.0 x1012.

anesthesia Total or partial loss of sensation from an injection, ingestion or inhalation of a drug. General anesthetics put a patient to sleep for a short time. Local anesthetics numb an area of your body without putting you to sleep (e.g., dentist's anesthetic for a tooth filling).

anesthesiologist A doctor specializing in providing an anesthetic during surgery and monitoring the patient's vital signs.

aneurysm A swollen or distended area in a blood vessel wall.

angina The pain that results from not enough blood going to the heart.

angiogram X-ray studies in which a dye is injected into the bloodstream to detect abnormalities in blood vessels, tissues and organs.

anorexia The loss of appetite experienced by most people near the end of their lives.

antacid A substance that neutralizes acid.

antibiotic Drugs that check the growth of bacteria but do not work against viruses.

antibody A substance produced in our bodies to fight against bacteria.

anticonvulsant A medication used to prevent seizures.

antitussive A drug used to relieve coughing.

apnea Extended periods when breathing stops during sleep.

apoplexy (See stroke)

arrhythmia An abnormal heartbeat.

aspiration Fluid that gets into the lungs.

asthma A tightening of the air passages that leads to wheezing and difficult breathing.

assets All of a person's properties, including real estate, cash, stocks and bonds, art, furniture etc., and claims against other people (e.g., loans).

asymptomatic Someone without any symptoms.

atrophy A wasting or withering away of part of the body.

autopsy An examination of a dead body to determine the cause of death; the post-mortem ordered by the coroner or medical examiner.

barbiturate A type of sleeping pill.

barium enema Radiopaque barium (visible by x-ray) is put into the lower bowel (colon) and rectum by an enema for an x-ray. Also called a Lower GI Series.

bedsore A sore that develops when pressure causes inadequate blood circulation to the skin. For persons confined to bed, good skin care, repositioning, cushioning and some limited activity are the best treatment. Also called decubitus ulcers.

beneficiary Person who receives a benefit from a will, insurance policy or trust fund.

benign Non-malignant self-limiting condition that is not life threatening.

b.i.d. abbrev. = twice a day.

biopsy An examination of body tissue with a microscope to help in diagnosis. Tissue is removed from the body by surgery, insertion of a needle into tissue and other methods.

blood gas test A blood test to determine the level of oxygen and carbon dioxide in the blood.

bolus An amount given all at once.

bone marrow test A needle is inserted into a bone (hipbone or breastbone) to remove a sample of bone marrow for diagnostic purposes e.g., to diagnose leukemia, aplastic anemia.

brain scan Also called carotid angiogram. A radioactive substance is injected into a neck artery for a brain x-ray using a scanning camera.

CAT (or CT) Scan A computerized axial tomography scan. X-rays of the body or head are taken using a computer to give a slice-by-slice view of the area.

CCU (Coronary Care Unit) Unit in a hospital which provides intensive care to heart patients.

cancer A malignant tumor that tends to invade healthy tissue and spread to new sites.

candidiasis A fungal infection known as 'thrush' in one's mouth, throat, esophagus or other dark, moist areas (e.g., vagina).

carbohydrates Best source of energy for your body. Found in most foods but especially sugars and starches. If you eat too much, however, your body changes and stores them as fats.

carcinogenic Something that can cause cancer.

cardiac Refers to the heart.

cardiac surgeon Doctors specializing in heart surgery.

cardiologist Doctor specializing in the diagnosis and treatment of heart conditions.

cardiovascular surgeon Doctor specializing in surgery of blood vessels of the heart.

caregivers include professional health care providers and volunteers. Primary caregiver is usually a family member or close friend who provides most of the physical care for a person at home (e.g., wife, husband, lover, best friend).

catheter A plastic or rubber tube that puts in or takes out fluids from your body. A common example is a bladder catheter (Foley) to allow urine to leave the bladder freely.

c.c. abbrev. = cubic centimeter; also can mean with meals or food.

cerebral palsy Impaired muscular power and coordination from failure of nerve cells in the brain.

chemotherapy Drug therapy against infection or cancer that can destroy bacteria or dangerous cells.

Cheyne-Stoking A pattern of breathing where the respiration rates increase and then decrease followed by increasing periods of not breathing.

chiropractor Doctors without a medical degree specializing in manipulation of the spine; cannot prescribe medication or perform surgery.

chronic A prolonged or lingering condition.

clinical nurse specialist (CNS) A registered nurse with a Master's Degree in Nursing who specializes in one aspect of health care and is involved in research and teaching.

codicil An appendix or supplement to a will (e.g., to change the name of your beneficiary).

colostomy A surgical opening from the body surface (usually through the abdomen) into the colon which acts as an artificial anus. Colostomy bags collect the body's waste. Depending on a patient's condition a colostomy may be temporary or permanent.

coma A deep, prolonged unconsciousness.

competence Legal competence to make decisions for one's self is difficult to determine because incompetence may not be permanent and definitions of legal competence depends on where one lives.

complementary therapies Includes therapies like: acupuncture, aroma therapy, art, autosuggestion, biofeedback, chiropractic, herbal, homeopathy, music, naturopathy, osteopathy and therapeutic touch.

congenital Something present since birth.

COLD Chronic Obstructive Lung Disease. (see COPD)

conjunctivitis A redness and irritation of the thin membrane that covers the eye.

COPD Chronic Obstructive Pulmonary Disease. Includes illnesses like emphysema. Also called COLD for chronic obstructive lung disease.

coronary Refers to the blood vessels that supply the heart.

CPR Cardiopulmonary resuscitation is used on patients who are not breathing and have no pulse. Trained professionals or volunteers use artificial respiration (mouth-to-mouth breathing) and manually pump the patient's heart by compressing the chest with their hands to simulate a regular pulse.

culture A test for infection or organisms that could cause infection.

CVA Cerebrovascular accident. Also called a stroke.

cystoscopy A long flexible tube, attached to a miniature camera, is passed through the urinary tract into the bladder.

d. abbrev. = give.

dd. in d abbrev. = from day to day.

dec abbrev. = pour off.

decubitus ulcer (see bed sore)

dehydrated Lack of moisture in the body.

dementia Deterioration of a person's mental capacity from changes in the brain.

depressant A drug to reduce mental or physical activity.

dermatologist Doctor specializing in skin conditions.

diagnosis (dx) An analysis of someone's physical and/or mental condition.

diastolic The lower number in the blood pressure reading. Refers to the resting phase of a heartbeat.

dil abbrev. = dilute.

disp. abbrev. = dispense.

diuretic A drug to increase urine output, relieving edema or swelling.

do not resuscitate (DNR) A written order that the doctor makes, usually with the patient-family's consent, not to resuscitate the person if they have a cardiac or respiratory arrest. This is usually written near the end of someone's life so that no CPR or treatments are done to prolong the person's life.

doctor Common title for a doctor.

doppler Sound waves. Also the name for a test that can detect a deep vein thrombosis (DVT).

dos abbrev. = dose

draw sheet A folded bed sheet placed sideways on the bed under a patient. Two people on either side of the bed can then lift the draw sheet and the patient to move them up or down in bed or to help them turn the person onto their side or back.

dur dolor abbrev. = while pain lasts.

dx abbrev. = diagnosis.

dysphagia Difficulty in swallowing

dysplasia Abnormal cells.

dyspnea Shortness of breat

ECG See EKG.

echocardiogram Sound wave test of the heart.

EKG (Electrocardiogram) A record of the electrical current produced by the heart. Diagnoses abnormal cardiac rhythm and damage to the muscle of the heart. Also ECG.

EEG (Electroencephalogram) A record of the electrical current produced by the brain.

edema Excess collection of fluid in the tissues.

electrolyte imbalance When salts or chemicals in the blood are not balanced correctly.

embolism Blockage of a blood artery by a clot. In the brain it can cause a stroke.

EMG (Electromyography) Test to evaluate the electrical activity of nerves and muscles.

emesis vomiting.

emp abbrev. = as directed.

empiric Based on experience.

emphysema A condition of the lungs with labored breathing and increased risk of infection. The lungs lose their elasticity and function.

endocrinologist A specialist in diagnosing and treating disorders of the endocrine glands (glands affecting hormones) and their secretions.

endoscopic exam Using a thin, lighted tube to examine an internal part of the body.

enema A fluid injected into the rectum to clean out the bowel or to give drugs.

enteral Something given by way of the intestines.

epidural anesthesia Medication given through a thin tube into your spine. Common in woman having babies as it allows the mother to be alert with pain relief.

estate All of one's assets and liabilities, especially those left by a deceased.

executor The person named in a will to dispose of the assets and pay, from estate funds, the liabilities of a deceased.

executrix The female noun for executor.

family Includes people who are part of one's immediate family and those we define as members of our family through friendship and love. In legal terms, each province and state has different definitions that may restrict family members to biologically related members.

family practitioner Doctor who diagnoses and treats the general illnesses and problems of patients and refers them to a specialist when necessary.

febris Latin for fever.

fibrillation Irregular heart beat or an involuntary muscle contraction.

gastroenterologist Doctor specializing in the digestive system: esophagus, stomach and bowels.

geneticist Specialist in genetic diseases -- hereditary disorders and abnormalities.

geriatrician (gerontologist) Specialist in the diagnoses and treatment of illnesses in older people.

GI (Gastrointestinal) Series An x-ray examination of the esophagus, stomach, colon and rectum.

GI Series--Lower (See Barium Enema)

gm. abbrev. = grams.

gr. abbrev. = grains.

gtt. abbrev. = drops.

h abbrev. = hour.

hallucination The feeling of seeing or hearing something that is not there.

hematologist Doctor specializing in conditions of the blood.

hematoma Swelling caused by bleeding into tissues as in a bruise.

hemiplegia One-sided paralysis of the body, usually from a stroke. A right-sided paralysis indicates left-sided brain damage.

hemoglobin The protein in red blood cells that carry oxygen to the body tissues. The normal count is 12-18 g/dL.

hemorrhage Extensive abnormal bleeding.

heparin lock A needle is placed in the arm with blood thinner to keep the blood from clotting inside the needle or tubing.

hepatoma Cancer or tumor of the liver.

hereditary Something inherited from parents.

high blood pressure (See Hypertension)

hodgkin's disease A form of lymphoid cancer that has high fever, enlarged lymph nodes and spleen, liver and kidneys and a dangerously lowered resistance to infection.

hormone A glandular excretion into the blood that stimulates another organ.

hospice (see palliative care) Also name for a free-standing institution where palliative care is given to people with a terminal illness. Programs often have major home care component and may also be part of an established institution such as a hospital.

h.s. abbrev. = at bedtime, before retiring. From the Latin hora somni.

huntington's chorea A hereditary condition with symptoms of uncontrolled movements and progressive mental disorder.

hypercalcemia/hypocalcemia Too high (more than 10.5 mg/dL), or too low (less than 8.8 mg/dL), calcium level in the blood.

hyperkalemia/hypokalemia Too high (more than 5.0 mEq/L), or too low(less than 3.8 mEq/L), potassium level in the blood.

hypernatremia/hyopnatremia Too high(more than 145 mEq/L), or too low(less than 136 mEq/L), sodium (salt) level in the blood.

hypertension High blood pressure The systolic number is usually above 140mmHg and the diastolic number is usually above 90 mmHg. Can lead to a stroke, heart failure or other serious condition if not treated. The pressure measures the force of the blood expelled from the heart against the walls of the blood vessels.

hypnotic A drug used to induce sleep.

hypnotism A treatment that puts a patient into a sleep-like trance to enhance memory or make the person susceptible to suggestion. Can be used in pain relief and to eliminate some negative habits.

hypotension Low arterial blood pressure.

hypoxia Low oxygen level in the blood.

I&O abbrev. = intake and output refers to fluids into and out of body.

iatrogenic disease A condition caused by a doctor or a hospital stay.

ICU Intensive Care Unit Unit within a hospital where seriously ill or postoperative patients receive intensive care.

incontinence Lack of bladder or rectal control.

in d abbrev. = daily. From the Latin in dies.

idiopathic Unknown cause.

infarct Death of tissue because of lack of blood supply.

infarction Blockage of a blood vessel especially the artery leading to the heart.

infection Inflammation or disease caused when bacteria, viruses and other micro-organisms invade the body.

infectious disease Disease which is passed from one person to another person.

inflammation Swelling or irritation of tissue.

insomnia An inability to sleep.

intern A recent medical school graduate undergoing supervised practical training.

internist Doctor who specializes in the nonsurgical treatment of the internal organs of the body.

intramuscular Something (e.g., medication) given into a muscle.

IV abbrev. = intravenous in which a needle is kept within a vein for the injection of medication or blood.

intraperitoneal Into the abdominal cavity.

intubate Putting a tube into a person's airway to help them breathe.

invasive procedure Anything that punctures, opens or cuts the skin.

laxative A drug that causes bowel movements.

lethargy Sleepiness.

leukemia Cancer of white blood cells in which these cells reproduce abnormally.

liabilities Debts owed to others such as a loan, mortgage, utility bills, credit card payments, etc.

life-sustaining procedures. These may include artificial means of keeping someone hydrated and fed, CPR, blood transfusions and mechanical ventilation.

life-threatening illness Any condition or disease that can lead to sudden or quicker-than-expected death.

lipid Fat.

living will A form of advance directives that lists what life-sustaining treatments the person does, or does not, want in situations listed in the document.

lumbar puncture A diagnostic procedure in which a hollow needle is inserted between two lumbar vertebrae in the spinal cord to remove some spinal fluid.

lymph glands Nodes of tissue that provide a system of protection against bacteria and other attacks against the body's immune system.

m et n abbrev. = morning and night.

malaise A vague feeling of discomfort; feeling bad.

malignant Progressive or terminal condition.

malnutrition Insufficient consumption of essential food elements whether by improper diet or illness.

mammography An x-ray of the breasts to detect tumors.

meningitis Inflammation of the membranes covering and protecting the brain and spinal cord.

metastasis The spreading of an infection or cancer from the original area to others in the body.

mg. abbrev. = milligrams.

MI abbrev. = myocardial infarction; a heart attack.

mor dict abbrev. = in the manner directed.

morbidity Serious disease; an undesired result or complication.

mortality Death or death rate.

mobility The ability to move.

MRI abbrev. = magnetic resonance imaging; a picture of the body that uses magnetic energy rather than x-ray energy.

multiple sclerosis A degenerative disease of the central nervous system where parts of the brain and spinal cord harden.

muscular dystrophy A degenerative muscle disease in which muscles waste away.

myalgia Muscle aches.

nasogastric tube A tube from the nose to the stomach to give nutrition and medication.

neoplasm A tumor or a new growth of abnormal tissue where cells multiply. (See cancer).

nephrologist Doctor specializing in kidney conditions.

neurologist Doctor specializing in the nervous system.

neurosurgeon Doctor specializing in surgery of the nervous system.

non rep abbrev. = do not repeat.

nosocomial pneumonia Pneumonia acquired in the hospital.

notarize A notary public authenticates or attests to the truth of a document (e.g., attests that a document was signed by a particular person).

notary public A public officer (can be a lawyer) who certifies documents, takes affidavits and administers oaths.

nurse practitioner Registered Nurse who has received additional training in order to perform more specialized care than other nurses.

o abbrev. = none.

obstetrician/gynecologist Doctor specializing in conditions of the female reproductive system. Obstetricians specialize in pregnancies and births.

occlusion Closing or an obstruction.

oncology The study of tumors or cancer.

oncologist Doctor specializing in tumors and cancer.

ophthalmologist Doctor who specializes in diseases of the eye.

opioids These drugs come from opium. They are generally used to relive severe pain. Heroin, methadone and morphine all come from the opium plant.

optician Non-doctor trained in filling prescriptions for eyeglasses and contact lenses.

optometrist Non-doctor trained to measure vision and make eyeglasses and contact lenses.

orthopedist Doctor specializing in bones.

osteopathy Diagnosis and treatment of disorders by manipulative therapy, drugs, surgery, proper diet and psychotherapy.

osteoporosis The bones become weaker because of a loss of calcium.

otolaryngologist A specialist in conditions of the ear, throat and nose.

palliative care Treatment to relieve symptoms, rather than cure, a disease or condition. Includes meeting the physical, emotional, spiritual and information needs of patients. Also called hospice care.

paracentesis Fluid drainage by inserting a tube into the body.

parenteral Administration of medication or nutrition into the body by injections.

parkinson's disease A progressive nervous disease. Symptoms are muscular tremor, slowing of movement, partial facial paralysis and impaired motor control.

pathogenesis The initial cause of a disease.

pathologist Doctor who examines tissue and bone to diagnose if there is a malignancy. They also perform autopsies.

pathology The scientific study of disease.

patient Someone who receives treatment. Sometimes called client, consumer or customer.

pc abbrev. = after meals.

pediatrician Doctor specializing in the care of children.

per os (po) abbrev. = by mouth.

percutaneous Through the skin.

pH test Determines the degree of acidity or alkalinity in the urine.

pharmacokinetics Study of how the body absorbs, distributes and gets rids of a drug.

phlebitis Irritation or inflammation of a vein.

physiatrist Doctor specializing in rehabilitative therapy after illness or injury.

physician A medical doctor as opposed to doctors with a Ph.D.

placebo A substance containing no medication. It can help a patient who believes that it will work. A practical and effective treatment for some people.

plasma The liquid part of blood (55% of total volume).

plastic surgeon Doctor specializing in reconstructive and cosmetic surgery.

platelets Small particles in the blood that help with blood clotting.

pneumonia An acute or chronic disease which inflames the lungs and fills them with fluid.

p.o. abbrev. = by mouth. From the Latin per os.

podiatrist Non-doctor who specializes in the care, treatment and surgery of feet.

powers of attorney There are two main types of legal powers of attorney documents that a person signs to delegate legal decision making to one or two people of their choice. The first gives someone financial and legal decision-making power from the time the document is signed until the document is revoked by the patient, and the second gives all health care related decisions away only if the patient cannot speak for themselves at the time. It is advisable to separate the two types of documents so that one person is not responsible for all decisions and not in a conflict of interest.

primary caregiver (See caregiver).

prn abbrev. = give as needed, as often as necessary.

proctologist Doctor specializing in diagnoses and treatment of disorders and diseases of the anus, colon and rectum.

prognosis (Px) A prediction of the future course of a condition or illness based on scientific study. It is only a prediction and should not be accepted as fact.

prophylaxis A drug given to prevent disease or infection.

prosthesis An artificial substitute for a part of the body such as an arm or leg.

protocol A plan of study.

psychiatrist Doctor who specializes in the diagnosis and treatment of emotional and medical disorders.

psychologist A professional with a Ph.D. in psychology who diagnoses and treats psychological disorders. They may not prescribe medication.

pt abbrev. = patient.

pulmonary Refers to the lungs.

px abbrev. = prognosis.

q abbrev. = every.

q.d. abbrev. = every day; daily.

q.h. abbrev. = every hour. From the Latin quaque hora.

q.i.d. abbrev. = four times a day. From the Latin quater in die.

qn abbrev. = every night. From the Latin quaque nox.

qod abbrev. = every other day.

qs abbrev. = proper amount, quantity sufficient.

quack Opportunist who uses questionable or worthless methods or devices in diagnosing and treating various diseases.

ql abbrev. = as much as desired. From the Latin quantum libet.

radiation therapy X-ray or cobalt treatment.

radiologist Doctor who interprets X-rays. Sub-specialties include nuclear medicine and angiography.

radiology A branch of science using radiant energy, as in x-rays, especially in the diagnosis and treatment of disease.

recombinant New combinations of genes.

refractory Not responding to treatment.

regimen A program or set of rules to follow for treatment of a condition.

relapse The return or reappearance of a disease.

remission Disappearance of evidence of cancer or other diseases.

renal Refers to the kidneys.

rep abbrev. = repeat.

resect Remove or cut out surgically.

resident Doctor receiving specialized clinical training.

respirologist Specialist who diagnoses and treats diseases of the lungs and respiratory (breathing) system.

respite care Time away for rest. This might mean that a family caregiver goes away for a few days or that the person who is ill goes to a hospice program.

rheumatologist Specialist who diagnoses and treats rheumatic diseases that cause by inflammation or pain in the joints and muscles.

rx abbrev. = prescription or therapy.

satiety (early) Feeling full or bloated quickly after eating very little food.

sedative A medication to calm a person or make them less anxious.

senility Loss of mental ability and memory (especially of recent events).

shiatsu (See acupressure).

shock Sudden, acute failure of the body's circulatory function.

sig abbrev. = write, let it be imprinted.

somnolence Sleepiness.

spinal tap (See lumbar puncture).

standard of care A treatment plan which the majority of health care providers accept as appropriate.

stat abbrev. = right away. From the Latin statim.

stomatitis Mouth sores or inflammation of the mouth.

stroke Sudden loss of muscular control, sensation and consciousness caused by the rupture or blocking of a blood vessel in the brain.

subclavian Under the collarbone.

subcutaneous Often refers to medication placed under the skin by a needle.

sublingual Often refers to medication placed under the tongue.

substitute decision maker This person is chosen by a patient in an advance directive document to make decisions about health care and treatment when a patient cannot speak for themselves.

supine Lying on the back.

supportive care General medical care that treats symptoms; not intended to improve or cure the underlying disease or condition. Sometimes called palliative care although not limited to people with a terminal or life-threatening illness.

suppository A medication given in solid form and inserted into the rectum or vagina. Dissolves into a liquid by body heat.

surgeon Doctor who treats a disease by surgery. Surgeons generally specialize in one or more types of surgery.

symptom An indication of a certain condition or disease.

symptomatic Having symptoms.

syndrome A group of symptoms that indicate a specific disease or condition.

systolic Top number in blood pressure; refers to the contraction phase of a heart beat.

TENS Trans-cutaneous electrical nerve stimulation. A device that provides mild amounts of electrical stimulus to different parts of the body as a way to reduce pain.

temperature Normal oral temperature is 97-99° Fahrenheit or 36-37.2° Celsius. Changes +/- one degree during the day.

terminal illness Often classified as any illness that will lead to death soon.

The length of time used is often between 3-12 months.

thoracic surgeon Doctor who specializes in chest surgery.

thrombosis Blood clotting within blood vessels.

t.i.d. abbrev. = three times a day. From the Latin tres in die.

titration Gradual change in drug dose to determine the best effect or dose of a drug.

tolerance Drug tolerance is when there is increased resistance to the usual effect of a drug as a result of long-term use.

topical On the skin or surface.

toxicity Side effects or undesirable effects of a drug.

toxin A poison or harmful agent.

transdermal Through the skin.

trauma An injury or wound.

tumor (See Neoplasm).

tx abbrev. = treatment.

ultrasound scan A picture of internal organs using high frequency sound waves.

urologist Doctors specializing in urinary tract and male prostate gland diseases plus male sexual dysfunction. ut dict abbrev. = as directed.

vascular surgeon Doctor specializing in blood vessel surgery.

venipuncture Going into a vein with a needle.

vital signs Measurement of temperature, pulse, respiration rate and blood pressure.

vomiting A reflex action that contracts the stomach and ejects the contents through the mouth.

x-ray Electromagnetic radiation used to create pictures of the body's internal structures.

x-ray dye A substance injected into a vein before an X-ray to highlight an area for examination. May cause an allergic reaction.

WBC White blood cells that fight infection. The normal count is 5,000 to 10,000.

Add your own definitions, descriptions and abbreviations here for future reference.

265

References

*The following is a selection of recommended books. Some were used to research and prepare this book. They certainly do not include all the books available on the various subjects in this book. **My first recommendation is that you check your local bookstore and library for the most recent and up-to-date books on the topic you are most interested in.***

When checking any source for health care information, expect to find information that might be unsettling. The information may tell you things you didn't expect or didn't want to know and it may have been written for a professional audience rather than for patients and families.

Some of the books in this reference list may have more recent, up-dated editions. If a particular author interests you, check the library for their other books.

The companion book to this one, by the same author, is *Caring for Loved Ones at Home* published by the Resources Suporting Family and Community Legacies Inc. in 1999. It provides basic home nursing suggestions to family members, friends and neighbors caring for someone at home.

Most bookstores can order books directly if they do not have a book in stock. Ms. Geri Leonard, owner of **Books for Caregivers,** has the most extensive catalogue of books in the home and hospice care fields that I know of as well as books in the area of self-help, gerontology, grief and bereavement. You can order directly from her by telephone or Internet:

Books for Caregivers   (416) 463-4461   Fax = (416) 461-4171

Her web page allows you to search her catalogue for specific titles, authors and topics. **www.interlog.com/~geri.** You can e-mail her at **geri@interlog.com.**

The Childhood Cancer Foundation -- Candlelighters Canada probably has the most extensive list of resources available in Canada for children of all ages who are dying or bereaved. Families can order a catalogue by calling 1 (800) 363-1062 or visit their web site at **www.candlelighters.ca.** Their resources are designed for children, teenagers, parents, siblings, and grandparents.

There are books in this Reference section that fit into more than one category. Please look in several categories for the books that will help you.

General Interest Books

Although these books are recommended for the general public they are also useful for caregivers involved in the care and treatment of people with terminal illness and their families. As well books listed in the section recommended for professional caregivers or advanced readers may also be of interest to the general public.

Adams, David W. and Deveau, Eleanor J. (1988). *Coping with childhood cancer: Where do we go from here?* Hamilton, Ontario: Kinbridge Publications.

Berry, Carmen Rene. (1989). *When helping you is hurting me: Escaping the Messiah trap.* New York: Harper and Row. Provides fresh insights into the problems of neglecting one's personal needs in order to help others.

Bliss, Shepherd (Ed.). (1985). *The new holistic health handbook.* Lexington, Mass.: Stephen Greene Press. Overview of holistic health practices and health centers in the U.S. and Canada.

Brody, Jane E. (1997). *Jane Brody's The New York Times Book of Health.* New York: Time Books.

Buckman, Robert. (1992). *I don't know what to say: How to help and support someone who is dying.* Toronto: Key Porter. A book written specifically for the friends and family of a dying person.

Carroll, David. (1991). *Living with dying: A loving guide for family and close friends.* New York: McGraw-Hill Book Company. Question and answer format covering the emotional and physical needs of the patient, family and friends.

Dass, Ram and Gorman, Paul. (1987). *How can I help?: Stories and reflections on service.* New York: Alfred A. Knopf. Using stories and quotes to help identify ways for professional caregivers to help those receiving services.

Duda, Deborah. (1987). *Coming home: A guide to dying at home with dignity.* New York: Aurora Press.

Etue, Elizabeth with P. D. Chalmers. (1985). *Take charge of your health: A personal health record and reference.* Toronto: Summerhill Press Ltd. A pocket size personal health record

Hanson, Peter G. (1985). *The joy of stress.* Toronto: Hanson Stress Management Organization. Examines physical and mental causes and effects of stress and how to turn stress into a positive, energizing force.

Harris, Dan R. (1998). *Aging sourcebook.* Detroit: Omnigraphics. Examines social, medical, legal, financial, elder care, lifestyles and dying.

Inlander, Charles B. with Ed Weiner. (1997). *Take this book to the hospital with you.* Emmaus, Pennsylvania: St. Martin's Mass Market Press. People's Medical Society consumer guide for patients going into hospital. Critical of the medical profession, describes ways to take control of your own medical care.

Kaufman, Barry Neil. (1979). *Giant steps.* New York: Fawcett Crest. Through personal histories this book gives a back-to-basic form of therapy that encourages people to take control of their lives. One story deals with a teenager learning to deal with his mother's terminal illness.

-----. (1977). *To love is to be happy with.* New York: Fawcett Crest. Describes "Option Process" as a process of self-fulfilment based on the assumption that we have choices and can choose happiness rather than depression, anger and pain.

Kavanaugh, Robert E. (1972). *Facing death.* Los Angeles: Nash. Sensitive account of a personal and professional approach to facing death and meeting the emotional needs of someone who is dying.

Lamm, Maurice. (1969). *The Jewish way in death and mourning.* New York: Jonathan David Publishers. The Jewish traditions re: preparation of the body after death for the funeral and burial, the funeral service, the mourning observances including year-long observances, special situations and life after death.

Linn, Erin. (1986). *I know just how you feel...avoiding the cliches of grief.* Cary, Illinois: The Publishers Mark.

Little, Deborah Whiting. (1985). *Home care for the dying: An authoritative, reassuring guide to physical and emotional care.* New York: Doubleday.

Mitford, Jessica. (1998). *The American way to death.* New York: Simon and Schuster. Critical review of the funeral industry in the United States.

Moore, Thomas. (1994). *Soul mates: Honoring the mysteries of love and relationship.* New York: Harper Perennial.

Morgan, Ernest and Morgan, Jenifer (Ed.). (1994). *Dealing creatively with death: A manual of death education and simple burial.* Burnsville, NC: Celo Press. Review of death education, home care, bereavement, right-to-die issues, simple (Memorial) burials and an annotated bibliography.

Mount, Balfour M. (1983). *Sightings in the valley of the shadow: Reflections on dying.* Downers Grove, Ilinois: InterVarsity Press.

Noyes, Diane Doan with Mellody, Peggy. (1988). *Beauty and cancer.* Los Angeles: AC Books.

Nulan, Sherwin B. (1995). *How we die: Reflections on life's final chapter.* New York: Vintage Books.

Raphael, Simcha Paul. (1996). *Jewish view of the afterlife.* New York: Jason Aronson.

St. John Ambulance. *The Complete Handbook of Family Health Care.* Ottawa: St. John Priory of Canada, (Latest edition). Review of home care, medication, bed care, cleaning and treatments.

Sobel, David and Tom Ferguson. (1985). *The people's book of medical tests.* New York: Summit Books. Sobel states that 25-50% of the 10 billion medical tests performed every year in the U.S. are not medically necessary. Describes over 200 tests including why the test should be done, how to prepare, what to expect, what the risks are and what the results may mean.

Stedeford, Averil. (1994). *Facing death: Patients, families and professions.* London: Oxford Sobell Publications. Explores some of the issues facing those involved when a person faces death. Concise, well presented and easy to read.

General Interest Books for Advanced Readers

The resources listed below are more technical in nature and often written specifically for professional caregivers but may also be interesting for non-professionals.

Adler, Robert (Ed.). (1981). *Psychoneuroimmunology.* New York: Academic Press. A study of the role of emotions and stress to the immune system and its effects on infection resistance, allergies and cancer.

Ainsworth-Smith, Ian and Speck, Peter. (1982). *Letting go: Caring for the dying and bereaved.* London: SPCK. Explores the pastoral role of the caregivers, both professional and informal and their needs for support and care.

Armstrong, Karen. (1993). *A history of God: The 4,000-year quest of Judaism, Christianity and Islam.* New York: Ballantine Books.

Byock, Ira. (1998). *Dying well: Peace and possibilities at the end of life.* New York: Riverhead Books.

Callahan, Maggie and Kelly, Patricia. (1997). *Final gifts: Understanding the special awareness, needs and communication of the dying.* New York: Bantam. Uses patient scenarios and discussions as a learning tool.

Cassel, Eric J. (1982). "*The culture of suffering and the goals of medicine,*" *New England Journal of Medicine,* 306 (11): 639-645. An important article on the nature of suffering.

Chidwick, Paul. (1988). *Dying yet we live.* Toronto: Anglican Book Center. Our response to the spiritual needs of people who are dying.

Columbia University Press. *Foundation of Thanatology Series.* Includes such topics as psychological aspects of terminal care, anticipatory grief, bereavement, nurse as caregiver and others.

Corr, Charles A. and Balk, David E. (Eds.). (1996). *Handbook of adolescent death and bereavement*. New York: Springer Publishing.

Corr, Charles A. and Corr, Donna M. (Eds.). (1996) *Handbook of childhood death and bereavement*. New York: Springer Publishing.

Corr, Charles A.; Morgan, John D.; and Wass, Hannelore. (Eds.). (1993). *International work group on death, dying and bereavement: Statements on death, dying and bereavement*. London, Ontario: Self-published through King's College.

Corr, Charles A.; Nabe, Clyde M.; Corr, Donna M. (1996). *Death and dying: Life and living*. New York: Brooks/Cole Publishing.

Corr, Donna M. and Corr, Charles A. (Eds.). (1990) *Nursing care in an aging society*. New York: Springer Publishing.

DeSpelder, Lynne and Strickland, Albert Lee. (1996). *The last dance: Encountering death and dying*. (4th edition). Mountain View, California: Mayfield Publishing. Standard 'death, dying and bereavement' text book.

Doka, Kenneth J. and Morgan, John. (Eds.). (1993). *Death and spirituality*. Farmingdale, New York: Baywood Publishing.

Dossey, Larry. (1995). *Healing words: The power of prayer and the practice of medicine*. San Francisco: HarperSanFrancisco.

Dossey, Larry. (1989) *Recovering the soul: A scientific and spiritual approach*. New York: Bantam, Doubleday, Dell.

Droege, Thomas A. (1987). *Guided grief imagery: A resource for grief ministry and death education*. New York: Paulist Press.

Fairchild, Ray W. (1980). *Finding hope again: A pastor's guide to counseling the depressed*. New York: Harper and Row. A review of pastoral counseling that examines different types of depression, the meaning of hope, working with health professionals, various strategies and work with the bereaved.

Feifel, Herman (Ed.). (1959). *The meaning of death*. New York: McGraw-Hill. One of the earliest collections of academic essays on the subject of death. Feifel has been called the 'grandfather' of the modern hospice movement.

-----. (1977). *New meanings of death.* New York: McGraw-Hill. Updated version of his earlier collection of academic essays.

Feinstein D., Mayo P. (1990). *Rituals for living and dying from life's wounds to spiritual awakening.* San Francisco: Harper.

Garfield, Charles; Spring, Cindy; and Ober, Doris. (1997). *Sometimes my heart goes numb: Love and caregiving in a time of AIDS.* San Francisco: Jossey-Bass.

Gentles, Ian (Ed.). (1982). *Care for the dying and the bereaved.* Toronto: Anglican Book Center. Discusses palliative care and dying at home plus bereavement, children with terminal illness, anti-euthanasia and Christian dying.

Kalish, Richard A. (Ed.). (1980). *Death and dying: Views from many cultures.* New York: Baywood Publishing.

Latimer, Elizabeth J. (Ed.). (1996). *When a patient is dying: A colloquium on the care of the dying patient.* Toronto: Ontario Medical Association.

Marrone, Robert. (1997). *Death, mourning and caring.* London: Brooks/Cole. Covers most aspects of death and bereavement with over 1,100 references.

Mead, Frank S. revised by Hill, Samuel S. (1995). *Handbook of denominations in the United States (10th Edition).* Nashville, TN: Abingdon Press.

Omega International Journal for the Psychological Study of Dying, Bereavement, Suicide and other Lethal Behaviours. Westport, Connecticut: Greenwood Press, Inc. 51 Riverside Avenue, 06880.

Ontario Multifaith Council on Spiritual and Religious Care. (1995). *Multifaith information manual.* Toronto: Self-Published.

Platt, Nancy Van Dyke. (1980). *Pastoral care to the cancer patient.* Springfield, IL: Charles C. Thomas. Spiritual care for patients with a terminal illness.

Smith, W. J. (1988). *AIDS: Living and dying with hope: Issues in pastoral care.* New York: Paulist Press.

Stack, Stephen and Feifel, Herman (Eds.). (1997). *Death and the quest for meaning.* New York: Jason Aromson.

Stillion, Judith M. (1985). *Death and the sexes: An examination of the differential longevity, attitudes, behaviours and coping skills.* New York: Hemisphere Publishing Corporation. Sexism in death, sex differences in longevity, sex roles and death attitudes, bereavement and grief, death education & counseling.

Tallmer, Margot, Peter N. DeSanctis et. al. (1984). *Sexuality and life threatening illness.* Springfield, Illinois: Charles C. Thomas.

Turnbull, Richard (Ed.). (1986). *Terminal care.* Washington, DC: Hemisphere Publishing. Symptom control, bereavement, staff stress and education plus terminal care in rural areas.

Vachon, Mary L.S. (1987). *Occupational stresses in the care of the critically ill, the dying and the bereaved.* New York: Hemisphere.

Wass, Hannelore, C.A. Corr, R.A. Pacholski and C.M. Forfar. (1985). *Death education: An annotated resource guide, II.* Washington, DC: Hemisphere Publishing Corp. Primarily for teachers in death education but also for other caregivers, with an extensive lists of resources. Part of a series of guides in Death Education.

Weisman, Avery D. (1972). *On dying and denying: A psychiatric study of terminality.* New York: Behavioral Publishing. Describes the stages a person with a terminal illness.

Weisman, Avery D. (1974). *The realization of death: A guide for the psychological autopsy.* New York: Jason Aronson. Examines psychological autopsies and how they can provide information on why a death occurred at a particular time and what events before the death may be related to it.

Weisman, Avery D. (1993). *The vulnerable self: Confronting the ultimate questions.* New York: Insight Books.

Woodward, J. (1990). *Embracing the chaos: Theological responses to AIDS.* London: SPCK.

Home and Hospice Care

Baycrest Center for Geriatric Care. (1996). *Visiting with elders: A guidebook for family and friends.* Toronto: Self-published.

Bennett, Laurie; Abrams, Barbara; and Cooney, Larry. (1996). *A practical guide for families when a loved one is dying.* Mississauga, Ontario: Hospice of Peel.

Buckingham, Robert. (1983). *The complete hospice guide.* New York: Harper Row, Publishers, Inc.

Carey, Deborah Allen. (1986). *Hospice inpatient environments: Compendium and guidelines.* New York: Van Nostrand Reinhold.

Deachman, Marilyn and Howell, Doris. (1998). *Supportive care at home: A guide for seriously ill patients and their families.* Markham, Ontario: Knoll Pharma.

Du Boulay, Shirley. (1984). *Cicely Saunders: The founder of the modern movement.* London: Hodder & Stoughton. Biography of Dame Saunders, founder   of St. Christopher's Hospice.

Hall, Beverly. (1988). *Caring for the dying: A guide for caregivers in home and hospital.* Toronto: Anglican Book Center. A practical guide for both professionals and volunteers.

Haller, James. (1994). *What to eat when you don't feel like eating.* Hantsport, Nova Scotia: Lancelot Press. A cookbook for cancer patients filled with delicious recipes and humor.

Hospice King. (1984). *Hospice King manual.* King City: Self-published. A practical guide to home care for non-medical hospice care workers including information on feeding and food suggestions.

Infeld, Donna Lind; Gordon, Audrey K.; and Harper, Bernice Catherine. (1995). *Hospice care and cultural diversity.* New York: Haworth Press.

Irish, Donald P; Lundquist, Kathleen F.; and Nelsen, Vivian Jenkins. (Eds.). (1993). *Ethnic variations in dying, death and grief.* Bristol, PA: Taylor and Francis.

Jones, Charmaine M. and Pegis, Jessica. (1994). *The palliative patient: Principles of treatment.* Markham, Ontario: Knoll Pharma Inc.

Krieger, Dolores. (1992). *The therapeutic touch*. New York: Simon and Schuster. A how-to book describing the therapeutic touch technique of natural healing taught in various universities in the U.S.

Lamerton, Richard. (1991). *Care of the dying*. New York: Pelican. Extensive bibliography of journal articles for professionals plus overview of hospice care and statistics.

Langley Hospice Society. (1994). *Death, dying and bereavement: A practical guide*. Langley, BC: Self-published.

Lepine, Lorraine. (September, 1982). *Palliative care in Canada*. Ottawa: Policy, Planning and Information Branch, Department of National Health and Welfare. Government of Canada report on palliative care in Canada.

Ley, Dorothy with van Bommel, Harry. (1994). *The heart of hospice*. Toronto: NC Press. Describes the founding principles of hospice care.

Manitoba Health. (undated -- mid 1990s). *Caring for the terminally ill person at home: An information booklet for caregivers*. Winnipeg: Manitoba Health

McDermott, Reena and Russell, Judy. (1995). *Palliative care: A shared experience--A nursing perspective of symptom management*. London: Parkwood Hospital Foundation.

Rhodes, Ann. (1994). *The eldercare sourcebook*. Toronto: Key Porter Books.

Rothstein, Jerry and Rothstein, Miriam. (1997). *The caring community: A field book for hospice palliative care volunteer services*. Burnaby, British Columbia: British Columbia Hospice Palliative Care Association.

Saint Elizabeth Health Care. (1988). *Caring across cultures: Multicultural consideration in palliative care*. Toronto: SEVNAO.

St. John Ambulance. (most recent edition). *First aid*. Toronto: The Priory of Canada of the Most Venerable Order of The Hospital of St. John of Jerusalem.

Saunders, Cicely. (1990). *Hospice and palliative care*. London: Edward Arnold. Written jointly by a team of experts in the field, this book offers good advice for setting up an interdisciplinary team on caring for the dying.

Saunders, Cicely. (1991). *Hospice: The living idea*. London: Edward Arnold. To help the health care professional understand how hospice care focuses on the quality of life left to the patient.

Saunders, Cicely and Baines, Mary. (1989). *Living with dying: The management of terminal disease.* Oxford University Press. A clinical examination of terminal illness.

Saunders, Cicely and Kastenbaum, Robert (Eds.). (1997). *Hospice care on the international scene.* New York: Springer Publishing.

Seibold, Cathy. (1992). *The hospice movement: Easing death's pain.* New York: Twayne Publishing.

Silverstone, Barbara and Hyman, Helen Kandel. (1989). *You and your aging parent: A family guide to emotional, physical and financial problems, 3rd edition.* New York: Pantheon Books.

Stoddard, Sandol. (1992). *The hospice movement: A better way of caring for the dying.* New York: Stein and Day. Thorough review of the hospice movement in the 1990s.

Taylor, Joan Leslie. (1989). *In the light of dying: The journals of a hospice volunteer.* New York: Continuum. A sensitive account of the loving relationships between hospice volunteers, patients and caregivers.

Tehan, Claire. (October 1985). *"Has Success Spoiled Hospice?"*, Hastings Center Report, pp. 10-13. Critical review of hospice movement.

Thompson, Wendy. (1987). *Aging is a family affair: A guide to quality visiting, long-term care facilities and you.* Toronto: NC Press.

van Bommel, Harry. (1999). *Caring for loved ones at home.* Scarborough, ON: Resources Supporting Family and Community Legacies Inc. Basic home nursing guide for family, friends and neighbors. Book available for free on the following Website: *www.inforamp.net/~harryvb*

van Bommel, Harry. (1993). *Choices for people who have a terminal illness, their families and their caregivers.* Toronto: NC Press.

van Bommel, Harry. (1992). *Dying for care: Hospice care and euthanasia.* Toronto: NC Press. An examination of the need for more hospice care programs (informal and formal) before society spends much time, effort and resources on the euthanasia debate. Includes detailed quotes from Canadian hospice care leaders.

Victoria Hospice Society. (1995). *Palliative care for home support workers.* Victoria, British Columbia: Self-published.

Zimmerman, Jack McKay. (1986). *Hospice: Complete care for the terminally ill.* Baltimore: Urban and Schwarzenberg.

Pain and Symptom Control

Many of the books listed in the section for professionals have specific chapters on pain and symptom control. The following deal specifically with pain and symptom control plus a list of pharmaceutical texts:

Angel, Jack E. (Publisher). (Use most recent edition). *Physicians' desk reference.* Oradell, N.J.: Medical Economics Company Inc. Includes supplements. Standard physicians' text on all prescription drugs, their purpose and their side effects.

Autton, Norman. (1989). *Pain--An exploration.* London: Darton, Longman & Todd.

Bruera, Eduardo and Fainsinger, Robin L. (1995). *Palliative care medicine: Patient-based training.* Edmonton, Alberta: Division of Palliative Care Medicine, University of Alberta.

Canadian Pharmaceutical Association. (1992). *About your medicines.* Ottawa. Consumer's guide to drugs.

-----. *Compendium of pharmaceuticals and specialties.* Ottawa. Choose most recent edition for professional information on drugs.

Doyle, Derek. (1994). *Domiciliary palliative care: A guide for the primary care team.* London: Oxford University Press.

Expert Advisory Committee on the Management of Severe Chronic Pain in Cancer Patients. (1984, 1987). *Cancer pain: A monograph on the management of cancer pain.* Ottawa: Ministry of Supply and Services. Excellent summary of modern pain control techniques; distributed to all Canadian physicians.

Fordham, Moira and Dunn, Virginia. (1994). *Along side the person in pain: Holistic care and nursing practice.* London: Saunders College Publications.

Goldberg, Ivan K., Austin H. Kutscher and Sidney Malitz (Eds.). (1986). *Pain, anxiety and grief: Pharmacotherapeutic care of the dying patient and the bereaved.* New York: Columbia University Press. Series of professional articles.

Hull, Robin. (1995). *A pocketbook of palliative care*. Rosewell, Australia: McGraw Hill.

Hull, Robin; Ellis, Mary; and Sargent, Vicki. (1989). *Teamwork in palliative care: A multidisciplinary approach to the care of patients with advanced cancer*. Oxford, England: Radcliffe Medical Press.

Librach, S. Lawrence. (1997). *The pain manual: Principals and issues in cancer pain*. Purdue Fredrick. A short and concise pocket handbook published in association with the Canadian Cancer Society.

Long, Don M. (1997). *Contemporary diagnosis and management of pain*. Newtown, PA: Associates in Medical Marketing.

Saunders, Cicely M. (Ed.). (1978). *The management of terminal disease*. London: Edward Arnold. Gives specific drugs and doses for pain control plus other forms of symptom control including radiation, chemotherapy, surgery as well as the philosophy of palliative care.

Seamore, Linda, D. (1996). *Symptom management algorithms for palliative care*. Yakina: Washington.

Twycross, Robert and Lack, Sylvia A. (1990). *Therapeutics in terminal care*. New York: Churchill Livingstone. A highly practical, quick reference book for all those involved in the care of cancer patients.

Twycross, Robert. (1994). *Pain relief in advanced cancer*. New York: Churchill Livingstone.

Woodruff, Roger. (1993). *Palliative medicine*. Australia.

World Health Organization. (1996). *Cancer pain relief (2nd edition)*. Geneva: WHO.A summary of the best current information on cancer pain. Much of the information applies to other types of terminal-illness pain.

Legal and Moral Rights and Responsibilities

Annas, George J. (1981). *The rights of hospital patients*. New York: AvonBooks.By the American Civil Liberties Union. This question-and-answer format bookexamines all areas of a patient's hospital rights.

Annas, George J, Glantz ,Leonard H. and Katz, Barbara F. (1981). *The rights of doctors, nurses, and allied health professionals.* Cambridge, Mass.: Ballinger Publishing Company. American Civil Liberties Union's examination of caregivers' rights to practice, the caregiver-patient relationship and liability and income rights.

Cohen, Cynthia B. (Ed.). (1988). *Casebook on the termination of life-sustaining treatment and the care of the dying.* Bloomington, Indiana: Indiana University Press.

The Hastings Center. (1988). *Guidelines on the termination of life-sustaining treatment and the care of the dying.* Bloomington: Indiana University. A record of cases which highlight medical, ethical, legal, psychological dilemmas.

Kerr, Margaret and Kurtz, Joann. (1999). *Facing a death in the family: Caring for someone through illness and dying, arranging the funeral, dealing with the will and estate.* Toronto: John Wiley and Sons. A must-have book that explains the legal and financial issues related to death and dying in Canada.

Robertson, John A. (1983). *The rights of the critically ill.* New York: Bantam Books. American Civil Liberties Union book in a question-and-answer format

Roy, David; Williams, John R.; and Dickens, Bernard M. (1994). *Bioethics in Canada.* Scarborough, Ontario: Prentice Hall Canada. Standard text for the study of bioethics in Canada.

Rozovsky, Lorne Elkin. (1980). *The Canadian patient's book of rights.* Toronto: Doubleday Canada Limited. Patient rights in Canada with a list of provincial licensing authorities, medical associations, nursing associations and a bibliography.

Storch, J. (1982). *Patients' rights: Ethical and legal issues in health care and nursing.* Toronto: McGraw-Hill Ryerson Limited. For health care professionals, this book reviews patients' rights, the ethics and law.

Grief and Bereavement

Many of the books listed in the general interest sections have specific chapters dealing with bereavement for adults and children plus the anticipatory grieving of patients. The following books deal more specifically with these concerns.

Buckman, Robert. (1988). *Care of the dying child: A practical guide for those who help others.* New York: Continuum. Deals with the care of the terminally ill child and family.

Buscaglia, Leo. (1983). *The fall of Freddie the leaf.* New York: Holt, Rinehart and Winston.

Caplan, Sandi and Lang, Gordon. (1993). *Grief -- the courageous journey: A step-by-step process for surviving the death of a loved one.* London, Ontario: Cor Age Books.

Coburn, John. (1986). *Anne and the sand dobbies.* Ridgefield, CT: Morehouse/Barlow. A story to help parents and children face the unavoidable fact of death squarely.

Coryell, Deborah Morris. (1997). *Good grief: Healing through the shadow of loss.* Sante Fe, New Mexico: Shiva Foundation.

Foehner, Charlotte and Cozart, Carol. (1988). *The widow's handbook: A guide for living.* Golden, CO: Fulcrum. A practical book full of basic information for a newly widowed individual.

Fassier, Joan. (1971). *My grandpa died today.* New York: Human Sciences Press. Picture book for children of all ages tells how a young boy adjusts to his grandfather's death.

Gatliffe, Eleanor D. (1988). *Death in the classroom.* Pembrooke Pines, FL: Tri Party Press. A resource book for teachers that offers realistic curriculum for death education.

Goodman, Michèle. (1991). *Vanishing cookies.* Toronto: The Benjamin Family Foundation. Suitable for junior grades.

Grollman, Earl. Has a series of books for patients, family members, children and professionals. Look for the most recent editions.

Hazen, B. (1985). *Why did grandpa die?* Racine: Western Publishing Company.

Krementz, Jill. (1988). *How it feels when a parent dies.* New York: Knoph. Eighteen children speak openly and honestly about their feelings when a parent dies.

Kushner, Harold S. (1981). *When bad things happen to good people.* New York: Avon Books. A distinguished clergyman's explanation of how God does not cause bad things but provides strength and courage to cope with difficult situations.

Levine, Stephen. (1989). *Meetings at the edge: Dialogues with the grieving and the dying, the healing and the healed.* New York: Anchor Press. Dialogues with emphasis on relief through meditation.

Lewis, C.S. (1966). *A grief observed.* London/Boston: Faber & Faber. A short, honest account of the author's experiences, emotional and spiritual, after the death of his wife. He argues against some of the conventional thoughts and behaviors of the time.

Martin, John D. and Ferris, Frank D. (1992). *I can't stop crying: It's so hard when someone you love dies.* Toronto: Key Porter Books.

O'Toole, Donna. (1989). *Aarvy Aardvark Finds Hope.* Rainbow, NC: Mountain Rainbow. A book for children to learn about the grief process. Used extensively in workshops and schools.

Panton, Elizabeth, and Allen, Louise. (1986). *Where's Linda?: A journal of grief.* Windsor, Ontario: Canadian Mental Health Association, Windsor-Essex County Branch.

Parkes, Colin Murray. (1987). *Bereavement: Studies of grief in adult life.* London: Tavistock and Pelican. A classic work in studying grief.

Parkes, Colin Murray with Laungani, Pittu and Young, Bill (Eds.). (1996). *Death and bereavement across cultures.* London: Routledge.

Parkes, Colin Murray; Stevenson-Hinde, Joan; and Maris, Peter (Eds.). (1993). *Attachment across the life cycle.* London: Routledge.

Rando, Therese A. (1984). *Grief, dying and death: Clinical intervention for caregivers.* Champaign, IL: Research Press. A clinically oriented examination of grief and loss for the professional caregiver, focusing on practical applications for caregiving.

Rando, Therese A. (1995). *Grieving: How to go on when someone you love dies.* New York: Lexington Books.

Rando, Therese A. (1986). *Loss and anticipatory grief.* New York: Free Press. This book helps those who work with the dying and bereaved to understand the many forms of anticipatory grief and use the forewarning of loss in a positive and creative way.

Rando, Therese, A. (1986). *Parental loss of a child.* New York: Research Press. An in-depth study of the unique needs of parents suffering from the loss of a child.

Rando, Therese, A. (1993). *Treatment of complicated mourning.* New York: Research Press.

Romond, Janis Loomis. (1989). *Children facing grief: Letters from bereaved brothers and sisters.* Saint Meinrad, IN: Abbey Press. A book for bereaved families, a tool to open communication between children and parents.

Rosen, Helen. (1986). *Unspoken grief.* New York: Free Press. A study of the effect of sibling death on a child and their family.

Sandford, Doris. (1985). *It must hurt a lot.* Portland, OR: Multnomah Press. For children between the ages of 5 and 11. A touching story about a boy whose puppy is killed by a car.

Schneiderman, Gerald. (1985). *Coping with death in the family.* Toronto: NC Press. Reviews death of an infant, child, adolescence, a parent's death, a grandparent's death and your own death.

Silverman, Phyllis and Campbell, Scott. (1987). *Widower: When men are left alone.* New York: Baywood. True stories of men left alone and how they coped.

Viorst, Judith. (1986). *Necessary losses: The loves, illusions, dependencies and impossible expectations that all of us have to give up in order to grow.* New York: Fawcett.

Worden, William J. (1991). *Grief counseling and grief therapy.* New York: Springer Publishing Company, Inc. A professional reference for counselors and therapists and often used as a starting reference for professionals.

Worden, J. William, and William Proctor. (1976). *PDA (Personal Death Awareness): Breaking free of fear to live a better life now.* Englewood Cliffs, N.J.: Prentice-Hall. Research Director of Harvard's Omega Project looks at terminal illness and suicide and how to rid yourself of the fear of death.

Wylie, Betty Jane and Webb, Jonathan (Ed.). (1997). *Beginnings: A book for widows.* Toronto: McClelland & Stewart. A book for widows written by a Canadian author with Canadian references.

Personal Stories

Bonisteel, Roy. *In search of man alive. (1980).* Toronto: A Totem Book. Interviews with celebrities including Mother Theresa, Elisabeth Kübler-Ross, and Elie Wiesel.

Brady, Mari. (1977). *Please remember me: A young woman's story of her friendship with an unforgettable 15 year old boy.* New York: Doubleday and Company Inc. Brady was a recreational aid who worked with young cancer patients.

Caine, Lynn. (1975). *Widow.* New York: Bantam Books. Her examination of how she grieved her husband's loss, her anger at his death and how she coped.

Callwood, June. (1990). *Jim: A life with AIDS.* Toronto: Lester & Orpen Dennys. Jim's story will inform and enlighten everyone who wants to better understand AIDS.

Callwood, June. (1986). *Twelve weeks of spring.* Toronto: Lester & Orpen Dennys. The story of Margaret Frazer's life ending in vitality and love, a triumphant experiment in palliative care.

Cameron, Jean. (1982). *For all that has been: Time to live and time to die.* New York: Macmillan Book by a hospital social worker with terminal cancer who describes her work on a palliative care unit, her struggle with cancer that keeps growing and bereavement concerns. She lives the Viktor Frankl observation that our last human freedom is our ability to choose our response to whatever the circumstances.

Cousins, Norman. (1979). *Anatomy of an illness As perceived by the patient.* Toronto: Bantam Books. How this magazine editor overcame a terminal illness using common sense, laughter, information and taking personal control over his health.

Craven, Margaret. (1975). *I heard the owl call my name.* Toronto: A Totem Book. Story of a young Anglican priest sent to an Indian Village in British Columbia. He doesn't know he is terminally ill yet learns "enough of life to be ready to die."

duBoulay, Shirley. (1984). *Cecily Saunders: Founder of the modern hospice movement.* London: Hodder and Stoughton.

Elmer, Lon. (1990). *Why her, why now: A man's journey through love and death and grief.* New York: Bantam.

Fynn. (1972). *Mister God this is Anna.* London: Collins. Story of a 5-8 year old girl genius and her adventures and discoveries before her death.

Kennedy, Betty. (1976). *Gerhard: A love story.* Toronto: Macmillan of Canada Limited. A journalist/broadcaster's sensitive story of her husband's last year and how they dealt with his dying.

Kramer, Herbert and Kay. (1993). *Conversations at midnight: Coming to terms with dying and death.* New York: William Morrow.

Liss, Robert E. (1980). *Fading rainbow: A reporter's last story.* New York: Methuen, Inc. Reporter, father of 3, 33 years old with leukemia and his description of symptoms, tests, doctors, hospitals, drugs, pain and other patients. Wife completed the book after his death.

Lund, Doris. (1974). *Eric.* New York: Dell Publishing. A mother's account of her son's last years of fighting cancer.

Meryman, Richard. (1980). *Hope: A loss survived.* Boston: Little, Brown and Company. Writer helps his wife die at home and how the family (two girls) survived the loss.

Mucciolo, Louis. (1992). *Eighty Something: Interviews with octogenarians who stay involved.* New York: Carol Publishing.

Pond, Jean. (1979). *Surviving.* New York: Ace Books. Well known network TV newscaster who reviews her triumph over a brain tumor but describes the process from a patient's point of view in a modern urban hospital.

Pope, Robert. (1991). *Illness and healing: Images of cancer.* Hantsport, Nova Scotia: Lancelot Press. Book of powerful and moving paintings and sketches by the Nova Scotian artist as he experiences the diagnosis and treatment of his cancer.

Radner, Gilda. (1989). *It's always something.* New York: Simon and Schuster.

Rollin, Betty. (1977). *First you cry.* New York: Signet. TV broadcaster who faced death when she had breast cancer and how she coped with her first of two mastectomies.

Rosenfeld, Stephen S. (1977). *The time of their dying.* New York: W. W. Norton and Company. Editorial writer and columnist who helps both his parents die within months of each other.

Sarton, May. (1981). *A reckoning.* New York: W.W. Norton and Company. A fictional account of a dying woman's examination of her life and relationships with family and friends.

Scrivener, Leslie. (1981). *Terry Fox: His story.* Toronto: McClelland and Stewart Limited. Based on Fox's daily journal, this is the story of his run across Canada to raise funds for cancer and how the run was cut short when his cancer returned.

Stewart, Fred Mustard. (1976). *Six weeks.* New York: Bantam Books. Story of a girl, her mother and the new man in their lives and how they cope with the girl's last six weeks of life.

Upson, Norma S. (1986). *When someone you love is dying: Sensitive, timely advice on providing primary care for a terminally ill loved one...from a woman who faced this challenge herself.* New York: Simon and Schuster.

Weingarten, Violet. (1977). *Intimations of mortality.* New York: Alfred A. Knopf. Journal of a writer's two year battle with cancer.

Weinman-Lear, Martha. (1980). *Heartsounds.* New York: Pocket Books. A journalist's story of her urologist husband's loosing battle with degenerative heart disease. It describes a surgeon's frustration and anger at being treated like a child by the medical profession and how he recognizes he might have done the same with his patients. His wife describes what it is like to help a spouse die.

Long-Term Care

Adams, Martha O. (1987). *Alzheimer's disease: A call to courage for caregivers.* Saint Meinrad, IN: Abbey Press. Written from personal experience, the author emphasizes the practical care of the Alzheimer's patient.

Bayly, Rich and Larue, Gerald A. (1992). *Long-term care in an aging society: Choices and challenges for the 90s.* New York: Prometheus Books.

Cleveland, Martha. (1989). *Living well: A twelve-step response to chronic illness and disability.* New York: Harper-Collins. Wisdom for millions who suffer from the distress and pain of chronic illness and disability.

Fabiano, Len. (1991). *Mother I'm doing the best I can: The families of aging parents during times of loss and crisis.* Seagrave, Ontario: FCS Publications.

Fabiano, Len. (1989). *Working with the frail elderly: Beyond the physical disability.* Seagrave, Ontario: FCS Publications.

Mace, Nancy and Rabins, Peter. (1991). *The 36-hour day: A family guide to caring for persons with Alzheimer's disease, related dementing illness and memory loss in later life.* Baltimore, MD: John Hopkins. A family guide to caring for persons with Alzheimer's Disease, dementia and memory loss in later life.

Maurer, Janet. R. and Strasberg, Patricia D. (1990). *Building a new dream: A family guide to coping with chronic illness and disability.* Redding, MA: Addison Wesley. A guide for patients, family and friends of people facing chronic illness. It provides practical and wise advice on coping with a changed life.

Miller, James E. (1996). *The caregiver's book: Caring for another, caring for yourself.* Minneapolis: Augsburg Fortress.

Miller, Judith F. (1992). *Coping with chronic illness: Overcoming powerlessness.* New York: Davis. A book offered as a resource for caregivers and patients to help combat the sense of helplessness in chronic illness.

Portnow, Jay with Houtmann, Martha. (1987). *Home care for the elderly.* New York: Pocket Books.

Rhodes, Ann. (1993). *The eldercare sourcebook.* Toronto: Key Porter Books.

Rhodes, Ann. (1997). *Take care: A practical guide for helping elders.* Toronto: HarperCollins Publishers.

Schwartzentruber, Michael. (1988). *From crisis to new creation.* Winfield, BC: Wood Lake. A terminally ill young man with cystic fibrosis probes "all that I would like to be", with hope, sensitivity and courage.

Books on Death

Aries, Philippe with translation by Helen Weaver. (1991). *The Hour of our death.* Oxford: Oxford University Press. A long-term study into western man's changing attitude toward death from earliest Christian times to the present.

Aries, Philippe with translation by Helen Weaver. (1975). *Western attitudes toward death: From the Middle Ages to the present.* Baltimore: John Hopkins University Press. Various views of western man's own mortality as seen through fine art, history, literature and religion.

Currie, Ian. (1993). *You cannot die.* New York: Somerville House. Examines evidence of an afterlife through apparitions, hauntings, out-of-body-experiences, deathbed visions, resuscitation experiences and reincarnation.

Levine, Stephen. (1989). *Who dies? An investigation of conscious living and conscious dying.* New York: Anchor Press. Examines evidence of reincarnation.

Moody, Raymond A., Jr. (1988). *Life after life: the investigation of a phenomenon, survival of bodily death.* New York: Bantam. Based on interviews with people who were "dead" but revived, Moody examines 15 points that bind all these peoples' experiences together.

-----. (1988). *Reflections on life after life.* Harrisburg, P.A.: Stackpole Books. Further interviews and conclusions on life-after-death issues.

The World Wide Web (Internet)

The following Internet links may be helpful for people interested in more information about hospice/palliative and home care. I have picked just a few sites that have excellent resources and extensive links to other related sites. These organizations deserve a lot of credit for the effort they have put into their Web sites.

A note of caution: There are thousands of Web sites offering health care information. The information on some sites may not be accurate or current. Check to see who produces the Web site, their qualifications and their credibility before assuming their information is correct.

Also, when checking the Web or other sources, for health care information, expect to find information that might be unsettling. The information may tell you things you didn't expect or didn't want to know and it may have been written for a professional audience rather than for patients and families.

For a searchable database of books in the fields of death, dying, bereavement and hospice care, **Books for Caregivers [www.interlog.com/~geri]** is a Canadian company that provides both the database and a mail-order business so that you can order any of the books at this site. Geri Leonard is the owner of this company. She provides an invaluable service.

For general health information, a good starting point is **www.sympatico.ca/healthyway**. This site includes thousands of reviewed health sites. Also, the **Health Canada** has an extensive resource base at **www.hc-sc.gc.ca** with links to other sites.

The **Edmonton Palliative Care Program** site is part of the University of Alberta, Oncology Department Palliative Medicine Program and the Regional Palliative Care Program for the City of Edmonton. The site has much information on palliative care with some special sections for Spanish-speaking people. [www.palliative.org]

The **Halton Peel Palliative Care Initiatives** site is a rich resource of other links and current information on educational events and conferences. [www.webhome.idirect.com/~sstreet]

The **Institute of Palliative Care in Ottawa** has an extensive links section to organizations around the country and globe [www.pallcare.org/links.htm]. Their whole site is worth a visit.

The **National Hospice Organization** in the U.S. [www.nho.org] provides many links to hospice programs throughout America and other organizations.

The **Association for Death Education and Counseling** [www.adec.org] is a useful site for those interested in teaching or learning more about death, dying and bereavement.

The **World Health Organization** is another extensive site for health related information [www.who.org].

Index

Notes

Notes

Notes

Notes

Notes

Notes

Notes

Notes

Notes

Notes

Family Hospice Care Contact List

Remove and photocopy this sheet.

Have one copy by each telephone and one in your pocket.

Patient's Name

_____

Phone

_____

Health Card #

_____

Next-of-Kin or Power of Attorney for Personal Care to call in emergency

_____

Doctors   Phone

_____

Home Care Coordinator   Phone

_____

Home Care Services   Phone

_____

Nursing   Phone

_____

Homemakers   Phone

_____

Hospice/Palliative Care Service   Phone

_____

Volunteers   Phone

_____

Pharmacist _____ Phone _____

Drug Store _____ Phone _____

Neighbors _____ Phone _____

_____ Phone _____

_____ Phone _____

_____ Phone _____

_____ Phone _____

Other Health Insurance

_____